A CRITICAL EDITION OF *I SIR JOHN OLDCASTLE*

edited, with an introduction, by

Jonathan Rittenhouse

The Renaissance Imagination

Volume 9

GARLAND PUBLISHING, INC.
NEW YORK & LONDON
1984

Library of Congress Cataloging in Publication Data

Sir John Oldcastle.
A critical edition of I Sir John Oldcastle.

(The Renaissance imagination ; v. 9)
Original ed. by Anthony Munday and others, published in 1600.
Ascribed to William Shakespeare in 1619 ed.
Originally presented as the editor's thesis (doctoral —University of Toronto)
Bibliography: p.
1. Oldcastle, John, Sir, d. 1417—Drama. 2. Henry V, King of England, 1387–1422—Drama. I. Rittenhouse, Jonathan, 1953– . II. Munday, Anthony, 1553–1633. III. Shakespeare, William, 1564–1616. IV. Title. V. Title: Critical edition of First Sir John Oldcastle. VI. Series.
PR2867.A2R 1984 822'.3 84-10135
ISBN 0-8240-5457-1 (alk. paper)

Printed on acid-free, 250-year-life paper
Manufactured in the United States of America

CONTENTS

Acknowledgments vii
List of Abbreviations ix

Chapter One : The Text
i. Textual History 1
ii. This Edition 10
iii. Copy Text 12

Chapter Two : Sources 21

Chapter Three : Date and Authorship
i. Date 43
ii. The Authors 46
iii. The Question of Authorship 50

Chapter Four : Critical Assessment 68

Chapter Five : Theatrical Background and Assessment
i. Stage History 84
ii. The Company 85
iii. The Stage and Staging 93

I Sir John Oldcastle 99

Appendices
I. Press Variants and Running-Titles of Q1 254
II. From Holinshed's *Chronicles* 265
III. From Foxe's *Acts and Monuments* 269

Bibliography 277

ACKNOWLEDGMENTS

This critical edition of *I Sir John Oldcastle* was, originally, a doctoral dissertation for the University of Toronto. My thesis advisor, Anne Lancashire, provided me with very useful guidance and help. For this Garland publication I have revised the dissertation's introduction, textual notes, and format. My wife, Rina Kampeas, has helped me enormously in this process. As well I would like to thank my typist, Paula de Man, for her excellent work.

The Huntington, Folger, Clark, and Biblioteca Bodmeriana libraries provided me with microfilm copies of Q1.

Finally, I would like to dedicate this work to the memory of my mother and father, two loving parents.

LIST OF ABBREVIATIONS

I. EDITIONS

Q1	*The First Part . . . of Sir John Old-castle,* printed by V.S. for Thomas Pavier, 1600
Q2	*The First Part . . . of Sir John Old-castle,* printed for T.P., 1600 [1619].
F3	*Mr. William Shakespear Comedies, Histories, and Tragedies,* 1664.
F4	*Mr. William Shakespear's Comedies, Histories, and Tragedies,* 1685.
Rowe	*The Works of Mr William Shakespear,* Nicholas Rowe, ed., 1709, Vol. VI.
Pope	*The Works of Shakespear,* Alexander Pope, ed., 2nd ed., 1728, Vol. IX.
Mal.	*Supplement to the Edition of Shakespeare's Plays Published in 1778,* Edmond Malone, ed., 1780, Vol. II.
Simms	*A Supplement to the Plays of William Shakespeare,* William Gilmore Simms, ed., 1848.
Tyrrell	*The Doubtful Plays of Shakespeare,* Henry Tyrrell, ed., n.d. (conj. 1851).
Hopk.	*The First Part of Sir John Oldcastle,* A.F. Hopkinson, ed., 1894.
Mac.	*The First Part of Sir John Oldcastle,* J.R. Macarthur, ed., 1907.
MSR	*The Life of Sir John Oldcastle,* Percy Simpson, ed., 1908.
Brooke	*The Shakespeare Apocrypha,* C.F. Tucker Brooke, ed., 1908.

Hebel	*The First Part of Sir John Oldcastle*, in *The Works of Michael Drayton*, J. William Hebel, Kathleen Tillotson, and Bernard H. Newdigate, ed., Vols. I and V, 1931 and 1941.

II. OTHER WORKS

Abbott	E.A. Abbott, *A Shakespearean Grammar*, 1869.
Annals	John Stow, *The Annales of England*, 1592.
Complete Peerage	Vicary Gibbs, et al., eds., *The Complete Peerage*; or, *A History of the House of Lords and all its members from the earliest times*, Vol. VI, 1926.
DNB	Sir Leslie Stephen and Sir Sidney Lee, *The Dictionary of National Biography*, 1921–22.
DWB	Sir John Edward Lloyd et al., eds., *The Dictionary of Welsh Biography Down to 1940*, 1959.
Elton	G.R. Elton, *The Tudor Constitution*, 1965.
Foxe	John Foxe, *The Acts and Monuments of John Foxe*, ed., Rev. George Townsend, 1843, Vol. III.
GHQ	Frank Taylor and John S. Roskell, translators and eds., *Gesta Henrici Quinti: The Deeds of Henry the Fifth*, 1975.
Hol.	Raphael Holinshed, *Holinshed's Chronicles*, R.S. Wallace and Alma Hansen, eds., 1923.
OED	*Oxford English Dictionary.*
Survey	John Stow, *Survey of London*, ed., Henry B. Wheatley, n.d.
Tilley	Morris Palmer Tilley, *A Dictionary of the Proverbs in England in the Sixteenth and Seventeenth Centuries*, 1950.
Waugh	W.T. Waugh, "Sir John Oldcastle," *English Historical Review*, 20 (1905), 434–56, 637–58.

III. PERIODICALS

ELR	*English Literary Renaissance*
MLN	*Modern Languages Notes*

N&Q	*Notes and Queries*
SB	*Studies in Bibliography*
SP	*Studies in Philology*

INTRODUCTION

CHAPTER ONE

The Text

i. Textual History

For such an obscure play, 1 Sir John Oldcastle has had a varied and tempestuous printing history. Primarily because the play became connected with the various works known as the Shakespeare apocrypha,[1] it has been printed eighteen times since its original 1600 publication date. As well, some eminent Shakespeare editors and scholars of the Elizabethan period--Edmond Malone, Percy Simpson, and J. William Hebel--have given their time and attention to solving some of its textual cruxes and elucidating some of the more obscure passages. Oldcastle presents the critic, then, with a series of interesting problems or controversies that span the centuries.

The play's printing history begins with this entry from the Stationers' Register, a list of books authorized for printing:

> 11 Augusti / 1600
> Thomas pavier Entred for his copies vnder the
> handes of master VICARS and the / wardens.
> These iij copies
> viz.
> The first parte of the history of the life of
> Sir John / OLDCASTELL lord COBHAM.
> Item the second and last parte of the history
> of Sir / JOHN OLDCASTELL lord COBHAM with his
> martyrdom

> Item ye history of the life and Deathe of Captaine / THOMAS STUCLEY, with his Mariage . . . xviij d[2]

1 Sir John Oldcastle was indeed published in 1600. Captain Thomas reached print in 1605, and 2 Sir John Oldcastle either never was printed or has simply disappeared.[3]

On the title page of the 1600 edition of 1 Sir John Oldcastle we read that "The first part / Of the true and hono- / rable historie, of the life of Sir / John Old-castle, the good / Lord Cobham" was "Printed by V.S. for Thomas Pauier". "V.S." refers to Valentine Simmes, a printer who worked with various publishers (A. Wise, W. Aspley, among others). This Simmes printed a number of plays in the late Elizabethan and early Jacobean period, but the appearance of the first quarto (Q1) of 1 Sir John Oldcastle in 1600 marks the only time that Simmes collaborated with the publisher Thomas Pavier.[4] A full discussion of Q1 follows in the "Copy Text" section of this "Introduction."

Another quarto of Oldcastle appeared with a slightly altered title page. On it we find that the play was supposedly written by "William Shakespeare" and that it was printed in 1600 in London "for T.P.". Not until the early twentieth century did research prove that Thomas Pavier, publisher of both quartos, was up to something irregular, and that the Shakespeare-attributed quarto was printed not in 1600, the same year as Q1, but in 1619. According to W.W. Greg and A.W. Pollard,[5] in 1619 Pavier and printer William Jaggard decided to print a number of Shakespeare plays and other plays to which they had the rights: The Whole Contention, Pericles, The Merchant of Venice, Sir John Falstaff, King Lear, Henry V, A Midsummer Night's Dream, A Yorkshire Tragedy, and 1 Sir John Oldcastle. The existence of bound volumes of these nine plays, as well as the general similarity in layout of their title-pages, the brief imprints, the use of the same device (gillyflower between rose and marigold) and the similarity in type led Greg and Pollard to conclude that Pavier and Jaggard intended some sort of collection designed, no doubt, to "scoop" the newly-planned Shakespeare folio. The intention to make a regular collection was apparently frustrated when a letter of May 3, 1619, was sent out from a court official, the Lord Chamberlain, in effect forbidding Pavier and Jaggard to anticipate the forthcoming Shakespeare folio. Both printer and publisher circumvented this prohibition by printing the plays using the old dates (in Oldcastle's case 1600) so that they could be passed off as old stock.[6]

Jaggard, the printer of the Shakespeare quarto Q2, plainly used Q1 as the basis for Q2. All evidence points to this, and there is no indication that the numerous changes between the two quartos are the result of playhouse alterations to a copy of Q1 subsequently used when printing Q2. Q2's major alterations or substantives, then, are regarded as no more textually valid than any later edition's might be. These substantives, however, have had a long textual history, for almost all later editions of Oldcastle used Q2 or an edition based on Q2 as their source.

Despite thousands of spelling modernizations and punctuation alterations, all clearly introduced by the Q2 compositor, Q2 is obviously a reprint of Q1. Up to the last three sheets Q2 is a page for page reprint. Some Q2 pages have one line more or less than Q1, and revealingly Q2 occasionally retains a wrong Q1 catchword (instead of "For" Q2 has Q1's "With" on E3r). In the earlier sheets, A3r-G4v, there are few substantive changes in the play's verse, the revision of Q1's pointing being Q2's main concern. The major substantive differences between the quarto texts come in the longer prose speeches where words are dropped or abbreviated, and phrases shortened. Excisions in both prose and verse become more pronounced in the later sheets, H1r-K4v. The Q2 compositor seems intent on saving time and space, and so from H1r he "edits" the remaining twenty-four pages of his copy into twenty-two and a half pages.

1 Sir John Oldcastle was printed twice more in the seventeenth century. Both the third and fourth folios of Shakespeare (published in 1664 and 1685) included the play in an addition of seven plays "never before Printed in Folio."[7] The third folio (F3) is based on Q2,[8] and it faithfully reproduces the variants of that quarto. The F3 printer also adds and subtracts still more words and phrases. Emendations are rare, but one useful example is the reassignment of two Constable speeches to the Aleman (iv.114-16, 119).[9] This edition also supplies a list of the characters' names. The fourth folio (F4) is no more than a reprint of F3[10] and repeats almost all of the earlier folio's emendations. However, F4's relineation into prose of original verse (i.1-2, 13-14, 42-43, 56-57) was often retained by later editors.

The eighteenth century saw more editions of Oldcastle. In Nicholas Rowe's edition of The Works of Mr William Shakespear (first edition, 1709) the play was printed in "Volume the Sixth" along with the other apocrypha dramas collected in F3 and F4. Added to Alexander Pope's 1728 second edition of The Works of Shakespear was a supplementary Volume IX in which Oldcastle was printed. Jacob Tonson came out with a single-volume edition of the play in 1734 (along with separate issues of forty-two other Shakespeare plays, published in this and subsequent years), and produced another issue in 1735. In the same year R. Walker came out with a single-volume edition of Oldcastle, of which only one copy exists. Apparently this was a pirated edition for on the verso of the title page of Tonson's edition there appears a piracy notice by Tonson against Walker.[11] Finally, in 1780 Edmond Malone edited a two-volume supplement for the 1778 Johnson-Steevens edition of Shakespeare's works, in which we find Oldcastle in Volume II.

The Rowe edition is a slightly edited reprint of the text found in the Shakespeare folios. Some attempt is made to expand on incomplete stage directions (vii.195.1), and a few changes from prose to verse are made (iii.66-67; vii.222-24). Rowe is also the first editor to recognize and correct the obvious confusion in the printing of the scenes at the Bell Inn and those with Sir John, Doll, and the Irishman (xvii-xxiv). Evidence suggests Rowe used F4 as he follows that text's unique alterations. For example, Rowe adopts F4's emendations in lineation in scene i, and its change of "old saw:" to "old say." (v.58).

The 1728 Pope edition of Oldcastle is a faithful copy of Rowe's text, with very few emendations. Later editors have followed its relineation to prose of the soldier's speech (iii.39) and relineation to verse of a Cobham speech in the same scene (ll.152-53). The Tonson edition offers no new emendations--only printing errors.

With the publication of Malone's supplement, Oldcastle gets its first thorough going over. In this scholarly edition Malone provides the reader with glossarial and explanatory notes to the text (some of which are attributed to other Shakespeare editors: Farmer, Percy, Reed, and Steevens), and general remarks on the play's authorship and connections with the Henry IV and V plays. Moreover, the text is spruced up. Malone carefully divides the play into acts (five) and scenes, each scene provided with a highly specific scene-heading: Eltham. / An anti-chamber in the palace, Kent. / An outer court before lord Cobham's house. A publick road / leading to it;

and an alehouse appearing at a little distance, and London. / A room in the Axe Inn, without Bishopgate. Most entrances and exits are expanded and clarified so that the reader can easily follow the action. Careful attention is paid to punctuation, lineation, and obscure passages, Malone endeavouring to turn Oldcastle into some readable and uniform whole. His intentions are laudable if overzealous.

Of greater importance is the crucial fact that Malone returns to the "original" edition of Oldcastle, basing his text primarily on this, thus rejecting the easier method of merely modifying a previous edition. The "original," however, was Q2, not Q1, and so all Malone produced was a relatively sound edition of the "Shakespeare" quarto. There is no doubt that Malone's source is Q2 as his text consistently incorporates the variants in Q2. Where he does provide an occasional Q1 reading, this is not due to any first-hand knowledge of Q1; rather it is a correct emendation of a corrupt Q2 reading. An example of this occurs at vii.19. The Q2 reading is "By fortune was to marry,"; Malone emends to the original Q1 "My fortune . . . ", but notes that "all copies concur" with the unemended reading. Obviously Malone never saw, or at least never referred to, a copy of Q1.

In the nineteenth century five editors turn their attention to Oldcastle. All used the Malone text, or an edition based on Malone, as their copy, occasionally (and intentionally) emending to a Q2 reading, or rarely (and unintentionally) emending to a Q1 reading.

In Volume I of The Ancient British Drama in Three Volumes (Edinburgh: James Ballantyne and Co., 1810) the compiler (conjectured to be Sir Walter Scott) provides us with a direct reprint of the 1780 Malone text, and only modernizes the spelling. Later on in the century William Gilmore Simms, the noted American writer and editor, produces his A Supplement to the Plays of William Shakespeare (New York: G.F. Cooledge & brother, 1848). His text is idiosyncratic, Simms allowing himself many creative and wild surmises. One lucky result of his technique comes with his emending the Malone and Q2 "pretensed" to "prepensed" (vi.39). He notes that the old copy has "pretensed," yet feels that "malice prepense or prepensed malice seems most legitimate." As "prepensed" is, in fact, in the original Q1, Simms, on this occasion, comes up with a fortuitously correct emendation.

Henry Tyrrell edits Oldcastle in his The Doubtful Plays of Shakespeare (London and New York: John Tallis and Co., n.d., conj. 1851). In contrast to the eccentric and more valuable Simms text, Tyrrell's edition of the play is an unoriginal modern-spelling reprint of Malone. Tyrrell's notes are taken from Malone and his historical and critical introduction (like Simms' before him) is derivative. William Hazlitt's edition of the play in the familiar-sounding The Doubtful Plays of Shakespeare (London: George Routledge and Sons, Limited) which was printed a number of times between 1852 and 1887, is cursorily edited. Hazlitt, however, does incorporate a few Malone conjectures into his text.

A.F. Hopkinson, the last of the nineteenth-century editors of Oldcastle, is also the last to modernize the spelling of the original, a practice adopted by every previous editor or printer and by none afterwards. In the last years of the century Hopkinson edited the plays of the apocrypha individually and produced his version of our play in 1894 (London: M.E. Sims and Co.). His text is merely a reprint of Tyrrell and Hazlitt, yet his introduction to the play is fresh. He is the first editor to make use of the knowledge gained from Henslowe's Diary that Oldcastle was written by Drayton,

Munday, Wilson, and Hathaway.[12] Indeed he sallies forth (in the tradition of F.G. Fleay) into the murky underworld of authorship and metric analysis, but is aware of the fallibility and limitations of his apportionment of Oldcastle amongst the four collaborators.

In the early twentieth century Oldcastle reached print four times. In 1907 the American scholar John Robertson Macarthur had his dissertation, an old-spelling edition of Oldcastle, published (Chicago: Scott, Foreman and Company). Unfortunately for him he had done all the work before the Greg-Pollard discoveries, and produced a faithful reprint of Q2. His introduction to the play is, of course, the most complete study of Oldcastle written. Here he spends a good deal of time trying to prove that the "Shakespeare" quarto is indeed the original quarto. To his credit, however, he provides the reader with all the "substantive variants" found in the non-Shakespearian quarto. He also discusses the play's sources, authors, and aesthetic qualities. The explanatory notes are useful from an historical or literary viewpoint, but scant attention is paid to dramatic issues.

In 1908 the Malone Society published a reprint of Q1 prepared by Percy Simpson, using as copy text the British Museum (C.34.1.2) and Bodleian (Mal. 768) copies. The text was scrupulously reprinted (I have found only five errors) and Simpson provides the reader with a useful listing of Q1 press variants and doubtful readings, and a collection of the substantive changes in the Q2 text, as well as a list of significant emendations found in the Shakespeare folios and Malone's text. A brief introduction to the play provides the bibliographical background to the Oldcastle text, and refers to the important Greg articles in The Library (1908) which established the correct printing date of the "Shakespeare" quarto and thus Q1's textual superiority over Q2.

In the same year C.F. Tucker Brooke came out with his The Shakespeare Apocrypha (Oxford: Clarendon Press). The text of Oldcastle found there is a critical old-spelling edition of Q1. Emendations in punctuation and lineation are freely made, Brooke incorporating later editions' improvements to Q1. In 1911 Q1 was photographically reproduced for the Tudor Facsimile Texts, John S. Farmer editor.

Oldcastle was once again published in Volume I of The Works of Michael Drayton (Oxford: Shakespeare Head Press, 1931) which was edited by J. William Hebel. The text is a reprint of Q1 though a few emendations are introduced into it. By the time of the printing of Volume V (1941), in which an introduction to the play and glossarial and explanatory notes appear, Hebel had died and Kathleen Tillotson and Bernard H. Newdigate had completed his work.[13] Nothing of great originality appears in the introduction, but much of what has been previously said on the play has been cogently summarized. Collation of five of the seven extant copies of Q1 is provided. Explanatory notes are good, but are more an exercise in compilation than original work.

Finally, William Kozlenko has recently edited the Disputed Plays of Shakespeare (New York: Hawthorn Books Inc., n.d., © 1974) in which we find Oldcastle. His text is a photographic reprint of Tyrrell's with nothing new added.

Oldcastle has been translated into German (three editions) and Danish (one edition). It first appeared in L. Tieck's Vier Schauspiele von Shakspeare (Stuttgart and Tübingen, 1836), then in Volume I of Ernst Ortlepp's compilation of Tieck's and Schlegel's translation of the apocrypha, Nachträge zu Shakspeare's Werken von Schlegel und Tieck (Stuttgart: L.F. Rieger, 1840), and in Heinrich Doring's Supplemente zu allen Ausgaben Shakspeare's sämtlicher Schauspiele (Erfurt: Hennings und Hopf, 1840). In 1913 a Danish translation by A. Halling was printed in Den Lystige Djaevel. Tre pseudo-Shakespeareske Skuespil (Kjobenhavn og Kristiania).

ii. This Edition

This edition is a critical modern-spelling version of 1 Sir John Oldcastle generally based on the editorial format of the Revels Plays. Details of spelling, punctuation, and italicization which do not affect sense, as well as obvious printing errors,[14] are silently emended. Copy text has been a microfilm of the Huntington Library copy of Q1. All other extant copies have been checked for press variants. (See Appendix I for lists of Q1 copies, press variants, and running-titles). Subsequent editions of Oldcastle have been collated but this edition does not supply a variorum collation. Only emendations adopted in my critical edition are noted in the collation notes, as well as important emendations which, while rejected in this text, are considered valid alternatives. All citings are printed as in the original texts, except that archaic i/j, u/v, and long s have been normalized.

The text, as stated above, is a modern-spelling version and archaic forms are only preserved where rhyme or metre requires them or when modernization obscures rather than clarifies the required sense of the word. However, in dialect passages (Welsh-English, Irish-English, and Lancashire-English--see scenes i, xvii-xix, xxi, xxiii-xxiv, xxvii) the practice is to retain the spelling of the original text, modernizing only where pronunciation seems unaffected. Throughout, the "-ed" form is used for non-syllabic terminations and "-èd" for syllabic.

Punctuation is modernized to reflect modern usage. For example, many of Q1's commas habitually placed at the end of a verse line or unnecessarily inserted between phrases or clauses have been eliminated in this edition. Attempts are made, though, to convey the rhetorical or dramatic effect of Q1 where the pointing seems trustworthy. Thus a colon, usually employed in Q1 either for purposes of emphasis or as an indication of a break in speech due to stage action, becomes an exclamation point in the first instance and a period in the second. In the collation notes punctuation is collated when changes involve a decision between alternative interpretations (see, for example, notes for Prologue.12, 13). Occasionally, where usage has changed since the time of an earlier editor, I have adopted the interpretive spirit of an emendation in pointing made by him, but used punctuation conforming to modern usage. In these cases my modified use of the earlier editor's emendation is identified without comment as deriving from him.

Lineation of the text has caused a few problems, primarily because of the indifferent nature of much of the verse in Oldcastle. Thus it is sometimes difficult to tell if an irregular or unrhythmic line set as verse, in a mixed scene of verse and prose, is indeed verse. In a number of scenes characters who normally speak verse are interacting with those who usually speak prose (for example, scenes iii, x, xi, xx); moreover, it would appear that certain characters are present in scenes written by different collaborators, who, of course, may approach these characters from different artistic viewpoints. The upshot of all this is that I have found it very difficult and not especially useful to be rigorously consistent in my lineation of the text.

I have attempted to follow Q1 where possible, emending prose to verse or *vice versa* only where Q1 seems demonstrably wrong, or, in some cases, where Q1's compositor seems to have manipulated his MS copy by "creating" prose or verse so that he could more easily set his type. Variations from Q1's lineation are indicated in the collation notes.

The practice with stage directions is to centre entrances and to place exits on the right, irrespective of their original positioning. Stage directions within speeches are marked off by parentheses. Editorial stage directions are printed in square brackets--[. . .]. Characters' names in stage directions are silently normalized: thus King Harry, Lord Cobham, and Sir John are always preferred over King Henry, Sir John Oldcastle, and Priest. In similar fashion speech headings are silently normalized. Asides are normalized thus--(*Aside*). They are always placed before the aside portion of the speech, irrespective of their position in Q1, and subsequent portions not spoken aside are preceded by (*To them*) or whatever is appropriate.

In this text the scenes are consecutively numbered in square brackets on the left hand side of the page. Line-numbering, in fives, is provided on the right-hand side of the text.

iii. Copy Text

Q1 of *1 Sir John Oldcastle* was printed in the shop of Valentine Simmes.[15] Simmes's press printed a number of Shakespeare quartos and some of the plays put on by the theatre company called the Admiral's Men, as well as other plays and projects. The 1597 and 1598 quartos of *Richard II*, the 1597 *Richard III*, the 1600 *The First Part of the Contention*, *2 Henry IV*, and *Much Ado About*

Nothing, the 1603 Hamlet, the 1604 1 Henry IV, and the 1611 Hamlet were done on the Simmes press. He was also responsible for the printing of the Admiral's Men's 1599 An Humorous Day's Mirth, the 1600 Oldcastle and The Shoemaker's Holiday, the 1604 Doctor Faustus, and the 1604 and 1605 1 Honest Whore. Other plays printed at his shop were the 1599 A Warning for Fair Women, the 1604 The Malcontent, the 1605 How to Choose a Good Wife from a Bad, the 1606 The Gentleman Usher, the 1607 The Taming of a Shrew, and the 1611 1 & 2 The Troublesome Reign of King John.[16]

Bibliographic research into the compositorial and spelling habits of the workmen in Simmes's shop has centred on the Shakespeare quartos. In a 1960 article, "The Compositors of Henry IV, Part 2, Much Ado About Nothing, The Shoemaker's Holiday, and The First Part of the Contention," SB, 13, 19-29, W. Craig Ferguson concluded that one workman, Compositor A, was responsible for all of 2 Henry IV and Much Ado, most of The Contention, and part of Holiday. For Ferguson the crucial identifying mark of Compositor A's work was his unique habit of not stopping unabbreviated speech headings, a compositorial quirk found only in Simmes-shop quartos. Alan E. Craven in a 1973 article "Simmes' Compositor A and Five Shakespeare Quartos," SB, 26, 37-60, concluded that all of the 1603 Hamlet was the work of Compositor A, identifying him through his preferential use of unabbreviated unstopped speech headings. Moreover, in the 1597 quarto of Richard II, Craven used this trait as the crucial distinguishing mark between the two workmen responsible for the play's printing.[17]

Analysis of the speech headings in Oldcastle shows that of 392 unabbreviated speech headings 353 are unstopped while only 39 are stopped. Unabbreviated unstopped speech headings occur on sixty-four of the seventy-six pages of text, and on three of the other twelve pages (B4r, H2v, and H3v) unstopped numbers are used as speech headings. Furthermore, only on C4r do unabbreviated stopped speech headings outnumber the unstopped (three to one), and two of the former, "Dol.", may be abbreviations for "Doll". From such evidence in Oldcastle it seems clear that the 1600 quarto was set by Compositor A.

Oldcastle was set by Compositor A in mid-career, so to speak, along with 2 Henry IV and Much Ado. In these 1600 Shakespeare texts, both substantive and set from manuscript or prompt-book, Ferguson and Craven noted shared compositorial and spelling traits. The dialogue in the plays is all set in roman type, italic being reserved for stage and speech directions. These directions, moreover, are placed on the page in a consistent manner. Spelling analysis also reveals a consistent pattern, as "heart", "eie", and "yong" are consistently preferred over "hart", "eye", and "young", while "-nesse", "do", and "go" are slightly preferred over "-nes", "doe", and "goe".

To a great extent the text of Oldcastle shows the same compositorial and spelling traits. The Oldcastle text has a very similar appearance to that of the Shakespeare plays, and its spelling also conforms to their norms (though a distinct preference for "-nesse" and "do" probably reflects the influence of such a preference in the MS copy).

And what is the manuscript copy for Q1? The evidence indicates that the MS is authorial rather than prompt copy (though some stage directions may be the additions of a playhouse reviser)[18] and that these "foul papers" are in good enough order to have provided the Oldcastle compositor with an acceptable copy.[19]

Primary positive evidence in favour of authorial copy for Q1 and evidence against prompt copy for Q1 is provided by the inconsistencies in characters' names in speech prefixes and stage directions. The Bishop of Rochester, called such in text and stage directions and "Bishop/Bish." in speech headings, becomes "Rochester" and "Roch." in stage directions and speech headings only in the middle of scene xv. Sir John of Wrotham is not only called by his full title but also referred to as "Parson" and "Priest" in the text and stage directions. However, in speech headings we find "Wroth." in scene iv., "Priest" in scene ix, and "Sir John/Sir Iohn" elsewhere. Lord Cobham is referred to in many different ways. In scenes iii, vii, xii, xxii, and xxiii he is denoted by "Cobham/Cobh./Cob.", while in scenes xii, xiv, xxv, and xxvii he is "Old-castle/Old-ca./Oldca./Old." in speech headings. In scene xx he is "L. Cobh." for the only time in the play and in some speeches of scene xiv (11.24, 26, 34, 39) he is confusingly referred to as "Sir Iohn" in the text and one speech heading. Variations in stage directions generally match those in speech headings. King Harry is called "King/king" or "Harry" and once "King Harry" in the text. In the stage directions he is termed "K. Harry/King Harry" in scenes ii, vi, and xvi; "King" in scenes x and xvi; and "Harry" in scene xii. In speech headings "Harry/Har." dominates (see scenes ii, vi, xi and xii, and xvi); but "King" is used consistently in the long scene x, and in the beginning of scene xi (11.0.1, 1, 4, 19) he is uniquely referred to in three speech headings as "K. Hen." and in one stage direction as "King Henry". As in the Cobham/Oldcastle, Sir John/Priest, and Bishop/Rochester cases, there is little confusion created by such inconsistencies in characters' names, yet the consistency of certain names in select scenes indicates a manuscript reflecting the collaborators' particular ways of designating characters (and so can be an aid in determining who wrote what), rather than a manuscript reflecting the prompt-copy quality of homogeneity.

It is possible that such variations would be acceptable in prompt-copy;[20] however, as can be seen from the evidence above and that to follow, the possibility is remote. Additional proof of the non-prompt-copy nature of Q1 exists in the following indefinite or permissive stage directions found in Oldcastle, which surely could not have appeared in prompt-copy: Enter Harpoole and the rest (vii.195.1--"the rest" including two characters never met before); Exeunt (xii.136.1--the stage direction should, in fact, refer to only certain people on stage); They rise from the table, and the King steps / in to them with his Lordes (xvi.25.1-2--only one lord having been mentioned in the scene-opening stage direction). There are also other instances in Q1 where there are no entrance or exit directions (see my editorial additions iii.76, iii.155, iii.174, iv.89, vii.188, xiv.19.1, and so forth).

Q1 is plagued by a number of truly confused episodes that would have been unacceptable in prompt-copy but would have been inevitable in foul papers composed by four writers. For example, it is difficult to tell whether Doll is present during scene x when Sir John robs King Harry. In scene xi, when King Harry recalls the robbery, he says Doll was present, and as well provides other details of the robbery that do not coincide with the scene x action.[21] Another good example is to be found in the Bell Inn scenes, where the events are hectic and, at one point, bewildering. At xxiv.32-33 the Mayor orders the Watch to "keepe fast that traiterous rebell his seruant there," meaning Cobham's servant. This must refer either to the Irishman, who is dressed as Harpool, or to Harpool disguised as the Irishman. The first alternative is impossible, for the Irishman was escorted offstage by the Mayor and others at the end of scene xxi and it would have been very confusing, as well as ludicrous, for the Mayor to have brought the Irishman back on stage. The second interpretation is equally absurd for the Mayor cannot know that Harpool is anyone but the Irishman whom he and the others captured in the preceding scene. The problem with Harpool continues in the last scene of the play when the servant, still in disguise, is in the same courtroom with Lord and Lady Cobham and all are accused of the same crime! In all these cases something consistent must have been presented to the original Oldcastle audience and, presumably, there must have been a prompt-book used by the Rose theatre's Admiral's Men that provided the acting company with a consistent version of Oldcastle; yet such a prompt-book did not serve as Compositor A's copy.

The one possible weakness in this argument is that a number of entrance or exit directions are oddly placed in the Q1 text a line or two above or below where one would expect to see them.[22] One could interpret some of the early entrance directions as pointing to the presence of prompt-copy characteristics; on this view, the directions are prompter's anticipations needed to warn the actors when to enter, but I believe that the more probable and compelling explanation for these irregularities is that Compositor A placed such stage directions wherever there was enough space to set them. All premature or haphazardly placed stage directions can be explained in this fashion. Indeed still other explanations are available for the odd placement of these directions. They could be the cursory additions of a playhouse reviser, an actor, or another author, or they could simply be authorial in nature. Because the evidence can lead plausibly to varying interpretations, such directions have not been treated with the customary respect given to authorial stage directions. Finally, the substantial length of Oldcastle, and each of the individual scenes, does not indicate that Q1 has been heavily cut, another quality of prompt-copy and texts based on them.[23]

In conclusion it can be stated with some authority that Q1 of Oldcastle was set from authorial manuscript. This MS is a good example of "foul papers" despite the problems in copy that theoretically could afflict a play written by four hands. A further conclusion is that Compositor A, an experienced worker for the Simmes press, noted for his idiosyncratic manner of not pointing unabbreviated speech headings, apparently set the whole of Q1.

[1] Plays such as Sir Thomas More, Edward III, The Yorkshire Tragedy, etc., attributed at one time or another to Shakespeare.

[2] Edward Arber, ed., A Transcript of the Registers of the Company of Stationers of London; 1554-1640 A.D., III (London : Privately Printed, 1876), 169.

[3] One possible reference to 2 Oldcastle was collected by W.W. Greg, A Bibliography of the English Printed Drama to the Restoration, III (London: Oxford University Press, 1957), 1348. In Kirkman's Catalogue (a bookseller's list) there is the listing: "Will. Shakespeare / Old castles life and death. / H". It would seem that Kirkman is merely referring to the 1 Oldcastle quarto which has "Written by William Shakespeare" on its title page. There is, however, the unlikely possibility that Kirkman possessed a copy of 2 Oldcastle, the part which deals with Cobham's death, his martyrdom.

[4] Greg, Bibliography of English Printed Drama, III, 1537-38, 1545.

[5] See Greg, "On Certain False Dates in Shakespearian Quartos," The Library, NS 9 (1908), 113-31, 381-409; and Pollard, Shakespeare Folios and Quartos (London: Methuen and Co., 1909), pp. 81-103.

[6] More recent bibliographical research further proved that these nine plays were printed upon a single mixed batch of paper containing a great variety of watermarks, Allan H. Stevenson noting that Oldcastle was printed on old paper dated "1608". ("Shakespearian dated Watermarks," SB, 4 [1951-52], 159-64.)

[7] Others were Pericles, The London Prodigal, The History of Thomas Lord Cromwell, The Puritan Widow, A Yorkshire Tragedy, and Locrine.

[8] Mac., p. 15.

[9] Unless otherwise stated, references such as these use the scene and line-numbering of my edition of Oldcastle.

[10] Mac., p. 15.

[11] William Jaggard, Shakespeare Bibliography (Stratford-on-Avon: The Shakespeare Press, 1911), p. 451.

[12] Malone, in his 1790 edition of Shakespeare, noted the reference in the Diary to Oldcastle in a section called "Emendations and Additions" (I Part 2, 317-18, 320). Malone does not venture into authorship analysis.

[13] Henceforth this edition of Drayton's works will be referred to as "Hebel."

[14] E.g., "imperfection" (xxv.61) and "bloody" (xxvii.74) are "imperfectoin" and "boudy" in Q1.

[15] According to H.R. Plomer in "The Printers of Shakespeare's Plays and Poems," The Library, NS 7 (1906), 153-55, Simmes was an Oxfordshire man who came to London in 1576 and worked as an apprentice to bookseller Henry Sutton. Simmes then switched to the printing side of the booktrade and eventually became a compositor. His career was chequered and eventful. He was arrested and thrown in the Tower of London in 1589 for being the compositor for the Martin Marprelate press. He established his own office at the sign of the White Swan in 1594, and the next year his press was seized for his printing of the "Grammar" and the "Accidence." He set himself up again but had more brushes with the law till finally in 1622 he was forbidden to work as a master printer.

[16] Greg, Bibliography of English Printed Drama, III, 1545.

[17] My investigation of speech headings in two non-Shakespearian Simmes quartos, An Humorous Day's Mirth and A Warning for Fair Women, reveals that primary positive evidence for the work of Compositor A is lacking in An Humorous, while the evidence seems to show that A Warning was divided up by two compositors (A and someone else) in the same fashion as Richard II.

[18] In Act Division in Elizabethan and Jacobean Plays 1583-1616 (Hamden, Conn.: The Shoe String Press, 1958), p. 221, Wilfred T. Jewkes has this to say about Oldcastle: "On the whole the text looks as if it were prepared from an authorial manuscript which had been prepared by a stage adapter or prompter for performance and from which the prompt-book had probably been transcribed." In his opinion some marginal stage directions (see vi.38, xi.39, and xxv.22.1) "are more clearly the type added by prompters or stage adapters" (p. 221). If Jewkes is right the stage adapter's preparation is minimal and perfunctory.

[19] W.W. Greg defines "foul papers" in The Shakespeare First Folio (Oxford: Clarendon Press, 1955), p. 106, as a rough draft "representing the play more or less as the author intended it to stand, but not itself clear enough to serve as a prompt-book."

[20] But this would not affect authorship analysis using the variations in names as part of its data, for the consistent inconsistency of the original authorial MS can still be detected in such a supposed prompt-copy.

[21] Also see explanatory note for x.33.1.

[22] For example see ii.26.1, ii.51, vii.80.1, xii.50.1, xvii.19.1, and xxi.21.

[23] Greg, The Shakespeare First Folio, p. 145.

CHAPTER TWO

Sources

The Oldcastle dramatists based their version of the story of the late fourteenth century and early fifteenth century Lollard Lord Cobham on two popular sixteenth century historical sources: Raphael Holinshed's Chronicles (1587) and John Foxe's Acts and Monuments (1563--first English edition), which was commonly called The Book of Martyrs.[1] Edited selections from these two works can be found in Appendices II and III.[2] These sources contain references to most of the events in the Cobham affair, as well as to other events of Henry V's reign used in 1 Sir John Oldcastle: the Ficket Field rebellion and the Cambridge conspiracy. Yet while the Oldcastle dramatists depend mainly on secondary historical sources, one can also discern in the play their significant dependence on a different kind of "historical" source--the history plays of Shakespeare. Certain incidents, characters, and turns of phrase are borrowed from Henry V and the two Henry IV plays. Thus study of the sources shows that Oldcastle is not just a straight dramatization of historical incidents but a slightly more complicated and self-conscious play, using (or perhaps abusing) Shakespearian touches for its own ends.

Holinshed is a comprehensive but not necessarily indispensible or unique source for the historical information dramatized in scenes ii, v, vii, viii, x, xii, xiii, xiv-xv, and xx-xxiv of Oldcastle. The chronicler begins his discussion of the Cobham controversy with his mention of the accusation of heresy laid by the Archbishop of Canterbury against the Lollard knight and presented to Henry V (see 11.1-5). The chronicle continues and we read of the king's original sympathy for Cobham as well as the subsequent meeting between the king and Cobham (11.5-14), events which are dramatized in scenes ii and vi. Cobham's imprisonment, examination and escape from the Tower of London are quickly sketched in Holinshed (11.15-26), and may be a general source for the Bishop's securing of Cobham's warrant in scene xiii as well as for the Tower scenes, xiv-xv. Holinshed's discussion of Cobham's near capture at St. Albans and the finding of the heretical books in English (11.152-166) are probably sources for two quite separate scenes in Oldcastle: the brief episode at the end of scene xiii where Clun, the Sumner, comes in bearing various English works both sacred and profane, as well as the Bell Inn scenes at St. Albans, xx-xxiv, where the Mayor, Constable, and Watch nab everyone in town except the good Lord Cobham. Finally, Holinshed details Cobham's capture on Lord Powis' lands and his summary execution (11.173-187), incidents which were surely treated in 2 Oldcastle.

Holinshed describes the events of the Ficket Field rebellion at some length. He mentions the leaders Sir Roger Acton, John Brown, and John Beverley, assesses their support, outlines King Henry's expeditious quelling of the rebellion, provides the anecdote of William Murley, the brewer who hoped to be knighted, and points out the supposed part that Lord Cobham played in the debacle, including the accusations made by the rebels that Cobham was their captain (11.27-70). The Holinshed account of the aborted rebellion, then, is the most convenient source for the Oldcastle collaborators' treatment of the rebellion in scenes v, viii, x, xi, and xii. Also, Holinshed's overall perspective of the affair, that a rebellion was, indeed, intended but that Cobham's participation is debatable, more closely matches the Oldcastle interpretation of events than does John Foxe's sarcastic conclusion in his Book of Martyrs that the whole event was much ado about nothing and that a rebellion was probably never planned or enacted (see Foxe, 11.262-274).

The story of the Cambridge conspiracy as set out by Holinshed, including his judicious weighing of the causes for the plot--the French bribery of Cambridge, Gray and Scroop, and Cambridge's belief in his rightful claim to the throne (11.90-121; 131-149) are effectively dramatized in scenes vii and xvi of Oldcastle.

The other primary historical source, Foxe's discussion of Cobham in his Book of Martyrs, is nothing more than a lightly edited version of John Bale's earlier Brief Chronicle of Sir John Oldcastle. The dramatists share with Foxe and Bale the sympathetic view that Cobham is loyal to King Harry and suffers unjustly through rumour and episcopal hatred. I believe, though, that the Oldcastle authors used not Bale's work but the more popular and readily accessible Book of Martyrs.[3] In support of this view we may note that we find in Foxe, alone, a clearly stated position on Cobham's "treason" (11. 217-279; 326-353) that the Oldcastle writers explicitly defend:

> As touching the pretensed treason of this lord Cobham, [it was] falsely ascribed unto him in his indictment, rising upon wrong suggestion and false surmise, and aggravated by rigour of words, rather than upon any ground of due probation . . . .

The historical details of the Cobham story as well as certain aspects of the Ficket Field rebellion sketched in by Holinshed are fleshed out in Foxe. All or parts of scenes i, ii, iii, iv, vi, and xiv-xv could have been based on references in Foxe's narrative. For example, it is Foxe who points out at length the accusation laid against Cobham for aiding rebellion in Hereford, as well as in Rochester and London (11.12-21), and it is probably this detail that serves as the source for the Lord Herbert-Lord Powis brawl in scene i. At greater length than Holinshed, Foxe writes about Henry V's original sympathy for Cobham and their meeting and conversation (11.34-55), and Foxe's account is the primary source for scenes ii and vi. Significantly, one notices direct and specific borrowing from Foxe in King Harry's reply to the Bishop in scene ii as well as in the King's and Cobham's conversation in scene vi. Foxe writes:

> The king gently heard those blood-thirsty prelates, and far otherwise than became his princely dignity: notwithstanding requiring, and instantly desiring them, that in respect of his noble stock and knighthood, they should yet favourably deal with him; and that they would, if it were possible, without all rigour or extreme handling, reduce him again to the church's unity. He promised them also, that in case they were contented to take some deliberation, he himself would seriously commune the matter with him.
>
> Anon after, the king sent for the said lord Cobham . . . Unto whom the christian knight made this answer: " . . . Unto you, next my eternal God, owe I my whole obedience, and submit thereunto, as I have done ever, all that I have, either of fortune or nature, ready at all times to fulfil whatsoever ye shall in the Lord command me. But, as touching the pope and his spiritualty, I owe them neither suit nor service, forasmuch as I know him, by the Scriptures, to be the great Antichrist, the son of perditon, the open adversary of God, and the abomination standing in the holy place."

The summoning of Cobham first by an episcopal summoner and second by John Butler, Henry V's doorkeeper of the Privy Chamber, discussed at some length in Foxe (11.58-85), is the basis for the Oldcastle episodes where Butler successfully summons Cobham to the king at the end of scene iii and where the Sumner comically fails to get past Cobham's servant, Harpool, in scene iv.[4] Foxe, like Holinshed, briefly mentions Cobham's escape from the Tower of London (11.209-213), and Foxe may be a general source for scenes xiv-xv.

Foxe also discusses the issue of the Ficket Field rebellion (11.197-209) but does not provide the same straightforward blow-by-blow account of the rebellion as Holinshed. Foxe does not detail any of Henry V's precautions on the eve of the rebellion nor does he mention the character of William Murley. Still, the dramatists responsible for writing the rebellion scenes adopt Foxe's attitude that Cobham is innocent.

The martyrologist retells the story of Cobham's eventual capture and execution (11.289-325) in greater detail than Holinshed. Obviously such discussion served as a basis for many scenes in 2 Oldcastle, but Foxe's emphasis on the motivation behind Lord Powis' taking of his friend Lord Cobham was probably used by the Oldcastle collaborators in their portrayal of Lord Powis in Part 1. The following critical explanation of Powis' actions by Foxe may help to explain the Oldcastle Powis' cowardly exit from scene i and his fearful quaking at the mention of the king's name by Harpool in scene iii:

> About the end of which four years being expired, the lord Powis, whether for love and greediness of the money, or whether for hatred of the true and sincere doctrine of Christ, seeking all manner of ways how to play the part of Judas, and outwardly pretending him great amity and favour, at length obtained his bloody purpose, and most cowardly and wretchedly took him, and in conclusion brought the lord Cobham bound up to London . . . .

There exist, beside Foxe and Holinshed, a number of historical treatments of the Cobham material. Robert Fabyan in his Chronicles (1516), Robert Hall in his Chronicle (1548), and John Stow in his Chronicle (1580) and his Annals (1592) discuss many of the historical details found in Holinshed. Samuel Daniel in The Civil Wars and John Hayward in The First Part of the Life and Reign of King Henry the Fourth (1599) discuss the Cambridge rebellion. The Mirror of Martyrs by John Weever is a verse version of the Cobham story as set out in the chronicles. It was published in 1601 but written, as the author says in his dedication, "some two yeares agoe" (that is, at the same time as Oldcastle was being written and performed). But only few details incorporated into Oldcastle are to be found in these works and not in Holinshed or Foxe. One significant example, which R.E. Bennett noted in "The Parson of Wrotham in Sir John Oldcastle," MLN, 45 (1930), 142-44, is that the character of Sir John probably owes his appearance in a play about a Lollard martyr to Fabyan's mention (p. 583) of Wrotham's imprisonment in Newgate in the same paragraph in which he refers to Cobham's execution:

> This yere [1416-17] sir Iohn̄ Oldcastell, lorde Cobham, . . . was . . . sent vnto London by the lorde Powys out of Walys, the which sir Iohn̄ for heresy and treason was conuict . . . and for the same drawen vnto Seynt Gyles felde, where he was hãged vpon a newe peyer of galowys with chaynes, and after cōsumed with fyre. And aboute that season, the persone of Wortham in Norfolke . . . had haunted Newmarket heth, and there robbyd and spoyled many of ẏͤ kynges subgettes, was nowe with his cōcubyne brought vnto Newgate where he lastly dyed.

A second example concerns the Annals accounts (p. 555) of the details of Cambridge's conspiracy where Stow describes Edmund Mortimer's tricking of the conspirators:

> . . . these [Cambridge and the rest] had made Edmond earle of March to sweare vpon a booke, not to disclose their counsell, and then tolde him that they thought to slay the king, and to make the saide Edmond king, the which if hee refused to take vpon him, they would slay him: whereupon, the earle praied them to giue him one houres space to take aduisement what was best to do, which being graunted, the earle went secretly and tolde the king thereof.

Finally there is an example in John Weever's The Mirror of Martyrs. It is impossible to prove whether Weever used Oldcastle as a source or, conversely, whether the Oldcastle dramatists read Weever's work in MS and were influenced by it.[5] Weever develops the character of Lady Cobham, ignored in the chronicles but dramatized in Oldcastle, and in three stanzas on E3v-E3r describes the entreaties and piteous tears she uses to melt the wrath of the abbot of

St. Albans:

> My men to treate the Abbot now begin,
> My Margarites beauty, streaming on his face,
> Fairnesse no fauour in his sight would win,
> Their wordes no pittie moue, their lookes no grace:
>   Then she gan speake, but spake vnto the wind,
>   Remorse did neuer lodge in clownish mind.
>
> Dumb stood my doue, and wrung her hands, whilst often
> Low kneeling downe, teares from her eies did shower:
> Hard is that hart which beauty cannot soften,
> Yet mourning beautie had on him no power:
>   Although her teares were like his christall beads,
>   Which melted, wash the place whereon he treades.
>
> Still she intreates, and still the pearles round
> Stil through her eies, and wel vpon her face,
> Such hony drops, on roses I haue found,
> When bright Apollo held the morne in chace:
>   But both the charmes, of teares and sugred words,
>   For their release no aide at all afordes.

This roughly parallels the confrontation between Lady Cobham and the Bishop at the beginning of scene xiii as well as Cobham's attempt to comfort his wife later on in the scene. What is distinctive in both the Oldcastle and the Mirror use of the historical event is their dramatic emphasis on Lady Cobham's pitiable situation. Weever then goes on to tell us that Lady Cobham is sent back to Cooling where she dies--an event which could easily occur in 2 Oldcastle. Weever's poem concludes with lines addressed to Hermes, wit, poets, and actors. The reference to actors is unexpected and perhaps suggests that Weever was aware that a play about Cobham was being written and performed. It is tempting to conjecture, then, that the correspondences already noted are more than coincidental.

I have also tracked down a relatively obscure historical source for a detail in scene vii. In this scene Cambridge says that Roger Mortimer's son, Roger, had four offspring--Edmund, Roger, Anne, and Eleanor. As far as I can tell this Roger is only mentioned in The Historie of Cambria (1584), p. 317:

> Roger Mortimer . . . maried Elianor . . . by whom he had issue Roger and Edmond, who both died without issue; and two daughters, Anne maried to Richard Plantagenet Earle of Cambridge; and Elianor . . . who died without issue.[6]

Despite the Oldcastle dramatists' use (evident in such details as these) of various historical sources and their obvious dependence on Holinshed and Foxe, the collaborators are not constrained by their sources and they are not above creating their own history. First of all they invoke poetic licence to fabricate a close relationship between Cobham and Powis out of the brief mention of Lord Powis' part in Cobham's capture noted in Foxe and Holinshed.[7] Secondly, they alter the historical order of Cobham's talk with Henry V and his subsequent summoning first by the Archbishop's summoner and then by John Butler. In Oldcastle the conversation with the king takes place after the summonings (which are also reversed), presumably to show that for the Oldcastle dramatists Cobham is completely loyal to King Harry and blameless in the mistreatment of the Sumner.

The collaborators also tinker with the historical sequence of events when they delay Cobham's imprisonment in the Tower till after the Ficket Field rebellion. They do this so as to make their case for the loyal Cobham as strong as possible by not having an AWOL Cobham wandering the countryside at the same time as the Ficket Field rebellion is underway. The authors also establish an important link between Cobham and the Cambridge conspiracy, a "fact" that has no more status than surmise in Holinshed (11.150-151). With respect to Cambridge's plot, historical time is considerably altered. In Oldcastle the conspiracy takes place at about the same time as the Ficket Field uprising, whereas the chronicles report that the Cambridge affair took place a good year after the Ficket Field revolt. The _Oldcastle_ dramatists adjust the time sequence for dramatic reasons, for they surely want to convey to the audience Cobham's near helplessness in the fact of all this treasonous activity springing up around him and his good name.

As stated earlier, the other primary sources for the _Oldcastle_ collaborators were Shakespeare's _1 & 2 Henry IV_ and _Henry V_. The four dramatists freely pillage these histories for situations, characters, and catch-phrases which presumably had become familiar to theatre-goers. _Oldcastle_'s King Harry, for example, owes a debt to both the strength exemplified by King Henry in _Henry V_ and the playfulness shown by Prince Hal in _1 Henry IV_. As well, Sir John of Wrotham's character slyly recalls the roistering Falstaff of _1 & 2 Henry IV_. But before detailing these and other Shakespearian borrowings I should make some comment about the exact purpose of these allusions.

It is, indeed, difficult to tell whether the _Oldcastle_ authors were transferring such popular dramatic figures as King Henry V to their own play to make their drama more palatable and popular or whether they wished to satirize those Shakespearian elements they borrowed. I suspect that they were doing a bit of both and that they cleverly incorporated these popular figures into their play while archly and self-consciously acknowledging their debt. The effect on an audience, then, would be to make them aware of the Shakespearian connections. Doing so would, perhaps, augment the rivalry between the Admiral's Men who performed _Oldcastle_ at the old Rose Theatre and Shakespeare's Chamberlain's Men who were performing at the new Globe Theatre. In this view the commercial theatre's principle that controversy and rivalry mean good box office would be one reason for the explicit and implicit references to Shakespeare's history plays in almost every scene of _Oldcastle_.

Scene ii of Oldcastle coyly alludes to Henry V, I.ii,[8] where the Archbishop of Canterbury discusses Henry V's claim to the French throne through the female line. Upon hearing Oldcastle's Suffolk say, "The king anon goes to the council-chamber, / There to debate of matters touching France" (ii.46-47), the frequent theatre-goer would realize that the characters in Oldcastle are trying to waylay King Harry before he gets into the Shakespearian scene. A similar type of allusion is the casual reference to the Battle of Shrewsbury by one of the maimed soldiers in scene iii ("Ha, were I but as lusty as I was at the Battle of Shrewsbury."). This allows the Oldcastle dramatists not only to introduce a realistic historical detail but also to connect these soldiers with those whom an audience saw in the dramatized Battle of Shrewsbury of 1 Henry IV.

Scene iv overflows with allusions to Shakespeare's Henry IV and V plays. Harpool's rough handling of the Sumner is very similar to Falstaff's rude treatment of the Chief Justice's servant in 2 Henry IV, I.ii. Steevens (Mal., p. 288) indicates the resemblance between Harpool forcing the Sumner to eat the summons and Fluellen making Pistol eat a leek in Henry V, V.i, and Poins threatening Falstaff with eating a letter steeped in sack in 2 Henry IV, II.ii. In the alehouse section of scene iv (ll.121-152) the "courtship" of Harpool and Doll owes something to Falstaff and Doll Tearsheet's conversation in the long tavern scene in 2 Henry IV, II.iv.258-63:

> Fal. Thou dost give me flattering busses.
> Doll. By my troth, I kiss thee with a most constant heart.
> Fal. I am old, I am old.
> Doll. I love thee better than I love e'er a scurvy young boy of them all.

Steevens (Mal., p. 292) also notes that Doll's speech, "I pledge you, sir, . . . and I pray you let it come" (ll.140-41), could be alluding to Silence's song, "Fill the cup, and let it come," in 2 Henry IV, V.ii.52.

The fight between Harpool and Sir John that concludes Oldcastle's scene iv cleverly recalls the many fight scenes in the Henry IV and V plays. The abusive language employed by the Oldcastle brawlers ("old fornicator", "whoreson stoned vicar", "old stale ruffian, you lion of Cotswold"--11.156, 161-62) is reminiscent of Hal and Falstaff insulting each other in 1 Henry IV, II.iv. 128, 133, 235-38):

> Prince. How now, woolsack! . . .
>
> Prince. Why, you whoreson round man, . . .
>
> Prince. This sanguine coward, this bed-presser, this horse-back-breaker, this huge hill of flesh . . .
>
> Fal. 'Sblood, you starveling, you eel-skin, you dried neat's tongue, you bull's pizzle, you stock-fish--. . .

The hurly-burly calls for peace in Oldcastle (11.164-67) are reminiscent of the Hostess' pleas during the Falstaff-Pistol scrap in 2 Henry IV, II.iv.194-97:

> Host. Here's a goodly tumult! I'll forswear keeping house afore I'll be in these tirrits and frights. So; murder, I warrant now. Alas, alas! put up your naked weapons, put up your naked weapons.

And, finally, the reconciliation of Harpool and Sir John, when Sir John whispers to Doll that he has plenty of "crowns" and the combatants quickly shake hands (11.177-82), recalls the peace established after the Nym-Pistol fight in Henry V, II.i.99-110:

> Bard[olph]. Corporal Nym, an thou wilt be friends, be friends; an thou wilt not, why then be enemies with me too. Prithee put up.
> Nym. I shall have my eight shillings I won of you at betting?

> *Pist*. A noble shalt thou have, and present pay;
> And liquor likewise will I give to thee,
> And friendship shall combine, and brotherhood.
> I'll live by Nym and Nym shall live by me.
> Is not this just? For I shall sutler be
> Unto the camp, and profits will accrue.
> Give me thy hand.

At the end of scene vii (11.204-216) Cobham's hasty exit, his urging Lady Cobham not to stop him, and his conversation with Harpool about his horse recall *1 Henry IV*, II.iii, where Hotspur prepares to go to Wales, asks his wife not to prevent him, and discusses with a servant the horse on which he will ride. One wonders how strong a connection the *Oldcastle* collaborators wished to establish, for if the audience was quick or interested enough they could either appreciate the irony or wonder at the inappropriateness of linking the rebel Hotspur going off to join Mortimer and the rest of the rebels with the loyal Cobham going off to warn the king of the treasonous plans of a relative of Mortimer.

Shakespeare's *Henry IV* and *V* plays are explicitly alluded to in scene x where Sir John robs King Harry. Both characters refer to Falstaff, Poins, and Peto, companions of King Harry (or rather Shakespeare's Prince Hal) in his wild oats days (x.52-55; 81-83):

> Where the devil are all my old thieves that were wont to keep this walk? Falstaff the villain is so fat he cannot get on's horse, but methinks Poins and Peto should be stirring hereabouts.
>
> How? Because he once robbed me before I fell to the trade myself, when that foul villainous guts that led him to all that roguery was in's company there--that Falstaff.

There are also numerous details in scene x that are reminiscent of situations and speeches from the Shakespeare plays. King Harry is in disguise when Sir John waylays him, or at least his kingly accoutrements are covered up. In *Henry V*, IV.i, the king borrows Sir Thomas Erpingham's cloak so that he can mingle unknown among his soldiers, and it is probable that *Oldcastle*'s King Harry also uses a cloak as a disguise. The parallels between the scenes seem intentional, the *Oldcastle* collaborators evoking the memory of Henry V stalking the soldiers' camp on the eve of Agincourt with their Harry, here and in scene xi, preparing to meet the rebels at Ficket Field.

Sir John's highwayman cry (x.34), "Stand, trueman, says a thief," is not an uncommon expression but the authors may be alluding to Falstaff's description of Poins in *1 Henry IV*, I.ii.105-106, "This is the most omnipotent villain that ever cried 'Stand' to a true man." King Harry's later playful and knowing reply (x.65), "Yes, that I am, and one of his chamber," to Sir John's query, "Art thou one of the king's servants?" seems a coy adaptation of Henry V's response, "Under Sir Thomas Erpingham," to Will's question, "Under what captain serve you?" in *Henry V*, IV.i.93-94. In both instances the kings are in disguise and both questioners are ignorant of this. In the very next speech of *Oldcastle* (ll.67-68) Sir John asks King Harry if "thou might'st get a poor thief his pardon," a speech that recalls Falstaff's in *1 Henry IV*, I.ii.60, where the fat knight tells Hal, "Do not thou, when thou art king, hang a thief." The conversation in scene x continues and Sir John and King Harry discuss Prince Hal's misspent youth. Sir John also complains that he was robbed by both Hal and Falstaff, alluding, no doubt, to the robbery scene at Gadshill in *1 Henry IV*. Finally, Sir John's breaking of an angel as "a token betwixt thee and me" (l.104) is one more example of the *Oldcastle* authors adapting familiar Shakespearian episodes for their own ends: the episode recalls *Henry V*, IV.i, in which the soldier Will gives his gage to King Henry so they will recognize each other.

Shakespearian allusions continue unabated in scene xi. King Harry tells the lords (11.19-20) "you do know of old / That I have been a perfect night-walker" referring to Henry V's walking among his soldiers in Henry V. As "night-walker" also meant "thief" (OED), a sly allusion to Hal's thieving in 1 Henry IV is also probable. The dumb joke on "cracked French crowns" in Oldcastle (11.74-75) was obviously a pun that every Elizabethan playwright fell prey to, but its presence in the play may recall King Henry's speech in Henry V, IV.i.222-23: "Indeed, the French may lay twenty French crowns to one they will beat us, for they bear them on their shoulders."

The exchange between King Harry and Acton in scene xii concerning Acton's claim that he rebelled because "my conscience urged me to it" (1.9) has a general link with King Henry's "conscience" soliloquy in Henry V, IV.i, as well as a more specific connection with Hotspur's Battle of Shrewsbury speech in 1 Henry IV, V.ii.86-89:

> An if we live, we live to tread on kings;
> If die, brave death, when princes die with us!
> Now, for our consciences, the arms are fair,
> When the intent of bearing them is just.

The Oldcastle collaborators are also borrowing from King Henry's long and complex speech to the Cambridge conspirators in Henry V, II.ii, when they have their King Harry lament the perfidy of conspirators. King Harry's outburst (xii.121-24), with its emphasis on the corrupting power of French gilt rather than on Cambridge's claim to the throne, may also show that the Oldcastle authors had in mind the Chorus speech in Act II of Henry V where "the gilt of France" (1.26) is highlighted. As Macarthur notes (p. 43) Oldcastle's scene xvi, where King Harry surprises the Cambridge conspirators, also borrows from Henry V, II.ii, and King Harry's long speech (11.27-49) again recalls King Henry's even longer speech although the Shakespearian original is far more philosophical than King Harry's pointedly sarcastic reply.

One feature of Oldcastle that recalls Henry V in a somewhat less specific way is the use of regional accents; the collaborators seem to be aping Shakespeare's exploitation of comic accents--unless they are simply showcasing the Admiral's Men's mimicking talents.[9]

Scene xix in Oldcastle, as Macarthur points out (pp. 43-44), is an abbreviated version of 1 Henry IV, II.i. The waiting for the Ostler and the topics of conversation between Club and the Ostler (horses and the weather) are reminiscent of the Shakespearian Carriers waiting for the Ostler to appear and Gadshill and Chamberlain's conversation. Steevens notes (Mal., p. 354) the similar complaints made against inn-fleas by both 2. Carrier in 1 Henry IV, II.i.13-14, and Club in scene xxiv.2-3.

The last major borrowing from the Henry IV and V plays comes in scene xxv. There a pastoral interlude, where Lord Cobham rests his head in Lady Cobham's lap, climaxes with the Lady's poetic speech (ll.57-70). Macarthur indicates (pp. 43-44) that the Oldcastle episode has a model in Glendower's speech to Mortimer in 1 Henry IV, III.i.213-21:

> She bids you on the wanton rushes lay you down,
> And rest your gentle head upon her lap,
> And she will sing the song that pleaseth you,
> And on your eyelids crown the god of sleep,
> Charming your blood with pleasing heaviness,
> Making such difference twixt wake and sleep
> As is the difference between day and night
> The hour before the heavenly-harness'd team
> Begins his golden progress in the east.

These numerous examples of explicit and implicit allusion to the Henry IV and V plays make clear that the Oldcastle collaborators did not hesitate to use Shakespeare's plays either to improve their own or to spice it up. It has to be granted, though, that the majority of Elizabethan plays were written quickly and perfunctorily: dramatists such as the Oldcastle collaborators often drew upon a limited set of stock characters, situations and catch-phrases. Thus close reading of Oldcastle, coupled with a knowledge of plays contemporary with it, shows the Oldcastle dramatists not only consciously utilizing historical sources and the Henry IV and V plays, but also consciously or unconsciously borrowing from or reflecting many other plays of the period. Such an osmotic process is inevitable and, probably, necessary in the commercial theatre, where last week's popular play is fair game for both the imitators and the rivals.

Over the years editors and critics have pointed out the resemblances between stock characters or situations in many other plays of the period and those in Oldcastle. The most extensive of these studies is Macarthur's comparison (pp. 44-48) of Oldcastle with the 1599 edition of George Peele's Edward I. He claims that many of the incidents and speeches in the Sir John parts of Oldcastle have been lifted from the recently published Peele play. He makes a case for his position, though he conveniently ignores the evidence that the Henry IV and V plays are also a major influence on the Oldcastle writers. In Peele's play there is a Friar Hugh ap David who has a wench, Guenthia. Twice the Friar fights with the Prince of Wales (B2r, F2v), once when the Prince is in disguise (B2r). By playing dice the Friar cheats a farmer out of his hundred marks, but then King Edward intercedes on the farmer's behalf (G4v-H2r). A few of the Friar's speeches in Edward I generally resemble the outbursts of Sir John in scenes x and xi: "My maisters and frends, I am a poore Friar, a man of Gods making, and a good fellow as you are" (B4r); "Mines for my owne turne I warrant, giue him his Tooles, rise and lets to it, but no charge an if you loue me, I skorne the oddes I can tel you, see fair play and you be Gentlemen" (F2v).

Other, somewhat less detailed analogue and source studies also reveal the age's shared conventions. In his Studien über Shakespeare's Wirkung auf Zeitgenössische Dramatiker (1905; rpt. Vaduz: Uranus Reprint Ltd., 1963), p. 88, E. Koeppel notes the similarity of Dogberry's mangling of English in Much Ado About Nothing to that of Oldcastle's Constable. R.S. Forsythe in "Certain Sources of Sir John Oldcastle," MLN, 26 (1911), 104-107, details various similarities between Oldcastle and the Henry VI plays. He compares scene i with 1 Henry VI, I.iii, where the Bishop of Winchester bars Gloucester and his servants from entering the Tower and the Lord Mayor enters reading the riot act in an attempt to pacify the fighters. He also compares Oldcastle's first Cambridge conspiracy scene (vii) with 2 Henry VI, II.ii, where York, son of Oldcastle's Cambridge, speaks to Salisbury and Warwick about his claims to the throne. He likens scene vii to Cade's first entrance in 2 Henry VI, IV.ii, and scene xxv to Cade's seeking refuge in Iden's garden in 2 Henry VI, IV.x. William Creizenach (The English Drama in the Age of Shakespeare [Philadelphia: J.B. Lippincott Company; London: Sidgwick & Jackson, Limited, 1916], p. 291), points out the tendency for jovial characters to speak in set phrases and indicates the shared popularity of such citizen figures as brewer William Murley in Oldcastle, Simon Eyre in The Shoemaker's Holiday, Old Curtis in Captain Thomas Stukeley, the Host in The Merry Wives of Windsor, and the Host in The Merry Devil of Edmonton.[10] Hebel (V, 45, 48) thinks Oldcastle's scene i recalls the opening fight sequence in Romeo and Juliet, and that the beggars of scene iii are indebted to those in Sir Thomas More. He believes there are resemblances between Murley, Betts the Clown of Sir Thomas More, and Jack Cade of 2 Henry VI, but he does not elaborate on this. He also finds similarities in tone and situation between the Cobham-Lady Cobham dialogue in scene xxv and the scenes between Robin Hood and Marion in The Downfall and The Death of Robert Earl of Huntington. Again Hebel does not elaborate with specific examples but here is an illustrative excerpt from Downfall (B1r):

> Rob. I like thy counsell. Marian, cleare these clouds,
> And with thy sunny beames of thy brighe eyes,
> Drink up these mistes of sorrowe that arise.
> Mar. How can I ioy, when thou art banished?

Continuing the hunt for resemblances, of course, merely serves to emphasize the obvious fact that the Oldcastle collaborators strove not for original but for conventional effects. However, I have rooted out other resemblances, borrowings, or outright steals in Oldcastle. Certainly as a dramatic pattern the comic ending of 1 Oldcastle, to be followed, assuredly, by a tragic conclusion to 2 Oldcastle, has a most obvious model in the Huntington plays on which Anthony Munday worked. Also, the costume switchings that dominate the scenes at the Tower of London (xiv-xv) and the Bell Inn (xx-xxiv) seem a voguish way of dramatizing vaguely historical events, and the dramatists probably introduced them into Oldcastle because of the popularity of just such scenes. Such switchings are sophisticatedly presented in the Henry IV and V histories and in The Merry Wives of Windsor and As You Like It. They are also the central motivating factor in the anonymous Admiral's Men comedy Look About You, and are either parodied or simply botched in those contemporary comedies, The Wisdom of Doctor Dodypoll and The Maid's Metamorphosis, performed by the new boys' companies.

One scene from Richard II--II.iii--seems to have made an impression on the Oldcastle collaborators when they wrote scene vii. In the Shakespeare play Northumberland, along with Bolingbroke and his forces, refers to their trip to Berkeley Castle as "beguiled" (1.11), an adjective used by Oldcastle's Cambridge (1.75) to describe the conspirator's trip to Cooling and Lord Cobham's castle. Northumberland also describes Ross and Willoughby when they enter as "bloody with spurring, fiery-red with haste" (1.58) which is recalled by Cobham's entrance (1.80.1).

Creizenach's discussion of the jovial citizen who speaks in catch-phrases and his inclusion of Murley in his treatment (noted above p. 37) is sensible enough but somewhat limiting because he ignores another character from The Merry Devil of Edmonton, Sir John, the Priest, who speaks a lingo that Oldcastle's Murley would surely understand: "Hem, Grasse and hay, we are all mortall, let's liue till we die and be merry and theres an end" (C1r-C1v).

In The Three Ladies of London (1584) there is a reference to the tendency of brewers to be stingy with their malt and plentiful with their water (Diiir). While such remarks were probably commonplace, one could conjecture that this complaint, also made by the Ficket Field rebels at the end of scene v, ("Was never bankrupt brewer yet but one, / With using too much malt, too little water.") is characteristic of the Robert Wilson who collaborated on Oldcastle and possibly wrote The Three Ladies.

There are also more conscious and unconscious borrowings from Anthony Munday's The Downfall and The Death of Robert Earl of Huntington and John a Kent and John a Cumber. In Downfall the Prior bribes Warman with a hundred crowns, "For your good will and furtherance in this" (A4r), a situation similar to the Bishop's gift-giving in scene ii of Oldcastle. A later scene in Downfall that begins with the Prior, Doncaster, and Friar Tuck conversing about Robin Hood's fate (F2r) is similar to scene ii where the Bishop, Suffolk, Butler, and Sir John discuss the charges to be laid against Cobham.

The last scene of Downfall, where everyone exits except for the "actors" Sir John Eltham and Skelton, is curiously echoed in the final scene of 1 Oldcastle where, unnaturally, Lord Powis and Lord Cobham are left on stage to wrap up the play.

In Death there are a few details that seem to have been adopted in Oldcastle. King Harry's desire in scene xi for his men, Suffolk and Huntington, to refrain from calling him by his royal name has a probable model in Prince John telling Scathlock to call him "plaine Iohn" (A2v) or King Richard having to pay a penalty to Friar Tuck for calling Robin Hood by his title (B3v-B4r). Hanging in chains seems to have been in theatrical vogue not only in 2 Oldcastle where, presumably, Cobham suffers his final punishment, but also in Death where Doncaster suffers a similar fate.

There are some slightly out of the ordinary phrases in John a Kent that appear in Oldcastle and which might show a Munday influence in the latter play. Turnop's speech (Fol. 8b, ll.1056-58) is the most noteworthy: " . . . harke ye Sir, I neuer kist wench or playd the good fellowe, as sometimes ye knowe fleshe & bloode will be frayle, but my wife hath knowen on it ere I came home . . . ." Sir John's discussion of his own good-fellowship and frailty in various speeches in Oldcastle may owe something to Munday's Turnop. Earlier on in John a Kent there are a couple of phrases, "Then Madame, to omit all ambages" (Fol. 4a, l.1419), and "Leaue me awhyle, to gratulate your feast" (Fol. 5a, l.520) that may help prove that there is a Munday influence in scene xxvii where "ambages" (l.89) and "gratulate" (l. 154) are employed.

The foregoing detailed source analysis of Oldcastle, admittedly a play of limited quality and historical importance, might seem to be a good example of critical overkill; but I would argue that such an investigation vindicates and throws light on the useful critical truism that in the Elizabethan era playwright and audience stood in a fascinatingly productive relation to each other. In tracing the allusions that Oldcastle exploits with more or less coyness and consciousness, we discern the theatrical literacy, the thirst for good stories, and the avidity for an epic treatment of history that permeated the culture of the Elizabethan populace from whose ranks came the audiences for the Admiral's and the Chamberlain's Men's plays. While this popular culture gave rise to the limitedly workmanlike, as with Oldcastle, it also gave rise to the transcendent, in 1 & 2 Henry IV and Henry V.

[1] In this edition of Oldcastle Edmond Malone had shown (p. 269) that Cobham's story could be found in Holinshed, but it is J. William Hebel who pointed out (V, 45, 46) the dramatists' reliance on either Foxe's Book of Martyrs or Foxe's own source, John Bale's 1544 Brief Chronicle of Sir John Oldcastle.

[2] For convenience's sake references to Holinshed and Foxe will be identified by the line-numbering provided for in the Appendices when the passage in question is reproduced there.

[3] Over the years various scholars have pointed out the Book of Martyrs as a source for such Elizabethan plays as Sir Thomas More, Thomas Lord Cromwell, The Conflict of Conscience, 1 & 2 Tamburlaine, The Jew of Malta, etc. (See Warren W. Wooden's bibliographic article, "Recent Studies in Foxe," ELR, 11 [1981], 224-232).

[4] See notes for ii.141-45; iv.7-8, 28, 43.

[5] Macarthur (p. 41) does not think that either Weever or the dramatists knew each other's work, but suggests (with no corroboration) that Weever might have influenced them.

[6] This text is in black-letter; the words underlined in the quote are in roman type.

[7] Powis calling himself an "old friend" of Cobham (iii.92) may also owe something to the fact that the chronicles state that both Powis and Cobham had gone over to France to support the Duke of Burgundy in 1411.

[8] References to scene and line-numbering in Shakespeare's plays follow Peter Alexander's edition of William Shakespeare: The Complete Works (London and Glasgow: Collins, 1951).

[9] Other Admiral's Men plays contemporary with Old. that require accents are Old Fortunatus (Spanish, Irish, and French), Patient Grissill (Welsh), The Shoemakers' Holiday (Dutch).

[10] F.G. Fleay in A Chronicle History of the Life and Work of William Shakespeare (New York: Scribner & Welford, 1886), p. 294, hints at this Merry Devil connection to Oldcastle.

CHAPTER THREE

Date and Authorship

i. Date

In Henslowe's Diary, a record kept by the Rose theatre manager Philip Henslowe, we find three revealing entries about 1 & 2 Oldcastle:

a) this 16th of october 99
Receued by me Thomas downton of phillipp
Henchlow to pay m^r^ monday m^r^ drayton & m^r^ wilsson
& haythway for the first pte of the lyfe of
Sr Jhon Ouldcasstell & in earnest of the
Second pte for the vse of the companyny
ten pownd I say receued.......................[1] 10^li^

b) as A gefte Receved of M^r^ hincheloe for Mr Mundaye &
the Reste of the poets at the playnge of S^r^
John oldcastell the ferste tyme.........[2] x^s^

c) Receued of m^r^ Henchlow for the vse
of the Company to pay m^r^ drayton
for the second pte of Sr Jhon ould
Casell foure pownd I say receud..
p me Thomas Downton.[3] iiij^li^

From entry (a) we see that on October 16, 1599, Anthony Munday, Michael Drayton, Robert Wilson, and Richard Hathaway had completed 1 Oldcastle and were in the process of completing 2 Oldcastle. Entry (b) is situated in the Diary between a November 1 and a November 8, 1599, entry, and so we can accurately pinpoint 1 Oldcastle's first performance date. Entry (c) is found between entries dated December 19 and December 26, 1599. This could mean either that the second part of Oldcastle was completed between those dates or that final payment for the second part was merely transacted then.[4] This sequence of entries proves one important point among others: if the first performance date of 1 Oldcastle was between November 1 and November 8, and the dramatists had received payment in earnest of Part 2 on October 16, then they had projected Part 2 before knowing how popular or unpopular Part 1 would be. The two parts, then, were conceived as a single dramatic unit. The content and structure of the extant Part 1 itself fully bear out this inference, as can be seen elsewhere in the "Introduction." The extant play with which the two parts have greatest dramaturgical kinship is probably the two-part The Downfall and The Death of Robert Earl of Huntington, for which Henslowe had paid Munday and Henry Chettle 10 pounds between February 15 and March 8, 1598 (see Diary, pp. 86-87).

The evidence of topical allusions, theatrical borrowings, and so forth, found in Oldcastle (noted in the "Sources" chapter of this "Introduction" and in the explanatory notes)[5] leads to the conclusion that Oldcastle was written in the fall of 1599. The play displays a strong antipathy to the controversial Earl of Essex, I believe, and that fractious lord's escapades in Ireland in the late summer of 1599 and his hasty return to England in September could have affected some episodes in Oldcastle. Both the first scene's rebellion and also the Murley scenes seem to be the ones most affected by the great musters of soldiers and horsemen who were in London in August to train for a possible Spanish attack.[6]

Entry (a) is the first reference in Henslowe's Diary to any of the Oldcastle collaborators since the notice that the actor Thomas Downton was given 40 shillings to pay Drayton for his play "w^{m} longserd" on January 20, 1599 (see Diary, p. 103). The latest reference to Hathaway preceding entry (a) is dated July 19, 1598 (*Diary*, p. 93), the latest mention of Munday is dated August 19, 1598 (p. 96), and the latest reference to Wilson is dated August 29, 1598 (p. 97). As none of the collaborators seems to have been at work on any Henslowe plays before the *Oldcastle* entry, and as no evidence exists to link any of them with other companies at this time, the four dramatists may have been able to spend a little more time composing *1 Oldcastle* than was normal for plays worked on in the heat of a theatrical season. As Henslowe's records indicate (p. 95), the Rose theatre closed on June 3, 1599, and only reopened in October. This also suggests that the *Oldcastle* authors did not necessarily have to hurry their writing of the play because of any pressing need for new plays. Still, the evidence is far from overwhelming and the collaborators could just as easily have put their history together in short order. Taken together, all evidence, including the possible dependence of *Oldcastle* on the publication of George Peele's *Edward I* (entered in the Stationers' Register on August 13[7]), points to the conclusion that *1 Oldcastle* at least was written no later than October 16, and certain portions no earlier than August.

As a matter of interest we may note the rate of pay on *Oldcastle*; entry (a) tells us that 10 pounds was paid for *1 Oldcastle* and "in earnest of the Second pte." As this is only partial payment for the two plays (see entry [c]) the rates are good. They are not necessarily unusual though; the two *Huntington* plays mentioned above cost Henslowe 10 pounds. The *Oldcastle* plays' collaborators got at least 4 pounds for *Owen Tudor* (see *Diary*, p. 129) and likely 8 pounds if the fragment dated January 10, 1600, for payment of 4 pounds to Hathaway, Wilson, and Munday (p. 267), indicates a different payment than the one for all four writers. Henslowe also paid 8 pounds for *2 Henry*

Richmond (p. 126). This piece of information, along with the fact that the second parts of both The Blind Beggar of Bednal Green (or Tom Stroud) and The Black Dog of Newgate cost Henslowe more than the first parts,[8] supports the hypothesis that Henslowe in effect paid 6 pounds for 1 Oldcastle and finally 8 pounds for 2 Oldcastle.

ii. The Authors

We do know a fair amount about two of the four collaborators on Oldcastle --Anthony Munday and Michael Drayton--and here I will provide brief biographical outlines of these two writers as well as some information on the other two--Robert Wilson and Richard Hathaway.

Anthony Munday (1560-1633) was a poet, dramatist, pamphleteer, translator, pageant-writer, and antiquary, among other things. He was apprenticed to the printer John Aldee for eight years in October 1576 but left after two years. He spent some time on the stage and in 1578 went to Italy to enter a seminary on the advice of his patron, the Earl of Oxford. He returned disillusioned with Catholicism, wrote about his experiences in The English Romayne Life, and then served as a pursuivant, or Queen's messenger. He was a witness for the prosecution at the trial of the Jesuit Thomas Campion and was also a vigorous hunter of the Marprelate press, whose compositor, coincidentally, was Valentine Simmes, printer of Oldcastle. During this period he was also translating romances. He wrote the extant plays Fedele and Fortunio in the eighties, and John a Kent and John a Cumber as well as parts of Sir Thomas More in the nineties. He worked for Henslowe during the late years of Elizabeth I's reign and is favourably mentioned by Francis Meres in Palladis

Tamia (1598) where he is noted as one of the good comic writers as well as "our best plotter" (see p. 283). During James I's reign Munday was one of the chief pageant writers for the city of London and was editor of Stow's Survey of London. He lived and died in Cripplegate, an area of London.[9]

From the Diary we know that he worked on the plays Mother Redcap, The Downfall and The Death of Robert Earl of Huntington, The Funeral of Richard Coeur de Lion, Valentine and Orson, and Chance Medley before Oldcastle, and afterwards on Owen Tudor, 1 Fair Constance of Rome, 1 Cardinal Wolsey (The Rising of Cardinal Wolsey), Jephthah, Caesar's Fall (or Two Shapes), The Set at Tennis, and perhaps The Widow's Charm by "antony the poyete."[10] For the Funeral, a play written, like Oldcastle, with three other collaborators (Drayton, Chettle, and Wilson), it is probable that Munday received 25 shillings, Chettle 30 or 40 shillings, Drayton 30 shillings, and Wilson 30 shillings (see Diary, pp. 90, 91, 92). The work then for Funeral would have been equally divided. The same holds true for Chance Medley, written by the same four collaborators. Munday earned 25 shillings, Chettle 30 shillings, Drayton 35 shillings, and Wilson 30 shillings (see pp. 96, 97).

Michael Drayton (1563-1631) was a successful poet who also turned his hand to playwriting during the later years of Elizabeth I's reign. He was born of yeoman stock in Warwickshire and served as a page in the household of Sir Henry Goodere. He eventually settled in London and during the nineties wrote eclogues, sonnets, and historical poems. His most popular work was England's Heroical Epistles (1597, 1st edition) which were fictitious letters between famous English lovers. Drayton, like Munday, is mentioned in Meres' Palladis Tamia (see pp. 280, 281, 282, 283, 284) where he is highly regarded for his lyrics, elegies, historical poems, and tragedies, as well as honoured for his virtuous disposition. Though he seemed to have stopped writing plays in James I's reign, Drayton was still affiliated with the theatre. In 1607 he was a backer of the boys' theatre company, the Children of the King's Revels, who performed at Whitefriars. Most of Drayton's later life was devoted to rewriting much of his earlier work and to composing his topographical paean to England, Poly-Olbion. He died in 1631 and was buried in Westminster Abbey.[11]

Drayton was very busy in 1598 writing plays for Henslowe and the Admiral's Men. Along with various collaborators he wrote Mother Redcap, The Famous Wars of Henry I and the Prince of Wales, 1&2 Earl Goodwin and his Three Sons, Pierce of Exton, 1 Black Bateman of the North, The Funeral of Richard Coeur de Lion, The Madman's Morris, Hannibal and Hermes, Pierce of Winchester, Chance Medley, 1&2&3 Civil Wars of France, and Connan, Prince of Cornwall.[12] As noted before (see p. 44) he was given 40 shillings for work on "w^{m} longserd" in January 1599. Then he worked on Oldcastle and Owen Tudor. In 1600 the Diary indicates that Drayton collaborated on only 1 Fair Constance of Rome, in 1601 on 1 Cardinal Wolsey, and in 1602 on Caesar's Fall.[13] We have noted previously Drayton's shares in the Funeral and Chance Medley; with some certainty we can say that Drayton received 20 shillings on July 9 and Dekker and Wilson each received 20 shillings on July 10 for their play The Madman's Morris (see Diary, p. 92). Earlier, on June 10, Drayton had received 30 shillings, Wilson 10 shillings, and Chettle 10 shillings as payment for 2 Earl Godwin (p. 90).

We know far less about the third Oldcastle collaborator, Robert Wilson, than we do about Munday and Drayton. But some information has been unearthed about him, since there has been controversy over whether only one or two theatrical Wilsons even existed.[14] In all likelihood our Wilson is the one mentioned in Meres' list of comic writers in Palladis Tamia (p. 283), as the list refers to a number of Henslowe playwrights. He is probably also the Robert Wilson who died in St. Giles, Cripplegate, in November, 1600, as Wilson's name disappears from Henslowe's *Diary* after June 1600.

There is no evidence to suggest that more than one Wilson is mentioned in the *Diary*, so we can safely conclude that he collaborated over a three-year period not only on *Oldcastle* but also on *1&2 Earl Godwin and his Three Sons*, *Pierce of Exton*, *1&2 Black Bateman of the North*, *The Funeral of Richard Coeur de Lion*, *The Madman's Morris*, *Hannibal and Hermes*, *Pierce of Winchester*, *Chance Medley*, *Catiline's Conspiracy*, *2 Henry Richmond*, *Owen Tudor*, and *1 Fair Constance of Rome*.[15] Wilson's shares in *Chance Medley*, *Funeral*, and *2 Earl Godwin* have already been noted. Of interest, however, is the fragment in the *Diary* (see p. 294), "Mr Willsons whole share wch is xjs" in a letter from the actor Shaw to Henslowe about payment for *1 Fair Constance*. Wilson's share is one tenth of the 6 pounds that seems to have been paid for the play, and one half of what one would expect he would have been paid if his contribution to the play was equal to those of his four collaborators. This is the only solid piece of evidence that points to any of the four *Oldcastle* collaborators receiving payment for collaborative work significantly higher or lower than an equal share.

We have no information about Richard Hathaway, the last of the collaborators, other than Meres' mention of him in the list of comedy writers (see p. 283) and what there is in the *Diary*. Before *Oldcastle* he worked on *King Arthur* and *Valentine and Orson*, and afterwards on *Owen Tudor*, *1&2 Fair Constance of Rome*, *Hannibal and Scipio*, *Scogan and Skelton*, *The Conquest of Spain by John of Gaunt*, *1&2 Six Clothiers*, *Too Good to be True*, *As Merry as May Be*, *The Boss of Billingsgate*, *1&2 The Black Dog of Newgate*, and *The Unfortunate*

General (The French History).[16] No evidence can be gleaned here about the nature of Hathaway's share in writing these plays, though we know that he wrote King Arthur alone.

iii. The Question of Authorship

If we turn away from what we do know about the Oldcastle collaborators to the task of saying something intelligent about who wrote what, we quickly see that there is no easy solution. In our favour, of course, is the simple fact that the four dramatists did write the play and therefore each must be responsible for some parts of it. So much for the positive side. All four were involved in a number of different plays for Henslowe and there is no compelling evidence that one of them commonly composed the major part of a collaborative play or that one was usually responsible for only a minor share. The important exception to this is Wilson's minor share in 1 Fair Constance mentioned before. Also, we do know that Hathaway's name appears far less frequently than those of his collaborators before the Oldcastle entries and this might mean that his work on the history was at least less important than that of Munday or Drayton. In possible support of this hypothesis is the fact that Hathaway is not called a "Master" in Henslowe's Oldcastle entry (see entry [a]). Such an hypothesis, however, is offset by the evidence that after Oldcastle his name appears in the Diary far more often that those of his collaborators.

If we accept the Meres evidence at face value and apply it to Oldcastle we could infer that it is probable that Munday, Hathaway, and Wilson were responsible for the comical parts of Oldcastle and that Drayton was responsible for some portion of the poetic and tragic scenes. Obviously, such "proof" has no more validity than hearsay when we consider Oldcastle, yet Drayton's absence from the comedy list, given Meres' fulsome praise of the poet in all types of writing, is a useful piece of circumstantial evidence.

Also in our favour is the fact that a number of Munday's plays have survived to the present day in manuscript form. John a Kent and Sir Thomas More, being MSS, have been analyzed by scholars for Munday's orthographical habits. In Muriel St. Clare Byrne's "Anthony Munday's Spelling as a Literary Clue," The Library 4th ser. 4 (1923), 9-23, she found that Munday will double a medial vowel as in "heere," "doone," "looue," "woorthy," and prefers the spellings of "doo," "goe," "Ile," "hart," "freend," and "Maister." In chapters five and seven of A.C. Partridge's Orthography in Shakespeare and Elizabethan Drama (Lincoln: Univ. of Nebraska Press, 1964), the writer concluded that Munday's punctuation in the MSS is often overdone, and that he characteristically places a colon at the end of a penultimate line in speeches. He avoids colloquial contractions and, in particular, always uses the "in faith" construction. He consistently uses adverbs without the "s" as in "beside" meaning "besides," prefers "yon" to "yond" or "yonder," and uses apostrophes in verbs as in "dream'ste" and "daunc'ste." With Oldcastle in mind, I have looked at Munday's John a Kent and discovered that he adopts the spelling "Powesse" throughout--an important clue for authorship analysis, since various spellings of this name occur in Oldcastle.

There is a lot of Drayton's poetry extant but very little in MS form. From an autograph letter transcribed in Bent Juel-Jensen's "Michael Drayton and William Drummond of Hawthornden: A Lost Autograph Letter Rediscovered," The Library, 5th ser. 21 (1966), 328-30, I find that Drayton uses the form "freind," employs the colon and semi-colon far more often than the period, and does not exhibit Munday's tendency to double medial vowels. In Poly-Olbion (Hebel, IV) the form "Powse" is used consistently. Wilson's autographs are confined to those found in the Diary and little can be extrapolated from them; Hathaway's autographs in the Diary reveal nothing distinctive.

Such bits and pieces of information are the only tools available to us in the attempt to detect signs of Munday, Drayton, or Wilson (Hathaway, of course, is an unknown factor) in any scene, character, or turn of phrase in Oldcastle. Such detection, unfortunately, does not lead to firm conclusions for there are so many variables in the equation. Hathaway, for example, may share many of Munday's orthographical traits. Moreover, frequent collaboration on plays could lead to elimination or scrambling of distinctive authorial features. Also, though we are fairly sure Q1 was set from authorial manuscript (see above, pp.14-18) authorial traits need not have survived the handiwork of Compositor A. It is also possible to theorize that the play was written by committee. Such a hypothesis, however, has nothing to recommend it with respect to Oldcastle, because the major positive result from such group writing, the elimination of inconsistencies in plot and characterization, is not apparent in the play.

Of greater importance, then, in the scrutiny of Q1 that follows is the discovery of just such inconsistencies in plot and characterization as mar Oldcastle and point to different authors being responsible for different scenes. As well we can judge which scenes depend on a particular historical source, which allude to Shakespeare's histories, and which are pure fiction. Such evidence can point to different authors being responsible for different types of scenes. Finally, we can point to the consistent inconsistency in naming characters in Oldcastle--in text, in stage directions, in speech headings--to show the varying attitudes that different authors have to the same character. Sensible conclusions and observations can be based on these types of evidence, and though the conclusions may be in nor more enlightening form than collaborator A wrote scene vi and collaborator A did not write scene ix, nevertheless they are the foundation upon which any conjectural theories of specific authorship must be constructed.

The Prologue was probably written when Oldcastle went to press for it seems addressed to a reader rather than to a member of an audience. The over punctuation of the Prologue and the use of apostrophes in "grac'te," "forg'de," and "defac'te" are traits noted in Munday's MSS. Munday, then, seems to be the best, even if not the certain, choice for composer of the Prologue.

There are a couple of interesting characteristics in scene i that may help to determine authorship. The scene was suggested by a mention in Foxe of Lollard problems in Hereford and owes nothing to the chronicles. Lord Powis, the only character in scene i who appears later on in the play, is always referred to as "Powesse," a spelling that Munday always preferred. Also we find "Iayle" at i.77 while in the first section of scene xxvii we find "Gaoler" is used consistently.

All six characters in scene ii are important figures in Oldcastle. The scene is more purely historical than scene i and is suggested by Foxe's and the chroniclers' detailed discussion of the accusations made against Cobham and his followers. King Harry and Butler appear in all the sources but the latter is only bribed in Foxe; Suffolk and Huntington are not specifically named in the sources. A Bishop of Rochester is referred to in Foxe but the Oldcastle character truly corresponds to Archbishop Arundel, a personage mentioned in all the sources. In contrast, Sir John, the parson of Wrotham, only appears in Fabyan's and Stow's works. Clearly, the dramatist(s) responsible for the scene is (are) familiar with the various historical sources. In the speech headings King Harry is "Harry/Har.", Sir John is "Sir Iohn/sir Iohn/sir Ihon", and Bishop is "Bishop/Bish.".

Scene iii is as unhistorical as scene i. John Butler's entrance at the end of the scene is the only event mentioned in the historical sources, and, even here, the Oldcastle authors have departed from historical fact, for in the sources Butler's summoning of Cobham comes after the summoners's visit and is unsuccessful. In direct contrast to the spelling in scene i, the form "Powis" is used in speech headings and one stage direction (1.86) while in the other stage direction (1.76.1) and one in-text reference (1.92) "Powes" is used.

The first half of scene iv adapts the historical incident of a summoner's attempt to cite Lord Cobham, fully described in Foxe, but quickly wanders afield into comedy and theatrical allusiveness. Later on in the scene, the action, now taking place in an Alehouse, becomes farcical and unhistorical. When Sir John enters (1.152.1) he is "Priest" in the stage directions and, for the only time in the play, "Wroth." in the speech headings.

All characters in scene v are historical though this episode is not based on any noted in the chronicles. The emphasis on Murley, however, shows that the writer(s) was (were) referring to the most complete treatments of this figure found in Holinshed and Stow's Annals.

Scene vi is directly based on Foxe's treatment of the important meeting between King Henry and Lord Cobham. All the characters who appeared in scene ii (minus Sir John) appear in this scene, and King Harry and the Bishop are denoted in the same way in speech headings and stage directions as they had been in scene ii. Unlike scene iii, where Cobham was called "Lord Cobham" in his one stage direction (1.23.1), Cobham is denoted as "Old-castle" in the opening stage direction of scene vi. The policy for speech headings is the same for Cobham in the two scenes and he is "Cobham/Cob." consistently, except for the section (iii.156-171) where he is "Cobh.". The name "Powesse" appears once in the text (vi.34).

As can be seen from the discussion of scene vii in the "Sources" chapter of the "Introduction" the story of Cambridge and his conspiracy is based on a wide variety of historical sources. Also, while other scenes in Oldcastle (iv, x, xi) more conventionally borrow from the Henry IV and V plays, a number of speeches and actions in scene vii recall, echo, or borrow from other Shakespeare history plays--Richard II and 2 Henry VI. There are also many dramatic inconsistencies in scene vii. Cambridge has, in terms of the play, a misguided sense of the "uneasy" relationship between King Harry and Cobham; the conspirator has, too, a greater knowledge of the Acton rebellion than would be logically possible. Furthermore, this is the only scene in the play that takes place at Cooling and not Cobham. Lady Powis' presence is quite uncalled for, and she appears in only one other scene in the play--the last. In speech headings Cobham is designated "Cobh.", as he had been in iii.156-71, Lady Cobham is "Lady Cob./Lady Cobh.", Lady Powis is "Lady Po.", and Powis is "Powesse/Powes." In the text Powis is once referred to as "Powesse" (1.210).

Scene viii is the second scene to deal with the Ficket Field rebellion, and its style, content, and characters are completely consistent with the first.

In the unhistorical scene ix we are reacquainted with Sir John and Doll.

In it he is "*Sir Iohn of Wrootham*" in the opening stage direction and, uniquely, "*Priest*" in speech headings.

Scene x begins with the king's orders to protect London (actions which are described in the most detail in Holinshed) but then develops into an unhistorical confrontation between a disguised King Harry and Sir John. Sir John, presumably, is in some disguise, for if he was not, King Harry would have recognized him. Uniquely King Harry is referred to as "*King*" in all speech headings. He is "*King*" in the opening stage direction, an appellation used one other time in *Oldcastle* (xvi.25.1). Interestingly Sir John, who was "*Priest*" in speech headings in scene ix, is again "*Sir Iohn*/*sir Iohn*" throughout.

The unhistorical scene xi, analogous to certain scenes in *Edward I* and *Henry V*, displays two significant inconsistencies that indicate a change in writers. As Sir John appears in his priest's costume once again in scene xi, it is inconsistent that Suffolk, in particular, and Huntington and King Harry, to a lesser extent, do not recognize him from their meeting in scene ii. Obviously, that meeting has been long forgotten or was never remembered by the writer(s) of scene xi. Secondly, King Harry's description of his encounter with Sir John (11.98-116) does not correspond with what occurred in scene x. Speech heading evidence suggests that scene xi may have been written by two different authors and neither would seem to be the author of scene x. In the opening stage direction King Harry is uniquely denoted as "*King Henry*" and in his first three speech headings as "*K.Hen.*". As the scene switches from the formal verse opening to the unhistorical, prosaic, comical confrontation between Sir John and King Harry, Harry becomes the familiar "*Har.*" in subsequent speech headings. Sir John is "*sir Iohn*/*sir Ihon*" in speech headings.

The action returns to the historical events of the Ficket Field rebellion in scene xii. Cobham's timely appearance and exculpation by these rebels, however, is pure fiction. The discussion of the Cambridge conspiracy and the emphasis in scene xii upon the corrupting power of French "gilt" on another set of rebels (see ll.121-24), as opposed to the emphasis in scene vii on Cambridge's anger at being denied his rightful claim to the throne, probably indicates that different authors were responsible for each scene. Bourne's absence from scene xii is another curious anomaly for he should have been captured with the rest of the rebels. (However, see "Theatrical Background and Assessment" chapter of this "Introduction" for discussion of doubling in _Oldcastle_.) King Harry is the usual "_Har_." in speech headings, but is uniquely denoted as "_Harry_" in the opening stage direction. Sir John is the usual "_sir Iohn_" in his one speech heading (l.40). Cobham is "_Cob_." at ll.82, 87, 96, 100 and "_Cobh_." at ll.118, 125.

There are some important inconsistencies in scene xiii. The action takes place in Cobham (see l.36) though it seems more reasonable to expect that it take place in Cooling, where the action in scene vii occurred and to which Cobham is supposed to return. It is possible that the writer(s) responsible for the last section of scene vii, from the entrance of Lady Cobham et al. (ll.195-224) is (are) also responsible for scene xiii but not for the section of scene vii specifically set in Cooling (see vii.87). According to this interpretation the collaborators would be consistent with their own scenes but not with respect to the play as a whole. Unfortunately, there is a further complication which makes the above hypothesis quite fragile: Lord Powis and Lady Powis, who were present at the end of scene vii and had promised to stay at Cobham/Cooling (see vii.220-24), have disappeared. The Powises are not even mentioned in scene xiii and so it is equally valid to hypothesize that there is no connection between the authors of scene vii and xiii. Another irregularity arises in connection with the date on the Bishop's warrant, which cannot antedate King Harry's subsequent pardoning of Cobham, for the two events occurred within a minute in stage and real time in scene xii. Also, the claim by the Bishop that Harpool is lucky to have been pardoned by King Harry (1.127) does not adequately describe the action in scene vi (11.56-85) to which the Bishop is alluding. Finally, the Sumner, who is nameless in scene iv, is called "Clun" by the Bishop at the end of scene xiii (1.149). For the first time in the play Cobham is "Oldcastle" in stage directions (11. 31.1, 107.1) and "Old-castle/Oldca./Old." in speech headings. Lady Cobham is "Lady Cob." in the opening stage direction and "Lady" in speech headings.

The Tower of London scenes, xiv and xv, are a comical interpretation of the historical sources' discussion of Cobham's escape from prison. Importantly, Cobham is called "Sir Iohn" a number of times in scene xiv (11.24, 26, 34, 39) and he is called this only one other time in the play (vii.114). Uniquely, a "sir Iohn" speech heading for Cobham occurs in scene xiv (1.50). In the one stage direction in scene xiv (1.32.1) Cobham is "sir Iohn Old-castle" and throughout the Tower scenes is denoted "Old-ca." in speech headings. In scene xiv the Bishop, as usual, is "Bish." in speech headings. The evidence suggests that when the Bishop reappears in scene xv (1.34.1), and is consistently called "Rochester" in his entrance direction and "Roch." in speech headings, a different author is responsible for this last section of the scene than the one who wrote scene xiv.

Scene xvi is based on the chronicles' account of the Cambridge conspiracy as well as on II.ii, Henry V, where King Henry confronts the traitors for their treason. In scene vii Cambridge had said the conspirators would meet again in Kent (see 1.179), but scene xvi is probably set in Southampton, for that is where the plot was historically discovered (it was called the Southampton Plot) and that is where the Bishop says King Harry is (see xiii.68). As usual King Harry is "Har." in speech headings.

As scenes xvii-xix are out of place in Q1, appearing after scenes xx-xxiv, it is likely that scenes xvii-xix were written on one sheet and that the sheet was wrongly placed in the MS. Circumstantial evidence indicates, then, that scenes xvii-xix might have been written by one author.

The unhistorical conversation between Doll and Sir John in scene xvii is similar to their conversation in scene ix. Unlike scene ix, though, Sir John is "Priest" in the opening stage direction and at 1.36, and "sir Iohn" in speech headings. In the brief scene xviii the Host is "Host" in speech headings.

Scene xix borrows various details from the Carriers' scene in 1 Henry IV. Here Club is "carrier" in the opening stage direction and "Club" in speech headings; the Ostler is "Hostler" in speech headings. The exact relationship between Club and Kate is difficult to pin down for it appears that different characters (and, perhaps, different authors) have varying assessments of the couple's familial and sexual connections. Kate calls Club "goff [i.e., old man] Club," in xix (1.4). In scene xx (1.4) the Host refers to Kate as the carrier's daughter. At xxii.8 she is called "his wench" by Harpool, and in the stage direction (xxiii.11.1-2) Lady Cobham is said to be in the "wenches apparrell". Two lines later the disguised Cobham calls to his "Kate" and calls her "wench". Finally, Kate calls Club "neame [i.e., uncle] Club" in the last speech of scene xxiv. Various collaborators, it would seem, have slightly varying attitudes to Kate and Club, though it is not impossible that one author could be responsible for the slight discrepancies.

The scenes at the Bell Inn, xx-xxiv, are, like the Sumner-Harpool confrontation in scene iv, fiction based on historical incidents. In this instance the chronicles mention Cobham's near capture in St. Albans at the hands of the abbot. In scene xx Cobham is "sir Iohn Old-castle" in the opening stage direction and uniquely "L.Cobh." in the one speech heading. Unlike scene xviii the Host is "Hoste" in speech headings.

In scene xxi we find out that the Watch is looking for Cobham and an Irishman who committed a murder. Assuredly the latter must be the Irishman of scene xvii and so the victim must be Sir Richard Lee's son, but it is very confusing that the body is not found until Sir Richard Lee's servant comes upon it in scene xxv (1.74). The Constable's discussion of the murder here in scene xxi, and later in scene xxiii (11.5-7), suggests that the body has already been found.

In scene xxii Harpool describes the Irishman's costume as a mantle and a pair of brogues (11.7-8), but in the last scene of the play the Irishman asks to have back his clothes, which Harpool is wearing, specifying "my strouces [i.e., trousers]" (1.123). In scene xxii Cobham is "Lord Cobham" in the opening stage direction and "Cobh." in the two speech headings. In the following scene Cobham is "Lord Cobham " in the stage direction (1.11.1) and "Cobham" in the two speech headings.

A major inconsistency occurs in scene xxiv when the Mayor tells his men to keep a good hold on Cobham's servant. It is impossible to tell whether he means Harpool or the Irishman. The Host, as he had been in scene xx, is "Hoste" in speech headings. The Ostler, who had been designated as "Hostler" in scene xix, is "Ostler" in speech headings here. As is the case in scene xix, Club is "Carrier" in his entrance stage direction (1.15.1) and "Club" in speech headings. One time, however, he is denoted as "Carier" in a speech heading (1.35).

In the final three scenes of Oldcastle, all of which are unhistorical, verse and artificial conceits return, in obvious contrast to the prosaic Bell Inn scenes. There are a number of irregularities in scene xxv. Cobham calls the Bishop "Winchester" (1.5), and he fears that Harpool has either fallen into the Bishop's hands or forgotten where they planned to meet (11.41-43). To all intents and purposes the Cobham of scene xxv seems ignorant of the St. Alban's escapades and is harking back to the plan that Harpool made in scene xv at the Tower of London. Cobham should know that Harpool had been captured by the Watch, and, obviously, the two would have had no time to make a plan at St. Albans. In speech headings Cobham is "Oldca." before Lee's entrance (1.70.1) and "Old-castle/Old." after; Lady Cobham is "Lady" before and "Lady Old." after.

Scene xxvi presents a number of logical problems. One cannot help wondering how it is that Harpool was brought to the Bishop of Rochester before the Irishman, as the Irishman was captured before Cobham's servant, and also why Harpool, supposedly a murderer, was taken to the Bishop and not to the secular authorities. Sir John is "sir Iohn of Wrotham" in the opening stage direction and "sir Iohn" in speech headings.

The last scene of the play is also marred by a few glaring inconsistencies caused, no doubt, by the collaborative nature of Oldcastle. The fact that Harpool is being tried in the same courtroom and for the same crime as Lord and Lady Cobham is ludicrous. It is also difficult to believe that

Cobham would remark on Harpool's being "i' th' briars" (1.12) but not on his being in Irishman's apparel. Probably the collaborator responsible for these opening lines was not aware that Harpool was in Irish attire. Harpool also says he is glad the Bishop had nothing to do with his sentencing (11.25-29), yet in the previous scene the Bishop said he had dealt with Harpool (xxvi.2-3). The Bishop of Rochester is correctly referred to as "Rochester" (1.27) but later on in the scene the same error that was made in scene xxv crops up again and the Bishop is confusingly called "Winchester" (11.107, 137). Cobham is "Oldcastle" in the opening stage direction and at 1.149, and "Oldca./Old." in speech headings. Lady Cobham is "Lady Old-castle" in her one stage direction (1.9.1). In the first episode with her husband Lady Cobham is "Lady" in speech headings, as she had been in scene xiii and the first part of xxv, but "Lady Cob." during the cross-examination episode, as she had been in scene vii. Powis is "Lord Powesse/lord Powesse" in the two stage directions (11.30.2, 149), "Lord Po." in speech headings (for the only time in the play), and "Powes/Powesse" in the text (11.33, 149 respectively). Lady Powis is "Lady Po." in speech headings, as she had been in scene vii. Sir John is "sir Iohn of Wrotham" in the stage direction (1.90.2) and "sir Iohn" in speech headings.

As can be seen from the above ten pages of information, the history play does not divide easily into neatly separate sections. We can look at the Acton-Murley scenes v and viii, and make a sensible conclusion that one writer was responsible for these scenes, but such commonsensical deductions cannot be simply applied to the Bell Inn scenes, the Tower of London scenes, the Sir John scenes, and so on, since there are jarring inconsistencies within these scene groups. Though I have come to the inevitable conclusion that there cannot be any truly convincing theory concerning the collaborators' division of labour, I have, nevertheless, arrived at some reasonably educated conjectures.[17]

First of all one can make a sensible case that one collaborator is responsible for the historically-based, mainly serious verse scenes in the first half of Oldcastle. These scenes--ii, iii, vi, xii--introduce us to the most important characters in the play. They also show us the very real threats to Cobham's reputation and his attempts to assert his loyalty. In these scenes Cobham is "Cobham/Cob." in speech headings, in contrast to the scenes in the second half that have "Oldcastle", or abbreviations or variations thereof, as their speech headings; King Harry is "Har."; Sir John is "Sir Iohn" or slight variations of this; the Bishop is "Bish.". Drayton, because he probably preferred to write in verse and to treat serious themes, is my candidate for authorship of these scenes. I also think the less serious scenes at the Inn (xxii-xxiv) can be assigned to him, for here the "Cobham" speech headings recur.

On the strength of the references to "Powesse" in certain scenes of Oldcastle--i, vii and xxvii[18] (from Powis' entrance, 1.30)--I would give Munday these scenes. The first and last scenes of the play are also similar in that one involves justices from Hereford while the other includes judges from Hertford. As well the conclusion of 1 Oldcastle, where two characters bring the play to a somewhat artificial, comic close, bears a strong resemblance to the ending of Munday and Chettle's The Downfall and Death of Robert, Earl of Huntington where the characters Eltham and Skelton conclude one play and hint at action to come. For reasons of plot connections and resemblances of style I would also grant Munday authorship of the second Cambridge conspiracy scene, xvi. For similar reasons, and because "Winchester" (instead of the correct

"Rochester") is used only in the last scene of the play and scene xxv, I would assign scene xxv to him.

I believe that one collaborator is responsible for the plot-linked scenes xiii-xv (to l. 35 and the Bishop's entrance), and the first section of xxvii, where Cobham, Lady Cobham and Harpool do not seem to be aware of the events of the Bell Inn scenes, that is, the actions intervening between the Tower of London scenes (xiv and xv) and the final episodes. The use of "Oldcastle" in speech headings for these second-half scenes is another reason to assign them to one collaborator. Also, because the plot involves both the Sumner and the irascible Harpool in scene iv and the xiii-xv block, I would assign scene iv to this collaborator.

Finally, I think that one collaborator is also responsible for the serio-comic Murley scenes--v and viii--as well as the block of Sir John-Doll-Irishman scenes--xvii-xxi and xxvi--where Sir John is consistently referred to as "Sir John" in speech headings. This collaborator is probably responsible for the plot-linked scenes ix and x. In ix, Sir John and Doll both use language noticeably echoed in scene xvii, and in x Sir John robs the disguised King Harry, just as he does the Irishman in the second half of scene xvii. That Sir John is referred to in scene ix speech headings as "Priest" is, I think, less important than these obvious connections of scenes ix and x with scene xvii. Perhaps the anomaly arose because scene ix is the first scene for this hypothetical collaborator, who had not yet settled on "Sir John" for speech headings, though he does refer in the opening stage directions to "Sir John of Wrotham." And since all this work adds up to a portion somewhat smaller than any of the other three, I would assign these scenes to Wilson, the only collaborator for whom there is any evidence of less than equal participation in other collaborative work.

Having made the preceding hypothetical division of Oldcastle, I find it difficult to assign scene xi to any one collaborator, for it not only switches focus three times but also bristles with plot inconsistencies. I would assign, however, the bulk of the scene (up to Butler's entrance) to Hathaway, the third collaborator, since the unique "K. Hen." speech heading would be understandable for a collaborator who only dramatizes the character once in the play. The switch near the beginning of the scene to "Har." speech headings can then be explained as reflecting King Henry's own wish at this point to be known as just plain "Harry". The slightly more serious conclusion of the scene, from Butler's entrance on, can be assigned to Drayton, since this section is concerned with the question of Sir John's treason, linking it up with the play's major thematic concern with Lord Cobham's supposed treason. Moreover, the Butler has appeared twice before in "Drayton" scenes, and the conclusion of scene xi naturally leads into the concluding scene of the Ficket Field rebellion (xii), which I have assigned to Drayton.

The second section of scene xv, with the unique "Roch." speech headings, is almost impossible to place in my hypothetical division of the play. Hathaway and Drayton refer to the Bishop consistently as "Bish." in speech headings; Wilson, the Sir John collaborator, only characterizes the Bishop once and also uses "Bish." as speech heading. Munday, who does not dramatize the Bishop and only refers to him, confusingly, as "Winchester," is my rather poor candidate for authorship of this brief episode, mainly because it comes before scene xvi, which I have assigned to him.

[1] R.A. Foakes and R.T. Rickert, eds., Henslowe's Diary (Cambridge: Cambridge University Press, 1969), p. 125.

[2] Ibid., p. 126.

[3] Ibid., p. 129.

[4] The reference to Drayton alone in entry (c) should not necessarily lead us to conclude that Drayton is primarily (or solely) responsible for 2 Oldcastle and that he alone collected the 4 pounds. The entry mentioned below concerning 2 Henry Richmond shows that Robert Wilson collected 8 pounds for the play. However an MS at Dulwich (see Diary, Art. 26, pp. 287-288), a letter from the actor Robert Shaw (Shaa) to Henslowe, indicates that Wilson was not the sole author.

[5] See notes for i.103, iii.154-55, xiii.144-57, and xxv.78.

[6] See E. Howes, The Abridgement of the English Chronicle (1610), pp. 407-09.

[7] Arber, Company of Stationers, III, 169.

[8] Diary, pp. 135, 163, 166, 167, 220, 221, 223, 224.

[9] This biographical information is culled from Celeste Turner Wright's Anthony Mundy: An Elizabethan Man of Letters in Univ. of California Publications in English, II (Berkeley: Univ. of California Press, 1928), 1-234, as well as from: M. St. Clare Byrne's "Anthony Munday and his Books," The Library, 4th ser. 1 (1921), 225-255; Wright's "Young Anthony Mundy Again," SP, 56 (1959), 150-68; and Leslie Hotson's "Anthony Mundy's Birth-Date," N&Q, 204 (1959), 2-4.

[10] Diary, pp. 74, 85, 86, 87, 91, 93, 96, 125, 129, 135, 183, 184, 200, 201, 202, 203, 204, 205, 206, 267.

[11] The source for biographical information on Drayton is Bernard H. Newdigate's Michael Drayton and his Circle (Oxford: The Shakespeare Head Press, 1941).

[12] Diary, pp. 74. 85, 86, 88, 90, 91, 92, 93, 94, 96, 97, 98, 100.

[13] Ibid., pp. 135, 183, 184, 201, 202.

[14] E.K. Chambers in The Elizabethan Stage (Oxford: Clarendon Press, 1923), II, 349-50, summarizes the Wilson issue. Those who have unearthed other useful information are: I. Gourvitch, "Robert Wilson 'The Elder' and 'The Younger'," N&Q, 150 (1926), 4-6; T.W. Baldwin, "Nathaniel Field and Robert Wilson," MLN, 41 (1926), 32-34; H.S.D. Mithal, "The Two-Wilsons Controversy," N&Q, 204 (1959), 106-09.

[15] Diary, pp. 88, 90, 91, 92, 93, 94, 96, 97, 125, 126, 129, 267, 294.

16 *Ibid.*, pp. 65, 89, 90, 93, 125, 135, 136, 138, 166, 167, 168, 183, 186, 187, 193, 206, 208, 220, 221, 222, 223, 267, 295.

17 Before me, F.G. Fleay in *A Chronicle History of the Life and Works of William Shakespeare*, p. 294, concluded that Drayton was chief plotter and composer, that Munday wrote i, xvii-xxvii, that possibly Wilson wrote ii, vi, and x, and that Hathaway was responsible for vii and xvi. In *A Biographical Chronicle of the English Drama* (London: Reeves and Turner, 1891), II, 116, Fleay modified his theory by dropping the question mark before the Wilson-attributed scenes and adding xii-xv. Slightly less capricious attributions were made by A.F. Hopkinson and J.R. Macarthur. Hopk. (pp. x-xii) gave Munday and Drayton the bulk. Scenes i, iii (from Powis' entrance), v, viii, xii (to Bishop's entrance), xvii-xxiv, xxvi, xxvii went to Munday and scenes ii, vi, x (to Sir John's entrance), xi (to Sir John's entrance), xii (from Bishop's entrance), xiii-xv, and xxv went to Drayton. Wilson received iii (to Powis' entrance), iv, ix, x (from Sir John's entrance), xi (from Sir John's entrance). Hathaway was again awarded vii and xvi. Mac. (pp. 60-64) was far more tentative in his assignment. He thought Munday was responsible for the straightforward historical scenes and that Drayton was the best choice for the opening Welsh scene and, perhaps, for the other dialect episodes. He also noted that there were two other groups of scenes: the Acton-Murley ones and the various scenes with Sir John or Harpool in them.

18 The form "Powis" appears in scene iii, the only other scene of the play in which this character appears.

CHAPTER FOUR

Critical Assessment

Before Edmond Malone lavished his editorial attention on 1 Sir John Oldcastle in the late eighteenth century, this history play had received little or no interest. One brief and obscure reference to Oldcastle comes in George Daniel's historical poem Trinarchodia. In this 1647 poem, Daniel alludes, when treating Henry V's reign, to Shakespeare's Falstaff, and also to a priest and malt-man who were probably Oldcastle's Sir John and Murley:

> Another Knight but of noe great Account
> (Soe say his freinds) was one of these new Saints
> A Priest! but the fatt Mault-Man! (if you[u] don't
> Remember him, S[r] Iohn has let his rants)
> Flye backward, the first Knight to be made
> And golden Spurres, hee, in his Bosome had.[1]

A second Oldcastle allusion appears in Jeremy Collier's A Short View of the Immorality and Profaneness of the English Stage (1698). Considering Oldcastle as Shakespearian, Collier discusses Shakespeare's treatment of the clergy and mentions Oldcastle's Sir John:

> In the History of Sr. John Old-castle, Sr. John Parson of Wrotham swears, games, wenches, pads, tilts, and drinks: This is extremely bad, and like the Author of the Relapse, &c. Only with this difference; Shakspear's, Sr. John has some Advantage in his Character. He appears Loyal and Stout; He brings in Sr. John Acton, and other Rebels Prisoners. He is rewarded by the King, and the Judge uses him Civilly and with Respect. In short, He is represented Lewd, but not Little; And the Disgrace falls rather on the Person than the Office.[2]

In his 1780 edition of Shakespeare's Works, Malone spent little effort on critically assessing Oldcastle; he merely concluded that the play showed no sign of Shakespeare (see p. 269). George Steevens, who provided many of the notes for the Malone edition of the play, was also reticent. He said, however, that he did not lament the loss of Part 2 (see p. 369). The noted German translator of Shakespeare, A.W. Schlegel, had a more favourable opinion of Oldcastle. First of all he believed that Shakespeare was responsible for the drama and, significantly, he held that both Oldcastle and Thomas Lord Cromwell were models of biographical dramas and among Shakespeare's best plays.[3]

Another German, Herman Ulrici, was far less enthusiastic about the play and cogently outlined Oldcastle's shortcomings. He concluded that the playwright was an imitator of Shakespeare far inferior in talent. He found Oldcastle full of wholly distinct and unconnected action, overloaded with subordinate characters, and interspersed with irrelevant comic scenes (the Sumner scene, for example) "devoid of genuine wit." He also held that while the leading characters were "ably sketched and correctly worked out" there was no "progressive development" or "roundness" to these figures.[4]

Later editors of Oldcastle or Shakespeare have generally upheld Ulrici's negative appraisal of the history. Charles Knight in 1839 followed Ulrici by complaining about the lack of dramatic unity in Oldcastle and noted the play's emphasis on plot over character development. He did, however, find the Sumner scene amusing and also praised the Lord and Lady Cobham episode (scene xxv) as "happily imagined and gracefully expressed."[5] William Gilmore Simms made an assessment similar to Knight's, and marked for praise Cambridge's allegorical description of the stag (vii.100-12).[6] Henry Tyrrell praised Oldcastle more generously. He liked the comic characters (Sir John, Harpool, Murley) but found the serious episodes "discursive, and not sufficiently worked out," though occasionally displaying "passages of rigour and beauty."[7] A.F. Hopkinson complained of the jumbling of historical events but also praised the characterization of the Bishop and Sir John.[8] In his thesis introduction J.R. Macarthur called Oldcastle a "medley," and thought it lacking in the essentials of a drama and marred by irrelevant comic scenes. Nevertheless, he had some praise for the collaborators' comic handling of Cobham's flight from justice and for their ingenuity in tying together all strands of the plot by the play's end.[9] Finally, J.E. Hebel adopted a relatively generous point of view on Oldcastle and concluded that the play did not tarnish Drayton's reputation and brought "no discredit to his total achievement as a writer." While noting, as others before him had done, the liveliness of certain scenes and the patchy quality of the whole, Hebel concluded that the characterization of Cobham, "strongly and consistently drawn, . . . raises the play out of the ruck of typical factory products."[10]

Like Hebel, and Tyrrell before him, I have a favourable impression of the overall work--despite its inconsistencies, distortion of historical facts, moral muddle-headedness, and hodge-podge aesthetic style. Undoubtedly one of the play's flaws is that while the simple tale of Lord Cobham's downfall is made superficially complex by many plot strands, the joining together of these strands is patently awkward. Moreover, Oldcastle presents a melodramatic world of black and white, though the authors knew the historical facts were far more complicated and less clear-cut. Still, the play is written with verve and dramatic skill in many of its prose and confrontation scenes, and, at its best, has the virtues of those relatively uncomplicated dramas of the medieval and Tudor periods which successfully used their black-white conflicts to engage the hearts and minds of their audiences.

In almost all aspects of plot, characterization, and theme the Oldcastle authors look backward and borrow from existing dramatic techniques or situations. Thus both the comic and serious villains of the play, Sir John and the Bishop, remind an audience of the medieval vice figure who revelled in his self-conscious villainy; while scene xx, in which the disguised Cobhams seek refuge at the Host's Bell Inn, would perhaps recall those Nativity plays where Joseph and Mary look for lodging in Bethlehem (see note to sc.xx.0.1). No new ground is broken in Oldcastle and in fact what charm the play possesses depends on an audience's appreciating the dramatists' skill in moulding their grab-bag effects into a coherent whole.

Comparing Oldcastle, moreover, to its contemporary counterparts in the biographical genre--Sir Thomas More, Thomas Lord Cromwell, Captain Thomas Stukeley, and The Downfall and The Death of Robert Earl of Huntington--shows our play off to distinct advantage. None of these other works would be called well-made. Each focuses on an individual and proceeds with an "and then" story that, while it may provide us with an occasional perspective glimpse of the central figure, is more concerned with simply dramatizing chronological incidents from the hero's life. Certainly neither Cromwell nor Stukeley, plays lamentably lacking in thematic focus, measures up to the Oldcastle presentation of a resolute hero caught up in a web of circumstantial evidence. The More and Huntington plays approach the relative sophistication of Oldcastle but neither work is as deliberate or compelling in its creation of the hostile world in which its hero lives. For these reasons and for the fact that from the outset of Part 1 Oldcastle is about something, about an innocent being destroyed, the play is head and shoulders above its biographical peers.

Cobham and his reputation are always the focus of the play: the comic Sumner, Murley, Tower of London, Bell Inn, and Hertford trial scenes are far from being extraneous to the plot. They provide examples either of how people acting in Cobham's name sully his reputation through their own actions, or of the rush and whirlwind of events in which Cobham is caught up. The Sumner, for example: this foolish, petty bureaucrat has the misfortune to meet up with Harpool, Cobham's family servant, and so the lord is blamed for his servant's impetuous actions. In the Murley scenes, we see the braggart Murley connecting his treacherous actions to the innocent Cobham. Moreover, we see a character whose conceptions of honour, conscience and loyalty (see in particular viii.29-52) are clearly contrasted and counterpointed to those of Cobham. Even the somewhat strange ending of 1 Oldcastle, where Cobham is brought to trial for a murder he did not commit, is connected closely to the play's concern with the question of innocence and reputation. In this case of a private crime, paralleling the cases of Cobham's alleged political and religious crimes, where hearsay is "proof," the purely circumstantial evidence of a bloody handkerchief and unsheathed knives is used against the blameless accused man.

Only the Sir John of Wrotham episodes do not provide any direct insight into, or information about, the central figure. But I would suggest that the Oldcastle dramatists are making an important if indirect comment on Cobham through their characterization of Sir John. In their depiction of the priest they create a comic parallel to Cobham. This character constantly lives a lie--he is a thief not a priest--and he is always ready to assume new disguises and shapes to abet his thievery. Cobham, on the other hand, is a forthright figure who tells the king the truth. He is, however, not only required to dissemble to the Cambridge conspirators; he must also suffer the misfortune of being slandered through rumour and innuendo. As we see in the Bell Inn and Hertford courtroom scenes, he is forced to adopt the same dissembling tactics that the amoral Sir John so readily uses. The historical fact that Cobham was hanged and burnt for his "sins" at about the same time that Sir John was sent to prison leads me to conclude that in the lost 2 Oldcastle the dramatists continued to parallel the lives of their moral hero and their amoral vice figure. Obviously, by the end of Part 2, Sir John has run out of disguises and excuses and Cobham has run out of friends and supporters. The thief-priest, presumably, will receive just punishment while Cobham, no doubt, will be unfairly executed. Interestingly, the punishment handed out to the Irishman in scene xxvii (see ll.119-122), where he is to be hung in chains near the venue of his crime, serves as a melodramatic foreshadowing of Cobham's historical fate. Lord Cobham was punished for his treason and heresy by being hung in chains and burnt in St. Giles in the Fields, the site of the Ficket Field rebellion. The Oldcastle dramatists, then, consciously intended all the disparate pieces of their play to fit together.

As possible further proof of this assertion I would point to that odd figure in Oldcastle, Lord Powis, who appears, seemingly haphazardly, in only certain sections of a few scenes in the play. His presence is substantial in the first half-hour, but he all but disappears until the final scene of 1 Oldcastle, when he is required to deliver the concluding speech.[11]

Now, although the first scene of the play is loosely based on an historical event (a Lollard uprising in Hereford) Powis has no historical connection with that incident. Moreover the entire relationship between Cobham and Powis is unhistorical, though we do know from the chronicles that they had fought together in France in 1411. The *Oldcastle* dramatists clearly intended, then, to establish a fictitious friendship between the two lords for thematic reasons. In *2 Oldcastle* the dramatists probably presented the historical capture of Cobham on Powis' lands (actually Powis' father-in-law's) as a tragic betrayal of the good Lord Cobham by his supposed friend Powis. So in *1 Oldcastle* we are shown Cobham's unwavering aid and loyalty to Powis--a person whose reckless actions at the beginning of the play have triggered superficially unconnected series of events that lead to Cobham's inevitable downfall. In this light Powis' scurrying away from the fray in Hereford and his cowardly quaking at Harpool's mention of the king's name in scene iii takes on ominous meanings not immediately apparent to the innocent viewer. Furthermore, Powis' great debt to Cobham for securing his pardon and his subsequent attempt to repay Cobham for his kindness at the end of Part 1 are, if this theory is correct, in ironic contrast to his ultimate betrayal.

In some respects the Powis-Cobham relationship is a variation on the betrayal of Robin Hood by the Prior and Warman in *The Downfall* and *The Death of Robert Earl of Huntington* (but in the *Oldcastle* instance the laying out of the lords' relationship in Part 1 is demonstrably subtler and more sophisticated than that attempted in the *Huntington* plays). I suspect that, as Munday and Chettle attempted to characterize Robin Hood as a Christ-like figure, so the *Oldcastle* dramatists portrayed Cobham in Part 2 (as they do to a certain degree in Part 1) as a Christ-like sufferer, and that they probably developed Powis in the mould of Judas Iscariot--in effect creating a dramatic figure out of Foxe's comparison of Powis to Judas (11.289-294). It is possible that the dramatists again rewrote a bit of history and had Lord Powis loyally protecting his friend Lord Cobham to the bitter end,[12] but I consider it far more probable that in Part 2 they presented their audience with Foxe's all-too-human Lord Powis, a weak man both cowardly and greedy.

Though the Oldcastle collaborators, as stated earlier, are generally careful to let their audience know whom to cheer or hiss, they have also written a number of scenes whose dramatic tone is, perhaps, more difficult to grasp. There is a real opportunity for the actors performing Oldcastle to play up the ironic and comic opening fight and the Acton-Murley episodes. Since Oldcastle is usually unambiguous in its point of view and presentation of historical material, it is perhaps unorthodox to take such an approach to these scenes. Yet it strikes me that the dramatists defuse the controversial qualities in their play. They make it palatable to censor and audience by emphasizing the comic and ironical aspects of the major scenes of riot and conspiracy. Thus the arresting and provocative spectacle of a play opening with a street fight and a death, while conveying a vivid sense of the factionalism and broils besetting the new monarch's kingdom, is significantly diminished in its overall seriousness through the foreground depiction of Lord Powis' quaint Welsh retainers, Owen and Davy. Though out of control and enflamed into brawling, these two followers cut ridiculous not menacing figures. Similarly, the murderous Irishman of the play is as much a ridiculous character as he is a threatening one.

An audience cannot take William Murley, brewer of Dunstable, seriously either. He is depicted as a fool, a braggart, a Captain Bobadill type whose "temptation" and "fall" at the hands of Sir Roger Acton, Bourne, and Beverley serves as a brief character study of such vain, foolish men as he. The three tempters, while more sinister and dangerous in their treasonous schemings than Murley, are, fundamentally, as naive and absurd as he is. Certainly an audience need not worry that Acton et al. could prove a real threat to King Harry when they so significantly depend on support from such an inadequate source as Murley. Even the grandiose numbers of supporters that Acton speaks about (see scenes v, ll.45-52, and viii, ll.65-72), there to keep alive the possibility of a rebel victory, can just as easily be perceived as one more ironic comment by the dramatists on the self-deluded blindness and inflated egos of all factionalists and conspirators. Furthermore, the potential threat of Murley's wealth and his anarchic inclination to kill one king and set up another are comically deflated through his conversation with his followers, Dick and Tom. Again, scenes of insurrection are undercut by the dramatists' depiction of events from a comic or satiric point of view.

The most serious-seeming scene of conspiracy in Oldcastle is the Cambridge scene vii. Indeed, the episode has been marked out by various editors (Simms, Tyrrell, Hebel) as possessing the best poetry of the play. Given their positive assessment of scene I assume that these critics would have expected the scene to be played in a conventionally dramatic manner. I (to foment an imaginary academic squabble) am not so sure: I believe that the scene was written primarily with ironic and satiric intent, and that Shakespeare's histories are its target.

As I read scene vii, the Oldcastle dramatists intended their audience to perceive the Cambridge conspirators as self-important figures, that is, less as legitimate threats to King Harry's throne than as bumbling fools. The dramatists borrow, lift, and pillage bits and pieces of Shakespeare's histories. Both the Archbishop's endless "Salic law" speech from Henry V and York's lineage speech to a pair of conspirators in a very similar scene from 2 Henry VI are "sources" for the scene vii writer. On this view, the beginning of scene vii is supposed to be comic, and the original audience probably laughed on many different levels. Simply, they laughed at the obtuseness of Scroop and Gray in failing to understand Cambridge's original genealogical explanation offstage, and at the long-windedness of Cambridge himself; knowingly, they laughed at the vague parody of formal "historical" scenes that they saw at Shakespeare plays. As noted before in the "Sources" section, Cobham's entrance and the last few speeches preceding it deliberately recall the scene from Richard II where Bolingbroke returns from exile, Northumberland remarks on the "beguiled" trip to Berkeley Castle, and Ross and Fitzwater enter "fiery-red with haste." I cannot see any reason for such obvious lifting of Shakespearian elements by the Oldcastle dramatists unless they intended some kind of parodic or pointed effect.[13]

The dramatists avoid polemicism by presenting Cambridge and his co-conspirators in as unthreatening a light as that in which they present Acton, Murley and Co. Cambridge is unwaveringly stupid--a conspirator in intent but absolutely lacking in style. Thus we see him eagerly sign his name to the "platform," a complete outline of his plot--something that no self-respecting conspirator would ever do, and something that no self-respecting audience would ever believe, except from a comic or satiric perspective.

If my premise and conclusions are valid, and the audience saw the Cambridge scenes from the distancing point of view of comedy or satire, then I would further point out that the elevated tone of the scene cannot be taken at face value and that such extended speeches as Cambridge's stag analogy are not serious poetry but rather instances of the fulsome eloquence to which this character seems addicted,[14] or, given the Shakespearian connections of the scene, parodic approximations of Shakespeare's verbal dexterity.

The few modern critics of the Elizabethan drama who have studied 1 Sir John Oldcastle in some depth have stayed clear of assessing the aesthetic merits or shortcomings of the play; certainly no-one has articulated a view on the style of the work. Other than the source-hunters, two scholars have discussed Oldcastle at length, M.G.M. Adkins and David Bevington: both have for the most part written from an historical and political perspective on the play. In her article "Sixteenth-Century Religious and Political Implications in Sir John Oldcastle," Univ. of Texas Studies in English, 22 (1942), 86-104, Adkins emphasized the collaborators' religiously motivated treatment of the Cobham story. She pointed out that the writers repeatedly assert Cobham's loyalty to the king and constantly defend and demonstrate Cobham's innocence. She concluded that the collaborators presented the Puritan Cobham in an unquestionably favourable light while they depicted the heretical rebels in a contemptuous manner. Collaboration and the over-riding need to make Cobham a hero were, for Adkins, two possible reasons for these discrepancies.

In Tudor Drama and Politics (Cambridge: Harvard Univ. Press, 1968), pp. 256-59, David Bevington fine-tuned Adkins' thesis, maintaining that the history play was "the moderate Puritans' warning to extremists of their own party." Moreover, he compared the play Sir Thomas More with Oldcastle and concluded that both upheld "integrity of conscience" but only so long as this individual integrity was "severely distinguished from all corporate aspects of nonconformism." Bevington identified the scheming attitude of the Bishop with that taken by conservative Anglicanism and Archbishop Whitgift, while Adkins conventionally assumed that Oldcastle's Bishop was a portrait of vindictive Catholicism.

As I have indicated above, the Oldcastle collaborators make pointed but not necessarily controversial statements through their play. The overt Prologue and the many scenes that recall Shakespearian episodes demonstrate that the four Henslowe dramatists were trying to sell or package their play as some kind of reply to the types of plays performed by the Chamberlain's Men. The recent building of the Globe theatre in the summer of 1599 was an obvious commercial threat to the Admiral's Men and their manager of the Rose theatre, Philip Henslowe. This is also the time of the war of the theatres and probably the writing of Oldcastle was designed to augment the rivalry between the two theatres so that in the fall of 1599 the audience would not desert the Rose theatre for the delights of the brand-new Globe.

Plainly the Oldcastle authors also tried to indicate their distinct and separate position from that adopted by the pro-Essex Chamberlain's Men. The authors, in the factionalized world of late Elizabethan London, writing for the Admiral's men whose patron was no supporter of the Earl of Essex, and perhaps supported by the Elizabethan Cobhams (who were also anti-Essex), were obviously aware of the revival of bastard feudalism spawned by Essex's creation of knights during his military campaigns: 21 at Rouen (1591), 58 at Cadiz (1596), and 81 in Ireland (1599) (Russell, The Crisis of Parliaments, pp. 251-52). These knights would be beholden to Essex in a way that would threaten Elizabeth's political control. Murley seems a caricature of such knights and the dangers they represented.[15]

But, as I have indicated above, they tiptoe around this controversial topic by having Murley and their Essex-like figures, Cambridge and to a lesser degree Acton, shown as bumbling failures rather than evil threats. The collaborators show scorn rather than hysteria when alluding to the Essex affair. It is possible that they grew more controversial in Part 2, and that their attacks became so obvious that Part 2 was deemed unpublishable, but such an hypothesis is extremely weak given the example of Part 1, a play that consistently holds its punches.

On the subject of religion, a more integral issue in Oldcastle than the peripheral Essex affair, the dramatists take care to maintain a relatively orthodox Church of England position. They do not support the rigid or doctrinaire application of church power, so they present Cobham as a maligned victim of an excessive church; but they are certainly no liberal Puritans supporting the principle of religious conscience when they put such ideas into the mouths of the treasonous participants in the Ficket Field rebellion. Unlike Bevington and Adkins, I don't think Cobham is presented as a Puritan. The collaborators could have used all sorts of historical information to present their Lollard as the radical he undoubtedly was, but they do not. Oldcastle's Cobham is a conventional Protestant of strong beliefs, bedevilled by a completely erroneous reputation as some kind of rabble-rouser.

The Oldcastle dramatists do seem critical, however, through their characterization of the Bishop of Rochester, of those conservative persons or groups in Elizabeth's established church who speak about doctrine but who are nevertheless motivated by personal enmity. But their position is, once again, not as critical or contentious as it could well have been. First of all, they are presenting us, of course, with a Catholic--for Elizabethans, an uncontroversial villain. Secondly, they present us with an individual, the Bishop, determined to punish Cobham, but not with a representative cross-section of the church. Pointedly, the Bishop is alone in his malice. Moreover, he always had a good case against Cobham for treason--he never has to fabricate evidence--nor would his harsh and vindictive treatment of Cobham have been considered inappropriate _if_ Cobham had indeed been a traitor. The problem with the Bishop is not merely that he is working from a false premise, that Cobham is a cunning traitor, but that he is blinded by his intolerance.

The dramatists even blunt their anti-clerical bias, exemplified in their characterization of Sir John, by making him more a lovable rogue than a symbol of priestly hypocrisy. In this, as elsewhere in _Oldcastle_, the collaborators move away from the eye of controversy and develop the comic aspects of events.

This is most obvious in scene xiv where the Bishop meets and talks with Cobham in the Tower of London (see ll.33-60). The authors avoid a scene of doctrinal questioning of Cobham, discussed at length in Foxe (pp.326-28 and elsewhere). They do so either for artistic purposes--such a scene would be wordy or boring, or perhaps steal the thunder of the final scene of _2 Old-castle_, which presumably climaxed in Cobham's self-defence as discussed in Foxe--or for reasons of propriety, in that such doctrinal issues would still be considered too controversial for dramatic presentation. Instead, they concentrate on Cobham's escape, and do so in a comic manner. With respect to the entire issue of religion in _Oldcastle_ the writers steer their story away from the touchy and immensely complicated questions of religious rebellion and freedom of conscience towards the relative calm of the personality conflict between Cobham and the Bishop and the clear-cut problem of civil disobedience.

All in all _Oldcastle_, despite its flaws, timidity, and confusions, has a theatrical and dramatic quality that does repay close reading. The _Oldcastle_ collaborators paint a disturbing, if simplistic, vision for their Elizabethan audience. This vision of the hounded innocent, Cobham, who is from the first moment of the play put on the defensive, is a compelling picture of a nervous society no longer able to simply accept a man's word. In _Oldcastle_ ambition and cynicism are in the ascendant. We see, then, in the conscious paralleling of the two conspiracies--ambition and money equal knighthood for Murley; ambition and money equal crown for Cambridge--an attempt to convey a disordered society. But the Oldcastle collaborators are also optimists, and though they show their hero beset by troubles they still believe in heroes and the traditional verities: they still believe that evil men will, in the end, be punished.

Though I suspect that in 2 Oldcastle the evil Bishop of Rochester would have justly met the same fate as his historical model, Thomas Arundel, Archbishop of Canterbury, who died of apoplexy, and that the corrupt Sir John would finally have been sent to jail, as the chronicles attest, I cannot help wondering how the collaborators did present the final punishment, hanging and burning, of their innocent, Lord Cobham. Probably they still balanced the negative with the positive, as they do in 1 Oldcastle, and dramatized a Cobham aware of present human injustice but sure of divine justice and his reputation's future exoneration.

[1] The Poems of George Daniel, ed. Rev. Alexander B. Grosart, (Boston, Lincolnshire: Robert Roberts, 1878), IV, 113.

[2] A Short View of the Immorality and Profaneness of the English Stage, 3rd ed. (1698; rpt. München-Allach: Wilhelm Fink Verlag, 1967), p. 125.

[3] Lectures on Dramatic Art and Literature, trans. John Black, 2nd ed. rev. by A.J.W. Morrison (London: George Bell & Sons, 1900), p. 445.

[4] Shakespeare's Dramatic Art, trans. A.J.W. Morrison (London: Chapman, Brothers, 1846), pp. 434-35.

[5] The Pictorial Edition of the Works of Shakespeare, III (London: Charles Knight and Co., 1839), 213, 215, 216.

[6] Simms, p. 89.

[7] Tyrrell, pp. 129, 131.

[8] Hopk., pp. xv-xx.

[9] Mac., pp. 52-53.

[10] Hebel,(V, 48).

[11] The importance of Lord Powis and the fact that he seldom appears on stage suggests that the actor playing Powis performed another role, probably a role of some significance like Acton, Bishop, or King Harry.

[12] Also, see note for vii.217-18.

[13] It is tempting to conjecture that the authors are alluding to the controversy over the Essex-Elizabeth parallels to Bolingbroke and Richard II in Shakespeare's play. The Oldcastle dramatists might have been making clear their support of Elizabeth by placing their conspirator Cambridge in a parallel situation to Bolingbroke's. Such a testament of support would contrast creditably with the pro-Essex attitude of Shakespeare's company, the Chamberlain's Men.

[14] From this perspective Cambridge's "weeds of ususpation" speech (vii. 53-60), as well as Scroop's reply-interruption, "No more of that," also assume a comic tone.

[15] See Robert B. Sharpe, The Real War of the Theatres. Monograph Series, Vol. V (London: Oxford University Press; Boston: D.C. Heath and Co., 1935), p. 146.

CHAPTER FIVE

Theatrical Background and Assessment

i. Stage History

In a footnote to their edition of Henslowe's *Diary*, editors Foakes and Rickert write that the entry commonly used to establish *Oldcastle*'s first performance date between November 1 and November 8, 1599 (see entry [b] in "Date" section of this "Introduction") was written in actor Samuel Rowley's own hand. Importantly, the editors also show that the side notation "as A gefte" is in the hand of the Rose Theatre manager, Philip Henslowe.[1] The indications are that *1 Oldcastle* was a popular play, for such a gift (ten shillings) was not common. I have found only one other instance of Henslowe's noting a gift to his dramatists during the period when the four *Oldcastle* collaborators wrote for him. Ten shillings was given to John Day "after the playnge of the 2 pte of strowde" (that is, *2 The Blind Beggar of Bednal Green*--*Diary*, p. 168). *Oldcastle* probably earned its bonus for its first night success.

Later entries in the *Diary* also indicate that the play and its sequel were no nine days' wonder. On March 17, 1600, Henslowe gave the actor Robert Shaw 30 shillings to pay the "littell tayller . . . to macke thinges for the 2 pte of owld castell" (see *Diary*, p. 132). Even more important are the references made in the *Diary* on August 17 and then on September 7, 1602, to another Henslowe playwright, Thomas Dekker, being paid 40 shillings and then ten shillings for additions to Oldcastle (see pp. 213, 216). As well there is the Diary notice of August 21, 1602 (see p. 214) for 12 pounds to be paid out "to by a sewt for owld castell & A sewt & a dublet of satten." These notices are clear evidence that Oldcastle was revived in 1602. They occur in that section of the Diary where Henslowe recorded his dealings, not with the Admiral's Men but with another company managed by him, the Worcester's Men, who were now set up at the old Rose Theatre. (The Admiral's Men were now playing in the new Fortune Theatre.) We may safely conclude, then, that the revival was staged at the Rose, where the Oldcastle plays were originally produced.

After these notices the plays disappear without a trace and it is unlikely that they have ever been produced since the closing of the theatres in the 1640s. Indeed, there is no hard evidence to suggest that 1 & 2 Oldcastle were kept in the repertoire of the Henslowe companies after 1602.

ii. The Company

After the brouhaha over the staging of The Isle of Dogs by the Pembroke's Men in the summer of 1597 had subsided, Elizabeth I's Privy Council decided to allow only two companies to perform in London, the Chamberlain's Men and the Admiral's Men.[2] As a result, the Admiral's Men company who performed at the Rose theatre for Philip Henslowe from late 1597 to summer 1600 was a relatively stable company. Thus the group who performed Oldcastle at the Rose in the 1599-1600 season were a company of experienced actors many of whom had been together for two years.

From information in the Diary (see pp. 64-136, 239-242) we find that John Singer, Richard Jones, Thomas Towne, Robert Shaw, Edward Juby, Thomas Downton, William Borne (Bird), Anthony Jeffes, Humphrey Jeffes, Charles Massey, and Samuel Rowley were the major actors in the Admiral's Men at this time and it was they who put on Oldcastle. Thomas Heywood, Richard Alleyn, and William Kendall were also hired by Henslowe in the 1597-98 season (see pp. 241, 268-69) and probably they performed in the play. James Bristow, a boy, was hired in late 1598 (see p. 241). Other names which appear in theatrical "plots" (i.e., a guide to entrances, exits, and role assignments) of plays possibly put on at the time of Oldcastle (see Diary, pp. 328-331) are Thomas Hunt in a major role in Troilus and Cressida, William Cartwright and Robin Taylor in The Battle of Alcazar and 2 Fortune's Tennis, and the boys John Pyk (Pig), Thomas Parsons, Richard Juby, and George Somerset each in some of the following: Frederick and Basilea, Troilus and Cressida, The Battle of Alcazar, and 2 Fortune's Tennis. Undoubtedly, in a play like Oldcastle, which has about sixty speaking roles, the personnel of the Admiral's Men would have been kept quite busy.

A reading of the play shows that well over half of the characters appear in only one or two scenes and only a handful of the rest (Sir John, Cobham, Bishop, and Harpool) make their presence felt in all sections of the play. King Harry, Powis, Acton, Murley, Suffolk, and Cambridge are other characters who have an important influence on Oldcastle but are absent from major sections of the drama. Presumably, the actors playing these roles would have been required to play other parts. Moreover, many characters who only appear in one scene or section of the play, like the Sheriff and 1. Judge of Hereford, Club, Sir Richard Lee, and 1. Judge of Hertford, have a significant burden on them in their section. Again, one must conclude that such roles were doubled, for the Admiral's Men did not have the luxury of allowing their major actors to appear in only one scene or section of Oldcastle. There are only four female roles in the play--Lady Cobham, Lady Powis, Doll, and Kate--and since none but Lady Cobham has a heavy line load the boys could have either doubled in the female roles or played minor roles where their smallness or slightness would not be noticed. A primary piece of evidence in support of this is Lady Powis' curious exit in the last scene of the play. She makes her appearance with her husband in the courtroom and then leaves, presumably because she would be too squeamish to hear the details of the murder case. More than likely she leaves the courtroom so that she can return as Doll, a character that the boy playing Lady Powis could have easily doubled.

The first and last scenes of Oldcastle require the most speaking roles, eleven in the first scene and fourteen in the last (including two boys playing Lady Cobham and Lady Powis). The only other scene in the play that has most of the major actors on the stage at the same time is scene xii where ten characters--King Harry, Suffolk, Butler, Huntington, Sir John, Acton, Murley, Beverley, Cobham, and Bishop--appear. Scene xiii requires two more new characters to appear--Lord Warden and Cromer. A number of interesting details in these two scenes may provide useful information as to how the Admiral's Men divided up the roles in Oldcastle. First of all, Bourne is unexpectedly absent from the group of prisoners brought before Harry in scene xii. Secondly, Harpool does not accompany Cobham in scene xii though he left with Cobham in scene vii and will return with his lord in scene xiii. Finally, Lord Powis does not appear in scene xiii, though he has to be somewhere in Cobham where the action takes place. If these irregularities are not due to collaborative slip-ups, then it is highly probable that the actors playing Bourne, Harpool, and Powis were performing other roles in these two scenes. The evidence from these middle scenes and from the beginning and concluding scenes shows that the dramatists made a conscious effort to prevent their major scenes from being burdened with more than a dozen characters.

Trying to work out a doubling system in Oldcastle, for clearly most of the actors played more than one role, is a difficult task. Certainty is impossible for many doubling variations can be hypothesized. What follows, then, is a list of Oldcastle characters and groups of characters. The letters beside each character or group refer to those other characters in the list which could have been performed by the same actors.

a) Herbert, Gough, Davy, Owen: d-cc
b) Bailiff, Mayor, Sergeant, Sheriff, 1&2 Judge: h-cc
c) Powis: e, f, h, i, o, q, u, v, x
d) Sir John: a, s, v
e) Bishop: a, c, n, q, t, x, y
f) Suffolk: a, c, m, n, x-cc
g) Butler: a, v-cc
h) King Harry: a-c, l-n, x-cc
i) Huntington: a-c, l-n, q, t-cc
j) Old man, 1&2&4 Soldier: a, b, m-cc
k) Cobham: a
l) Harpool: a, f, h, i
m) Sumner, Butler of Cobham: a, b, f, h-j, o-t, w-cc, 3-5
n) Constable, Aleman: a-c, e-j, r-cc
o) Acton, Beverley: a-c, j, m, r, s, v-cc
p) Murley: a-c, j, m, v-cc
q) Bourne: a-c, e, i, j, m, r, s, u-cc
r) Cambridge, Scroop, Gray: a, b, j, m, n, o, q, u, x-cc
s) Chartres: a, b, d, j, m, n, o, q, u-cc, 1, 4, 5
t) Dick, Tom: a, b, e-j, m, n, u-cc, 4, 5
u) Lord Warden, Cromer: a-c, j, m, n, q-t, w-cc
v) 1&2&3 Serving-men, Lieutenant of Tower: a-d, g, i, j, m, q, s, t, w-cc, 1, 3, 4, 5
w) Irishman: a, b, g, i, j, m-q, s-v
x) Host, Club, Ostler, Officer: a-c, e-j, m-v, aa-cc
y) Mayor: a, b, e-j, m-vv, bb
z) Constable: a, b, f-j, m-v

aa) Lee: a, b, f-j, m-v, x
bb) 1&2 Serving-men: a-c, f-j, m-v, x, y, cc, 3-5
cc) Jailer, 1. Judge, 1&2 Justice: a, b, f-j, m-v, x, bb
1) Doll: m, s, 3
2) Lady Cobham:
3) Lady Powis: m, v, bb, 1, 4, 5
4) Robin: m, s, t, v, bb, 3
5) Kate: m, s, t, v, bb, 3

What appears below is a hypothetical and speculative doubling list of the major characters in Oldcastle that allows eleven major actors, two hired men, and four boys to perform the play comfortably. Probably more hired men were employed in speaking parts so that the other actors need not have had to double so many roles; but even if more hired men were not used, the play could go on.

Major Actors

Herbert, Suffolk, Harpool

Powis, Bishop, Host

Gough, Butler, Lieutenant, Mayor

Davy, King Harry, Club, 1. Justice

Owen, Huntington, Bourne, Irishman

Sheriff, Old Man, Murley, 1. Serving-man (Bishop's), Lee

Mayor, 2. Soldier, Acton, Ostler, 2. Justice

1. Judge, Aleman, Cambridge, Lord Warden, 1. Judge

2. Judge, Constable, Scroop, Cromer, Constable

Sir John

Cobham

Hired Men

Bailiff, 1. Soldier, Butler of Cobham, Gray, 1. Servant (Lee's)

Sergeant, 4. Soldier, Chartres, Beverley, 2. Serving-man (Bishop's), Jailer

Boys

Lady Cobham

Lady Powis, Doll

Sumner, Tom, Kate, 2. Servant (Lee's)

Dick, Robin, 3. Serving-man (Bishop's)

Those extant plays which were performed during the Admiral's Men's last season at the Rose--Oldcastle, The Shoemaker's Holiday, Old Fortunatus, Patient Grissill, Look About You, and 1 Blind Beggar of Bednal Green--have a recurring interest in the theme of the suffering hero. Mumford in Blind Beggar, Gloucester in Look About You, Fortunatus and Andelocia in Old Fortunatus, Grissill, and, in a complementary manner, Rafe and Lacy in Holiday all endure suffering and indignities. More importantly, most of the aforementioned, like Cobham in Oldcastle, are forced to assume disguises either to survive or achieve their reasonable ends. These plays, then, share a theatrical basis. The emphasis is on disguise and reflects either the commercial success of this device or the Admiral's Men's special skill at exploiting it. Significantly, these plays are also ensemble pieces that demand a group of about fifteen actors (boys included) to carry the burden of the numerous important speaking parts.[3]

Unfortunately very little information is available about what roles the individual actors in the Admiral's Men customarily performed. The Diary, the extant "plots" (playhouse casting lists and exit-entrance notices for a particular play), and the occasional mention of one of the actors in documentary records of other theatre companies are the only sources.

We do know that Richard Jones and John Singer had been in companies since the eighties,[4] and these men, along with Thomas Towne, Edward Juby, and Thomas Downton, were the major actors in the Admiral's Men where Edward Alleyn was leading the company in 1594-97.[5] Since Singer and Jones were, presumably, the oldest actors in the company they might have played those roles requiring older men in the plays put on in 1599-1600. From the Battle of Alcazar "plot" we find Jones playing the role of the Portuguese Luis de Silva. From this same plot we find Humphrey Jeffes playing the triumphant Muly Muhamet Xeque. Acting roles of lesser importance are Anthony Jeffes as the son of Muly Muhamet the Moor, Charles Massey as Zareo, Thomas Downton as Adbolmelec, Edward Juby doubling as Calsepius Bassa and Avero (the latter having a major soliloquy), Thomas Towne as the bluff Englishman Thomas Stukeley, Robin Tailor and William Kendall as Stukeley's Italian aides, Robert Shaw as the Irish Bishop, and Samuel Rowley doubling in various roles.[6] From various entries in the Diary (see pp. 76, 82) we see that William Borne played the villainous Duke of Guise in The Massacre at Paris.

Obviously, from such scant information one cannot make any brilliant reconstruction of the original casting of Oldcastle. Still, as with the problem of authorship responsibility, one is tempted to try to connect two known factors: the actors and the characters. Moreover, there are added enticements. There are five other plays which one can be relatively sure were performed by the same actors during the same theatrical season. These plays rely, for the most part, on familiar character types. The Oldcastle collaborators were fully cognizant of the personnel of the company. It is difficult, then, to resist formulating (or conjuring à la Friar Bacon) the same kind of equation--actor A = character-type A--as T.W. Baldwin did in his study of the Chamberlain's-King's company, The Organization and Personnel of the Shakespearean Company (1927; rpt. New York: Russell and Russell, 1961).

Fortunately, I have overcome this temptation. There are, to be sure, figures in Oldcastle who resemble in one way or another characters in the other five plays, and so hypotheses about the type-casting quality of the Admiral's Men plays could be made. As noted above Cobham has his counterpart in the other disguise heroes. Sir John, the comic vice figure of Oldcastle has his near doubles in Look About You's Skink, Holiday's Firk, and Old Fortunatus' Shadow or Andelocia. The evil-generating force in Oldcastle encompassed in the figure of the Bishop has his parallels in Sir Robert Westford of Blind Beggar, the Young King of Look About You, and Marquess Gwalter of Patient Grissill. Usually two older men are required in these plays. Apart from Fortunatus, Old Fortunatus needs two old men to open and end the play. Blind Beggar has the two older figures Old Strowd and Old Plainsey, Look About You has Old King and Fauconbridge, Holiday has Lord Mayor and Lincoln, and Oldcastle has Harpool and Sir Richard Lee. Invariably, the plays also have two contrasting female figures, one pure and good, the other evil, domineering, or common. In Old Fortunatus the subtle match-up is between the characters Vice and Virtue (though Fortune provides some variation to the symmetry). In Patient Grissill, where the use of the contrast is not only crude but downright repellent, Grissill is the shining example to impatient Gwenthyan; in Blind Beggar good Bess Mumford contrasts to bad Lady Eleanor;

and in Look About You Lady Fauconbridge plays nice woman to vindictive and cruel Queen Eleanor. In Holiday the plot is sweetened somewhat by the doubling of important female roles and thus we have romantic Rose and loyal Jane complementing Margery and knowing Sybil. In Oldcastle the opposites are Lady Cobham and Doll.

From the foregoing it would not be difficult to work up an argument to support the theory that Drayton, Munday, Wilson and Hathaway wrote Oldcastle with certain character types in mind. It is impossible, however, to assess whether the creation of these types was the result of writing with specific actors in mind, or the product of literary conventions outside the context of writing for particular actors at a particular theatre, or the reflection of widespread popularity in those theatrical types which were easily identified and enjoyed by an audience. Overwhelmingly, the odds are that the Oldcastle characters were created and formed by all of these and other considerations. I might have a strong feeling that Borne (Bird) played the villain Bishop, and so on, but such feelings would be, at best, educated hunches. The question of who acted what in Oldcastle, then, is unanswerable.

iii. The Stage and Staging

With respect to the staging of Oldcastle at the Rose theatre something more than educated hunches can be offered. The play does not require many props, intricate stage machinery, or costume finery, and one can envision most of the play being performed on a bare stage in front of the tiring-house façade. Still, there are incidents called for in the stage action that indicate something slightly more complicated is occurring.

The opening fight scene is arresting and certainly requires most of the company to appear on stage, but, apart from the portrayal of Herbert's injuries and the possibly unusual presence of welsh-hooks (see 1.36), the scene evolves in a straightforward manner.

The lame soldiers of scene iii are an effect that the Admiral's Men also employed in Dekker's _Holiday_. The _Oldcastle_ group approaches the lord's gate (see 1.31) and sits (1.32). Presumably "the gate" is one of the entrances in the tiring-house façade. Obviously the group came in from a different entrance than "the gate" and then moved towards it. This kind of stage movement is repeated in scene vii where Cambridge and friends enter and eventually end up near Lord Cobham's castle. (See 11.74-76.)

In his 1965 unpublished dissertation, "The Staging of Elizabethan Plays at the Rose Theatre" (Stanford University), Harvey Scott McMillin, Jr. makes a case (pp. 54-55) for the existence of three exits and entrances in the Rose theatre's tiring-house façade, maintaining that the middle entrance was probably a curtained alcove. He says that the three are needed in the scenes at Cobham's castle (iii and iv); and three entrances are needed in the Bell Inn episode to indicate a barn, an inn, and an undesignated entrance. I suspect all three entrances would also be necessary in the Tower scenes (xiv and xv).

Another interesting bit of stage business happens in scene iii. The stage direction requires Lord Powis to enter and then "_shroud himself_" (1.76. 1); at 1.86 there is the direction "_The Lord Powis comes on_". Cobham says that Powis "comes along the grove" (1.77) and intends "to shroud himself among the bushes" (1.80). This could mean that Powis enters and then leaves, to approximate being in the bushes and returning, but he could just as easily remain on stage and hide himself behind one of the two posts that were on the

Rose stage.

Action, no doubt, takes place on both sides of the Rose stage in scene iv, to indicate a slight switch in locale from Cobham's house to the alehouse. Near the beginning of the alehouse section at least one chair or stool is needed, for both Harpool and Doll mention that they were sitting (11.157, 172). One stool could suffice because Doll could have been sitting on Harpool's knee. Someone has to bring it in, and if a non-actor did not place it on the stage during the interval between scenes iii and iv, the Aleman is the best candidate for the job. In my text (see 1.131.1) I have Doll leaving and entering with the ale that Harpool asks for, but the Aleman could conceivably do this.

Indication that a significant amount of time has passed between scenes x and xi, and that the action in scene xi is to take place in the dead of night, is given through the entrance of the two men "with lights" (xi.0.2). The use of lights in public theatres like the Rose, where performances took place during the day, was the conventional way to indicate night-time. A passage of time, in this case a brief skirmish, is indicated in the opening stage direction of scene xii where an "alarum" or signal to fight is given off stage. Presumably some break in real time as well as stage time occurs between scenes xiii and xiv, for to have many of the same characters immediately reappear in a distant place at an obviously much later time is clumsy dramaturgy indeed. One way the awkwardness may have been diminished is by having the Bishop and the rest leave sometime during Harpool's last speech in scene xiii and to have the Sumner and Harpool alone on the stage at the end of the scene.

In scene xvi the conspirators are required to sit at a table "as in a chamber" (1.0.1) while King Harry and Suffolk listen "at the door" (1.0.3). For the scene to be staged a table and three chairs were set up either on stage or in a recessed area in the tiring-house façade. In the former case King Harry and Suffolk would be upstage of the conspirators and the audience would see the two looking out from one of the entrances in the façade. In the latter, King Harry and Suffolk would have been downstage of the conspirators and the audience would see them peering into the recessed area. With McMillin (p. 75) I find the first hypothesis more satisfactory because an appropriate focus would be on the conspirators in this first part of the scene; moreover, there would be no problems with sight-lines, an inevitable snag of recessed-area staging.

In scene xvii the Irishman drags in his slain master (see 1.19.1). There is, however, no information given as to where he takes the body. He has to "rifle" him on stage (1.22.1) but, of course, the body can't remain on stage when the scene is over. Also, the body must eventually be rediscovered in scene xxv (1.74) by one of Sir Richard Lee's servants. Probably the Irishman dumps the body near an entrance way or in a trapdoor on the stage.[7] The Irishman also wears a costume that is distinctly Irish and recognizable as such, for Harpool is automatically taken for an Irishman by the St. Albans constabulary when he wears the costume in scene xxiii.

The action in the Bell Inn scenes is hectic as characters change costumes and constantly enter and exit. The play demands fancy head-gear for Lady Cobham, for when the country Kate comes out in Lady Cobham's costume (xxiv.15.1) she can't figure out the head-gear or "gee-gaw." Scene xxiv also requires a character to appear above the stage; here Club speaks to the Ostler from an area above the stage and then he enters on to the main stage with Kate a few lines later.

For the most part the action is straightforward in the remaining three scenes of Oldcastle. Sir Richard Lee's son's body has to be found in scene xxv, and the stage was probably set up for the final courtroom scene. In the stage direction (xxvii.30.3) the judges are to "take their places" and at 1.1 the Jailer tells his man, "See the court prepared." Attendants, then, brought out a bench or chairs and they might have brought in a "bar," for 1. Judge says (1.63), "Call the prisoners to the bar." This may not be a statement of literal fact: rather it may merely be designed to create verbally the atmosphere of the courtroom; but as McMillin notes (p. 75) A Looking Glass for London, another play probably performed at the Rose, requires justice seats and a bar.

[1] Diary, p. 126.

[2] Bernard Beckerman, Shakespeare at the Globe, 1599-1609, (New York: Macmillan Co., 1962), p. 3.

[3] In this respect they are quite different from the earlier 1590 Admiral's Men's plays that so obviously concentrated on displaying the talents of that great actor, Edward Alleyn--Doctor Faustus, The Jew of Malta, The Blind Beggar of Alexandria, etc.

[4] Chambers, The Elizabethan Stage, II, 324, 339.

[5] Ibid., p. 149.

[6] W.W. Greg, Henslowe Papers (London: A.H. Bullen, 1907), pp. 138-41.

[7] McMillin (p. 57) concludes that there was one large trap in the Rose stage.

The First Part of the True and Honourable History of the Life of Sir John Oldcastle, the Good Lord Cobham

[Dramatis Personae

Lord Herbert--i
Lord Powis--i, iii, vii, xxvii
Gough; servant of Herbert--i
Davy; servant of Powis--i
Owen; servant of Powis--i
Sheriff of Hereford--i
Bailiff of Hereford--i
Mayor of Hereford--i
Sergeant of Hereford--i
2 Judges of Hereford--i
Suffolk--ii, vi, x, xi, xii, xvi
Bishop of Rochester--ii, vi, xii, xiii, xiv, xv, xxvi
John Butler--ii, iii, vi, x, xi, xii
Sir John of Wrotham--ii, iv, ix, x, xi, xii, xvii, xxvi, xxvii
King Harry--ii, vi, x, xi, xii, xvi
Huntington--ii, vi, xi, xii
Old man--iii
3 Soldiers--iii
Sir John Oldcastle, Lord Cobham--iii, vi, vii, xii, xiii, xiv, xv, xx, xxii, xxiii, xxv, xxvii
Harpool--iii, iv, vii, xiii, xiv, xv, xx, xxii, xxiii, xxiv, xxvii
Sumner--iv, xiii
Butler; servant of Cobham--iv
Constable of Cobham--iv
Aleman--iv
Doll--iv, ix, xvii, xxvi, xxvii
Sir Roger Acton--v, viii, xii
Beverley--v, viii, xii
Bourne--v, viii
Murley--v, viii, xii
Earl of Cambridge--vii, xvi
Lord Scroop--vii, xvi
Sir Thomas Gray--vii, xvi
Chartres, a French factor--vii
Lady Cobham--vii, xiii, xx(?), xxiii, xxv, xxvii
Lady Powis--vii, xxvii
Dick; Murley's man--viii
Tom; Murley's man--viii
Lord Warden--xiii
Cromer, a Sheriff--xiii
3 Serving-men of Bishop--xiv, xv
Lieutenant of the Tower--xiv, xv
Irishman--xvii, xviii, xxi, xxvi, xxvii
Host of the Bell Inn--xviii, xx, xxiv
Robin; a servant--xviii
Club--xix, xxiv
Kate--xix, xxiv
Ostler of the Bell--xix, xxiv
Mayor of St. Albans--xxi, xxiii, xxiv, xxvii

Constable of St. Albans--xxi, xxiii, xxiv, xxvi, xxvii
Officer of Watch--xxi, xxiii, xxiv
Sir Richard Lee--xxv, xxvii
2 Serving-men of Lee--xxv
Jailer of Hertford--xxvii
1 Judge of Hertford--xxvii
2 Justices of Hertford--xxvii

Non-speaking parts:

Sheriff of Hereford's man--i
(?) Lord Herbert's and Lord Powis' men--i
Townsmen of Hereford--i
Messenger--ii
(?) Attendants--vi
2 Attendants "with lights"--xi
Attendants--xiii
Lieutenant of the Tower's men--xv
Watch of St. Albans--xxi, xxiii, xxiv
Body of Sir Richard Lee the younger--xvii, xxv
Jailer of Hertford's man--xxvii
Attendants--xxvii]

Dramatis Personae] this edn. after MSR. A character-list was first given in F3. Scene numbers are provided as an aid to the discussion of authorship and the doubling of acting roles in the "Introduction."

Lord Powis] (c.1385-1421) John Gray married Joan (eldest daughter and co-heiress of Edward Cherleton [1371-1421], Lord of Powis), and in her right, Gray, for a few months, enjoyed half the lordship of Pool. Gray was a soldier who fought at Agincourt, Caen, etc. When Cobham was captured in 1417, Gray escorted him to London. (DNB, DWB)

Suffolk] (1316?-1415) Michael de la Pole, second Earl of Suffolk, was one of the commissioners for the Cambridge conspiracy trial (August, 1415). Michael de la Pole, third Earl of Suffolk (1394-1415), served with his father at Harfleur and was then killed at Agincourt. Drayton mentions him in The Ballad of Agincourt. (Hebel, III, 54-55, ll.1809-1848; DNB)

Bishop of Rochester] Based on Thomas Arundel (1353-1414) who had a tempestuous career in church politics. He was an ardent opponent of Lollardy and after Henry V's succession in 1413, as Archbishop of Canterbury, he examined Lord Cobham at length and condemned him for a heretic. (DNB)

John Butler] In 1413 he was the Usher of King Henry's chamber. In that year he attempted to summon Cobham to appear before an ecclesiastical court. (Waugh, p. 449)

Sir John of Wrotham] A parson of Wrotham who robbed on Newmarket Heath was captured in 1418. See "Sources" chapter, p. 26.

King Harry] (1387-1422) King of England from 1413-1422. On becoming king he had to quickly deal with Lord Cobham and other Lollard heretics, but he failed to persuade Cobham to recant his anti-church positions. When he heard of the Ficket Field rebellion (Jan. 1414) he quickly acted and successfully stopped that uprising. He also uncovered the Cambridge conspiracy (Aug. 1415). See notes for Cobham and Cambridge. (DNB)

Huntington] (1395/96-1447) John Holland was the second son but first surviving heir of his father the Earl of Huntington who was beheaded in Jan. 1400. He, too, is mentioned in Drayton's The Ballad of Agincourt (see notes for Suffolk). John Holland was restored in 1417 and so became Earl of Huntington. (Complete Peerage)

Sir John Oldcastle, Lord Cobham] (1387?-1417) He was the eldest son of Sir Richard Oldcastle of Almeley in Herefordshire. In 1408 he married Joan, Lady Cobham, and became Lord Cobham of Cooling. By 1410 he was suspected by Archbishop Arundel of having a chaplain who advocated Wycliffite views. He was on good terms with the Prince of Wales, however, and in 1411 served as one of the commanders sent to France to relieve the Burgundian party. By 1413 the clergy were strongly distrustful of Cobham, and in a June meeting with the new king at Kennington, at which Cobham was present, the lord confessed to owning a book of heretical tracts. The clergy then supplied the king with more damning information, and Henry V met Cobham again and attempted to turn the Lollard back towards the Catholic church. Henry did not succeed and Cobham left for Cooling. He was cited variously by an archepiscopal summoner, by John Butler (qv), and then through the affixing of a citation to the doors of Rochester Cathedral. As Cobham failed to appear he was excommunicated by the Archbishop in absentia. Cobham was finally taken to the Tower of London and on Sept. 23 he was brought by the keeper to St. Paul's where he was questioned by Arundel and other clergymen. At this meeting, Cobham presented a confession of faith in English. At a tribunal at Blackfriars on Sept. 25, Cobham was excommunicated but not before he denounced his judges. He was given forty days respite, presumably to recant, but during his imprisonment in the Tower he escaped, probably through the aid of William Parchmyer who was accused and convicted of this crime in Oct. 1416. On Jan. 9, 1414, Cobham, Sir Roger Acton, and their supporters met at St. Giles in the Fields probably to attempt an armed uprising. Hearing that the king knew of their plans, Cobham left the field and eventually escaped to Wales. Henry V offered a pardon at the end of 1414 but Cobham did not make a reply. In Aug. 1415, perhaps taking advantage of Cambridge's plot against Henry V, Cobham rebelled against Lord Aburgavenny. Henry reordered the proclamation for Cobham's arrest in late 1416. Cobham was in Nottinghamshire in Dec. 1416, near St. Albans in 1417 where he was almost captured by the abbot, in Northamptonshire in July 1417, and then at his own manor at Almeley in summer and early fall. In Nov. 1417 Cobham was finally apprehended near Broniarth by Sir Griffith Vaughan, his brother Ieuan, and servants of Lord Cherleton of Powis. He was transported to the Tower by Cherleton's son-in-law, Sir John Gray. He was taken before Parliament on Dec. 1417 and condemned to death but not before he claimed that Richard II still lived. He was drawn, hung, and burnt hanging in St. Giles in the Fields. (Waugh, passim; GHQ, pp. 183-85; DWB)

Sir Roger Acton] He was the son of a Shropshire weaver and, supposedly, his achievement in various Welsh wars won him his knighthood. In late 1413 and early 1414 he joined with Lord Cobham and they with their supporters met in St. Giles in the Fields probably to begin a rebellion. The plan failed and Acton was taken prisoner by the king's forces. He was tried and executed in St. Giles in early 1414. (Waugh, pp. 640-44)

Beverley] John Beverley, a priest who took part in the Ficket Field rebellion, was executed for his crime. (Waugh, p. 644)

Bourne] A John Brown, an esquire of Cobham's who supported the Ficket Field rebellion, was executed for his treason. (Waugh, p. 644)

Murley] William Murley, a rich brewer of Dunstable was captured near Harengay Park by Henry V's men during the aborted Ficket Field rebellion. Murley had his horses decked in gold and also had a pair of gilt spurs on his bosom since he thought he would be knighted after the battle. (Hol. 11.61-68; Annals, p. 551)

Cambridge] (1375?-1415) He was the second son of Edmund Langley, fifth son of Edward III and first Duke of York; he married Anne, grand-daughter of Lionel, Duke of Clarence, fourth son of Edward III. He became Earl of Cambridge in May 1414 and soon after conspired to place his wife's brother on the throne or, if that proved impossible, to place a pseudo-Richard II on the throne. As Henry V prepared to sail for France from Southampton in July 1415, the conspirators told Edmund Mortimer of their plan. Mortimer told Henry V. Cambridge was subsequently tried, convicted and executed on Aug. 5. (GHQ, p. 188)

Scroop] (c.1373-1415) A close friend of the Prince of Wales, he took care of important foreign negotiations upon the accession of Henry V. He was possibly drawn into the conspiracy because he had married Cambridge's step-mother. After the conspiracy was uncovered he pleaded that he too was intending to betray the plot. He was executed along with Cambridge on Aug. 5. (DNB; GHQ, p. 188)

Gray] (1384-1415) He was the younger brother of John Gray (see notes on Powis). He became involved in the Cambridge conspiracy and, upon the plot's discovery was tried by a Hampshire jury in Southampton on Aug. 2 for treason. He was convicted and executed. (DNB; GHQ, p. 188)

Cromer] A William Cromer was Mayor of London during the Ficket Field rebellion and it was to him that Henry V sent orders for the safeguarding of the city. As Mayor of London he also signed the "Commission against Lord Cobham," a warrant made out for Cobham's arrest after the aborted rebellion. (Waugh, p. 640; Foxe)

Lieutenant of the Tower] Sir Robert Morley was Lieutenant or Keeper of the Tower at the time of Cobham's imprisonment--Sept. and Oct. 1413. After Cobham's escape from the Tower, Morley was removed from his office and imprisoned, but a fortnight later was released. (Waugh, pp. 451, 453, 638)

The Prologue

The doubtful title, gentlemen, prefixed
Upon the argument we have in hand,
May breed suspense and wrongfully disturb
The peaceful quiet of your settled thoughts,
To stop which scruple, let this brief suffice.
It is no pampered glutton we present,
Nor agèd counsellor to youthful sin,
But one whose virtue shone above the rest,
A valiant martyr and a virtuous peer,
In whose true faith and loyalty expressed

The Prologue] It was probably written for the publication of Q1 and not for the stage, for it addresses itself to the discerning reader who has the leisure ("peaceful quiet") to reflect and consider the play's thesis. It is also forensic in tone: the authors use legal language to present the case for Cobham and the play and so reinforce the "truth" of the "true and honorable historie" that follows.

1-2.] referring to the title on the title page. The authors coyly allude to the controversy over the name "Oldcastle", the name Shakespeare originally gave to Falstaff. They indicate the seeming inconsistency of writing both a "true" and "honorable" history about the disreputable Falstaff-Oldcastle.

1. doubtful] uncertain, ambiguous (OED 1.a); or "giving cause for apprehensions" (OED 4).

2. argument] evidence (OED 1); or "a process of reasoning" (OED 3.a); applied figuratively to the play.

5. brief] a short statement or account of something (OED 5); in law "a summary of the facts of a case" (OED 7); or, quasi-adverbially, "in brief" (OED C.b.).

6-7.] indicating Falstaff's influence on Prince Hal in 1 Henry IV (Mal., p. 267). The other specific references to Falstaff in Old. (x.53-54, 82-83) also concern themselves with Falstaff's grossness.

Unto his sovereign and his country's weal,
We strive to pay that tribute of our love
Your favours merit. Let fair truth be graced,
Since forged invention former time defaced.

12. love] Q2; Love, Q1. 13. merit. Let] Q2; merite, let Q1.

12-13.] Here a "that" is in ellipsis before "your favours" and "merit" is in the indicative. If Q1's punctuation is retained it could mean that the authors strive to do the three things listed, and that "pay," "merit," and "let" are in the infinitive.

13. favours] a superior's good will (*OED* 1); or "partiality towards a litigant" (*OED* 4).

The True and Honourable History of the Life of Sir John Oldcastle, the Good Lord Cobham

[i] *[Enter Lord Herbert, Lord Powis, Davy, Owen, Gough, and other followers of the Lords Herbert and Powis; they fight.] In the fight enter the Bailiff, the Sheriff, and his man.*

Sher. My lords, I charge ye in his highness name
To keep the peace, you and your followers.

Herb. Good Master Sheriff, look unto yourself.

Pow. Do so, for we have other business.

[*All*] *proffer to fight again.*

Sher. Will ye disturb the judges and the assize?

0.1-2. *Enter . . . fight*] *Mal. subst.* 0.2-3. *In . . . man*] *This ed.*; *In the fight, enter the Sheriffe and two of his men Q1.*

0.2] *In*] during (Abbott, #161).

0.3. *Bailiff*] an officer of justice under a sheriff, who executes writs and processes, distrains and arrests (*OED* 3).

Sheriff] responsible for "executing most judicial writs, for keeping the county gaol, and especially for supervising elections to the Parliament" (Elton, p. 451).

1. highness] In Elizabethan usage the possessive inflection in disyllables ending in a sibilant is expressed neither in writing nor in pronunciation (Abbott, #217).

4.1. *proffer*] make an attempt (*OED* 3.a).

5. assize] periodically held county sessions, for the purpose of administering civil and criminal justice (*OED* II.12).

Hear the king's proclamation, ye were best.

Pow. Hold, then, let's hear it.

Herb. But be brief, ye were best.

Bail. O yes.

Davy. Cosson, make shorter "O," or shall mar your "yes."

Bail. O yes.

Owen. What, has her nothing to say but "O yes?"

Bail. O yes.

Davy. O nay. Py coss plut, down with her, down with her, a Pawess, a
Pawess!

Gough. A Herbert, a Herbert, and down with Powis!

Helter skelter again.

13-14. O . . . Pawess] *F4*; O . . . her, / A . . . Pawesse *Q1*.

---

6. king's proclamation] issued only from the king and council, proclamations could create offences with penalties but could not create felonies or treasons (Elton, p. 22).

8. O yes] more commonly "Oyez." It is a call by a public crier or court officer (generally thrice uttered) to command silence and attention (*OED* A).

9. Cosson] Welsh-pronounced English for "Zounds," i.e., "God's wounds" (Hopk. p. 1). In *Shakespearian Pronunciation* (New Haven and London: Yale Univ. Press, 1953), p. 37, Helge Kökeritz states that stage dialects were "synthetic" dialects, "employing only the most conspicuous peculiarities in pronunciation and grammar." In *Old*. Welsh dialect is indicated by replacing "ow" with "aw" (11.13, 22, 37, 42, etc.); replacing "b", "t", "k", "j", with "p", "d, "g", "sh" (11.13, 37, 42, 62, etc.) or *vice versa* (11.13, 43, 67, etc.); using "her" indiscriminately for various pronouns (11.11, 13, 42, 43, etc.); and pronouncing the silent "k" (11.17, 66).

13. Py coss plut] i.e., "By God's blood."

15.1. *Helter skelter*] i.e., confused action (*OED* adv. "in disordered haste").

Sher. Hold, in the king's name, hold!

Owen. Down, e' tha kanave's name, down!

In this fight the Bailiff is knocked down, and the Sheriff and the other run away.

Herb. Powis, I think thy Welsh and thou do smart.

Pow. Herbert, I think my sword came near thy heart.

Herb. Thy heart's best blood shall pay the loss of mine.

Gough. A Herbert, a Herbert!

Davy. A Pawess, a Pawess!

As they are lifting their weapons, enter the Mayor of Hereford, and his officers [*(including a Sergeant)*] *and townsmen with clubs.*

Mayor. My lords, as you are liege men to the crown,
True noblemen, and subjects to the king,
Attend his highness proclamation,
Commanded by the judges of assize,
For keeping peace at this assembly.

Herb. Good Master Mayor of Hereford, be brief.

Mayor. Sergeant, without the ceremony of "O yes"
Pronounce aloud the proclamation.

Ser. The king's justices, perceiving what public mischief may ensue this private quarrel, in his majesty's name do straightly charge and

---

17. e' . . . name] i.e. "in the knave's name."

31-36.] The proclamation seems based on the statute quoted in Foxe (pp. 353-55) passed in the second year of Henry V's reign (*after* the Ficket Field rebellion--sc. v., viii, xii), which provided local officials of the crown command all persons of what degree soever to depart this city of Hereford, except such as are bound to give attendance at this assize. And that no man presume to wear any weapon, especially welsh-hooks, forest-bills--

Owen. Haw? No pill nor wells hoog? Ha?

Mayor. Peace, and hear the proclamation.

Ser. And that the Lord Powis do presently disperse and discharge his retinue, and depart the city in the king's peace, he and his followers, on pain of imprisonment.

Davy. Haw? Pud her Lord Pawess in prison? A Pawess, a Pawess, cosson, live and tie with her lord!

Gough. A Herbert, a Herbert!

In this fight the Lord Herbert is wounded and falls to the ground, the Mayor and his company go away crying clubs, Powis runs away, Gough and other of Herbert's faction busy themselves about Herbert.

42-43. Haw . . . lord] *F4*; Haw . . . Pawes / A . . . Lord *Q1*.

---

the power to deal quickly and efficiently with Lollard-inspired activities. This scene conventionally implies that there is a need for just such "law and order" legislation, while realistically portraying the difficulties of making it effective.

36. welsh-hooks, forest-bills] forms of bill-hooks: "a heavy thick knife or chopper with a hooked end" (*OED*).

44.3. *crying clubs*] calling for support (*OED* "club" 1.c).

other] In Elizabethan usage "other" was used as the singular and plural (Abbott, # 12).

Enters the two Judges in their robes, the Sheriff
and his bailiffs afore them, [*the Mayor,*] *etc.*

1. Jud. Where's the Lord Herbert? Is he hurt or slain?
Sher. He's here, my Lord.
2. Jud. How fares his lordship, friends?
Gough. Mortally wounded, speechless, he cannot live.
1. Jud. Convey him hence, let not his wounds take air,
And get him dressed with expedition.

Exeunt Herbert and Gough.

Master Mayor of Hereford, Master Shrieve o'th' shire,
Commit Lord Powis to safe custody
To answer the disturbance of the peace,
Lord Herbert's peril, and his high contempt
Of us, and you, the king's commissioners.
See it be done with care and diligence.
Sher. Please it, your lordship, my Lord Powis is gone
Past all recovery.
2. Jud. Yet let search be made
To apprehend his followers that are left.
Sher. There are some of them. [*To bailiffs*] Sirs, lay hold on them.

54. us, . . . commissioners.] *Simms*; us; . . . commissioners, *Pope*; us, . . . commissioners, *Q1*.

44.5. *Enters*] In Elizabethan usage the -s ending for 3rd person plural was occasionally used (Abbott, #333). See also xxv.70.

54. king's commissioners] either generally being applied to the Mayor and Sheriff as local men of importance, or referring to justices of the peace commonly called "commissioners."

Owen. Of us, and why? What has her done, I pray you?

Sher. Disarm them, bailiffs.

Mayor. Officers, assist.

Davy. Hear you, Lor' Shudge, what resson is for this?

Owen. Cosson, pe 'puse for fighting for our lord?

1. Jud. Away with them.

Davy. Harg you, my lord.

Owen. Gough my Lord Herbert's man's a shitten kanave.

Davy. Ise live and tie in good quarrel.

Owen. Pray you do shustice, let awl be preson.

Davy. Prison, no!
Lord Shudge, I wool give you pail, good surety.

Both at once all this

2. Jud. What bail? What sureties?

Davy. Her coozin ap Rees, ap Evan, ap Morrice, ap Morgan, ap Llewellyn, ap Madoc, ap Meredith, ap Griffen, ap Davy, ap Owen, ap Shinken Shones.

2. Jud. Two of the most sufficient are enow--

---

63. pe 'puse] i.e., be abused (Hebel, V, 48).

67. Ise] colloquial variant of "I shall" (Kökeritz, Shakespearian Pronunciation, p. 39).

68. preson] i.e. "imprisoned."

70. surety] a person who undertakes some specific responsibility on behalf of another who remains primarily liable (OED 7).

72. ap] Welsh ap, from map son (OED).

74. Shinken Shones] i.e. "Jenkin Jones."

Sher. And't please your lordship, these are all but one.

1. Jud. To jail with them and the Lord Herbert's men,
We'll talk with them when the assize is done.

Exeunt [*Herbert's and Powis' factions attended*.]

Riotous, audacious, and unruly grooms,
Must we be forced to come from the bench
To quiet brawls which every constable
In other civil places can suppress?

2. Jud. What was the quarrel that caused all this stir?

Sher. About religion, as I heard, my lord.
Lord Powis detracted from the power of Rome,
Affirming Wycliffe's doctrine to be true
And Rome's erroneous. Hot reply was made
By the Lord Herbert: they were traitors all
That would maintain it. Powis answered:
They were as true, as noble, and as wise

---

76. these . . . one] Probably "these" refers to the names listed and the Sheriff is informing 2. Judge that the list merely refers to one person (Owen). This provides a joke at the expense of Welsh nomenclature where one person's name includes names of that person's ancestors up to half a dozen generations (Basil Cottle ed., *Penguin Dictionary of Surnames* [Great Britain: Penguin Books, 1967], p. 11).

79. grooms] serving-men (*OED* 3).

86. Wycliffe's doctrine] Foxe (pp. 324-25) includes "The Christian Belief of the Lord Cobham." In this confession Cobham enunciates Wycliffite doctrine by confirming his belief in the apostles' creed; maintaining that Christ, not the Pope, is the head of the church, that only those church customs based firmly on scripture are to be followed, that priests are to be confessed to only if they are virtuous, and that at the sacrament at the altar the bread and wine are both material and immaterial, not material before consecration and immaterial after.

As he, that would defend it with their lives.
He named for instance Sir John Oldcastle,
The Lord Cobham. Herbert replied again,
"He, thou, and all are traitors that so hold."
The lie was given, the several factions drawn,
And so enraged that we could not appease it.

<u>1. Jud</u>. This case concerns the king's prerogative
And's dangerous to the state and commonwealth.
Gentlemen, justices, Master Mayor, and Master Shrieve,
It doth behoove us all, and each of us
In general and particular, to have care
For the suppressing of all mutinies,

---

95. The lie was given] "To give the lie" means to accuse a person to his/her face of lying (<u>OED</u> "lie" 2). Here Herbert accuses Powis.

97-123.] 1. Judge's speech further articulates the intent of the statute noted above (see note 11.31-36): "And moreover, that the justices of the king's bench, the justices of peace, and justices of assize, have full power to inquire of all such which hold any errors of heresies, as Lollards, and who be their maintainers, receivers, . . . of such books, as well of their sermons, as schools, conventicles, congregations, and confederacies, and that this clause be put in the commissions of the justices of the peace."

97. king's prerogative] those rights and privileges exclusively the domain of the monarch. In this instance used anachronistically to refer to the civil disorder caused by religious controversy which would come under Elizabeth I's control as supreme governor of church and state.

99-117. justices] Likely 1. Judge is referring to non-speaking justices of the peace who came on either when the Mayor entered (1.22.1-3), or when the two judges of assize arrived on the scene (1.44.5-6); it is possible that 1. Judge is referring to the Mayor and Sheriff (see note 1.54) who could also be justices of the peace. Justices had many responsibilities, and after the revision of the commission of the peace in 1590, they were required to enforce all statutes concerning the peace, to take sureties for good behaviour (which 2. Judge does in <u>Old</u>.), to hear cases, and so on (Elton, pp. 454-55).

And all assemblies, except soldiers' musters
For the king's preparation into France.
We hear of secret conventicles made,
And there is doubt of some conspiracies
Which may break out into rebellious arms
When the king's gone, perchance before he go.
Note, as an instance, this one perilous fray:
What factions might have grown on either part,
To the destruction of the king and realm.
Yet, in my conscience, Sir John Oldcastle
Innocent of it, only his name was used.
We therefore from his highness give this charge:
You, Master Mayor, look to your citizens;
You, Master Sheriff, unto your shire; and you,
As justices, in everyone's precinct,
There be no meetings. When the vulgar sort

117. justices, . . . precinct,] Simms; Justices . . . precinct Q1; justices, . . . precinct Mal.

---

103. except soldiers' musters] This exception is not in the statute quoted by Foxe, and so may be a topical reference to the soldiers in London who had been on the alert since August 1599 (E. Howes, The Abridgement of the English Chronicle [1610], pp. 407-09).

105. conventicles] clandestine or illegal meetings (OED 3); or, anachronistically, "a meeting of (Protestant) Non-conformists or Dissenters from the Church of England for religious worship" (OED 4.b). See note 11.97-123 for use of "conventicles" in Foxe.

112-13.] 1. Judge's fair-minded opinion of Cobham is one of many examples of the authors' careful but simplistic colouring of their audience's response. This authority figure is used, much like King Harry is used in later scenes, as a character witness to underline Cobham's innocence.

Sit on their ale-bench with their cups and cans
Matters of state be not their common talk,
Nor pure religion by their lips profaned.
Let us return unto the bench again,
And there examine further of this fray.

Enter a Bailie and a Sergeant.

Sher. Sirs, have ye taken the Lord Powis yet?

Bail. No, nor heard of him.

Ser. No, he's gone far enough.

2. Jud. They that are left behind shall answer all. Exeunt.

[ii] Enter Suffolk, Bishop of Rochester, Butler, [Sir John the] parson of Wrotham.

Suff. Now, my Lord Bishop, take free liberty
To speak your mind. What is your suit to us?

Bish. My noble lord, no more than what you know
And have been oftentimes invested with.
Grievous complaints have passed between the lips
Of envious persons to upbraid the clergy--
Some carping at the livings which we have,
And others spurning at the ceremonies

0.1. Sir John the] Rowe.

123.1. Bailie] variant of bailiff.

7. livings] church positions (OED 5).

That are of ancient custom in the church--
Amongst the which, Lord Cobham is a chief.
What inconvenience may proceed hereof,
Both to the king and to the commonwealth,
May easily be discerned, when like a frenzy
This innovation shall possess their minds.
These upstarts will have followers to uphold
Their damned opinion, more than Harry shall
To undergo his quarrel 'gainst the French.

Suff. What proof is there against them to be had,
That what you say the law may justify?

Bish. They give themselves the names of Protestants,
And meet in fields and solitary groves.

Sir John. Was ever heard, my lord, the like till now?
That thieves and rebels--'sblood, heretics,
Plain heretics, I'll stand to't to their teeth--
Should have, to colour their vile practices,
A title of such worth as Protestant?

Enter one with letters for the Bishop and exit.

26.1.] *This ed*.; *enter one wyth a letter Q1*.

---

17. his . . . French] i.e., King Harry's claim to the throne through the female line. Archbishop of Canterbury at I.ii, *Henry V* (also Hol., pp. 9-10) discusses Henry's claim and Salic law.

19. justify] condemn to punishment (*OED* 2).

26.] It is, of course, inconsistent and anachronistic that any of these Catholics would consider "Protestant" a worthy title.

Suff. Oh, but you must not swear; it ill becomes
One of your coat to rap out bloody oaths.

Bish. Pardon him, good my lord, it is his zeal:
An honest country prelate who laments
To see such foul disorder in the church.

Sir John. There's one, they call him Sir John Oldcastle.
He has not his name for nought, for like a castle
Doth he encompass them within his walls;
But till that castle be subverted quite
We ne'er shall be at quiet in the realm.

Bish. That is our suit, my lord, that he be ta'en
And brought in question for his heresy.
Beside, two letters brought me out of Wales,
Wherein my Lord Hereford writes to me
What tumult and sedition was begun
About the Lord Cobham at the 'sizes there
(For they had much ado to calm the rage),
And that the valiant Herbert is there slain.

Suff. A fire that must be quenched! Well, say no more.

---

30. prelate] See note for Sir John in Dramatis Personae.

35-36.] Sir John shows his love of punning by playing on "Oldcastle" and "quite/quiet."

39-44.] These letters conveniently connect the first two scenes and provide relatively realistic exposition. For purposes of plot unity, the authors are careful in keeping this tumult at Hereford in the foreground, letting it serve, in this scene, as the clinching argument for letting King Harry know of the problems Cobham has supposedly caused.

The king anon goes to the council-chamber,
There to debate of matters touching France.
As he doth pass by, I'll inform his grace
Concerning your petition. Master Butler,
If I forget, do you remember me.

But. I will, my lord.

Bishop offers Suffolk a purse.

Bish. Not for a recompense,
But as a token of our love to you,
By me my lords of the clergy do present
This purse, and in it full a thousand angels,
Praying your lordship to accept their gift.

Suff. I thank them, my Lord Bishop, for their love,
But will not take their money. If you please
To give it to this gentleman, you may.

Bish. Sir, then we crave your furtherance herein.

But. The best I can, my Lord of Rochester. [*Refusing purse*.]

Bish. Nay, pray ye take it, trust me but you shall.

51. S.D.] *This ed.*; *Offer him a purse Q1*; *Offers the Duke a purse Mal., after 1.55*.

---

50. remember] remind (Mal., p. 267).

51. recompense] compensation for services (*OED* 4).

54. angels] an old English coin (*OED* 6).

59. furtherance] assistance (*OED* 1). As with "recompense" above the Bishop uses formal language, perhaps to disguise his bribery.

Sir John. [Aside] Were ye all three upon Newmarket Heath,
You should not need strain court'sy who should ha't.
Sir John would quickly rid ye of that care.

Suff. The king is coming. Fear ye not, my lord,
The very first thing I will break with him
Shall be about your matter.

Enter King Harry and Huntington in talk.

King. My Lord of Suffolk,
Was it not said the clergy did refuse
To lend us money toward our wars in France?

Suff. It was, my lord, but very wrongfully.

King. I know it was, for Huntington here tells me
They have been very bountiful of late.

Suff. And still they vow, my gracious lord, to be so,
Hoping your majesty will think of them
As of your loving subjects, and suppress
All such malicious errors as begin

62-64.] This brief aside of Sir John's not only lets the audience see and hear the "real" Sir John, but also further undermines our attitude to the Bishop, and thus his claim against Cobham, for the Bishop is retrospectively seen as a fool tricked by Sir John's mask.

62. Newmarket Heath] a notorious place for highwaymen. See notes for Sir John in Dramatis Personae.

67-72. My . . . late] Foxe believes (see Appendix III, ll.188-96) that the Church had hoarded money, and then under the threat of a government bill (Parliament considering to divest the Church of its temporalities) the Church cynically turned Henry V's attention to France and gave him money to aid his efforts. Old. does not take so cynical a line, and seems to follow Hol. (pp. 10-11, 12, 14) which neutrally notes the Archbishop's skill at turning attention away from the Church to France, and the Church's subsequent generosity towards the king.

To spot their calling and disturb the church.

<u>King</u>. God else forbid! Why, Suffolk, is there
Any new rupture to disquiet them?

<u>Suff</u>. No new, my lord, the old is great enough,
And so increasing, as if not cut down,
Will breed a scandal to your royal state
And set your kingdom quickly in an uproar.
The Kentish knight, Lord Cobham, in despite
Of any law or spiritual discipline,
Maintains this upstart new religion still.
And divers great assemblies by his means,
And private quarrels, are commenced abroad,
As by this letter more at large, my liege,
Is made apparent.

<u>King</u>. We do find it here
There was in Wales a certain fray of late
Between two noblemen. But what of this?
Follows it straight Lord Cobham must be he
Did cause the same? I dare be sworn, good knight,
He never dreamt of any such contention.

<u>Bish</u>. But in his name the quarrel did begin
About the opinion which he held, my liege.

<u>King</u>. How if it did? Was either he in place
To take part with them, or abet them in it?

If brabbling fellows, whose enkindled blood
Seethes in their fiery veins, will needs go fight,
Making their quarrels of some words that passed
Either of you, or you, amongst their cups,
Is the fault yours, or are they guilty of it?

<u>Suff</u>. With pardon of your highness, my dread lord,
Such little sparks neglected may in time
Grow to a mighty flame. But that's not all.
He doth beside maintain a strange religion
And will not be compelled to come to mass.

<u>Bish</u>. We do beseech you, therefore, gracious prince,
Without offence unto your majesty
We may be bold to use authority.

<u>King</u>. As how?

<u>Bish</u>. To summon him unto the Arches,
Where such offences have their punishment.

<u>King</u>. To answer personally, is that your meaning?

<u>Bish</u>. It is, my lord.

<u>King</u>. How if he appeal?

<u>Bish</u>. He cannot, my lord, in such a case as this.

<u>Suff</u>. Not where religion is in the plea, my lord.

---

100. brabbling] riotous (<u>OED</u> c).

103. amongst their cups] while drinking liquor (<u>OED</u> 10).

113. the Arches] an ecclesiastical court of appeal (<u>OED</u> 6).

King. I took it always that ourself stood on't,
As a sufficient refuge, unto whom
Not any but might lawfully appeal.
But we'll not argue now upon that point.
For Sir John Oldcastle whom you accuse,
Let me entreat you to dispense awhile
With your high title of pre-eminence. *In scorn*.
Report did never yet condemn him so,
But he hath always been reputed loyal,
And in my knowledge I can say thus much,
That he is virtuous, wise, and honourable.
If any way his conscience be seduced
To waver in his faith, I'll send for him
And school him privately. If that serve not,
Then afterward you may proceed against him.
Butler, be you the messenger for us,
And will him presently repair to court.

Exeunt. [*Manet Sir John and Bishop*.]

Sir John. How now, my lord, why stand you discontent?
In sooth, methinks the king hath well decreed.

Bish. Yea, yea, Sir John, if he would keep his word,

119-21.] The authors are attempting to modernize King Harry's reactions in accordance with the Elizabethan Royal Supremacy, where the monarch was supreme over church and state. It is implied that Harry has significant control over church affairs, though only a general personal action is indicated.

137. In sooth] in truth (*OED* 4).

But I perceive he favours him so much
As this will be to small effect, I fear.

Sir John. Why then I'll tell you what y'are best to do.
If you suspect the king will be but cold
In reprehending him, send you a process too
To serve upon him; so you may be sure
To make him answer't, howsoe'er it fall.

Bish. And well rememb'red; I will have it so.
A sumner shall be sent about it straight. _Exit_.

Sir John. Yea, do so. In the mean space this remains
For kind Sir John of Wrotham, honest Jack.
Methinks the purse of gold the bishop gave
Made a good show; it had a tempting look.
Beshrew me, but my fingers' ends do itch
To be upon those ruddocks! Well, 'tis thus:
I am not as the world does take me for.
If ever wolf were clothèd in sheep's coat,

141-45.] Sir John's advice to the Bishop is suggested by the reference in Foxe (see 11.58-61) to the Archbishop taking advice from the clergy with Cobham.

143. reprehending] reprimanding (_OED_ 1).

process] summons (_OED_ 7.b).

147. sumner] a messenger employed to summon persons to appear in the ecclesiastical court (Mal., p. 279); variant of "summoner."

152. Beshrew me] curse me (Mac., p. 145).

153. ruddocks] a cant term for money--gold coins (Mal. [Steevens], p. 279).

Then I am he, old huddle and twang, i'faith:
A priest in show, but in plain terms, a thief.
Yet let me tell you too, an honest thief,
One that will take it where it may be spared,
And spend it freely in good-fellowship.
I have as many shapes as Proteus had,
That still when any villainy is done
There may be none suspect it was Sir John.
Besides, to comfort me (for what's this life
Except the crabbèd bitterness thereof
Be sweetened now and then with lechery?)
I have my Doll, my concubine as 'twere,
To frolic with--a lusty, bouncing girl.
But whilst I loiter here the gold may 'scape,
And that must not be so. It is mine own.
Therefore I'll meet him on his way to court
And shrive him of it: there will be the sport. *Exit*.

---

156. old huddle and twang] an obscure phrase defined as a term of contempt (*OED* "twang" sb3). Probably Sir John uses it as a knowing or jocular synonym for the plainer "thief."

160. good-fellowship] the convivial manner of the "good fellow"--a roisterer (*OED*).

161. Proteus] Greek and Roman sea-god fabled to assume many shapes (*OED*).

172. shrive] in dual sense (as befits a priest-thief) of relieving someone of his sins as well as his purse (Mal. [Steevens], p. 280).

Enter four poor people, some soldiers, some old men.

1. [Sold.] God help! God help! There's law for punishing,
But there's no law for our necessity!
There be more stocks to set poor soldiers in
Than there be houses to relieve them at.

Old man. Faith, housekeeping decays in every place,
Even as Saint Peter writ, still worse and worse.

4. [Sold.] Master Mayor of Rochester has given commandment that none shall go abroad out of the parish, and they have set an order down, forsooth, what every poor householder must give towards our relief: where there be some cessed, I may say to you, had almost as much need to beg as we.

0.1. *Enter four*] *Q2*; *Enter three or foure Q1*. 1. S.H.] *Mal.*; *I Q1*.
1. help! God help!] *Simms*; help, God help! *Mal.*; help, God help, *Q1*.

Sc. iii.0.1. *four*] The evidence is that four people enter--three soldiers and an old man; *more* could enter but only four would speak. The fact that Q1 has no "*3.*" as a speech heading should cause no problems as "*Old man*" serves as a replacement.

1-14.] The plight of needy soldiers was a commonplace topic in Elizabethan literature. The Poor Laws of 1597 and 1601, instituted in part because of the miserable weather of the decade and subsequent famine and drastic increase in needy poor (including lame soldiers), set up overseers who, with the parish churchwarden, would levy a poor rate (Wallace Notestein, *The English People on the Eve of Colonialization, 1603-1630* [New York: Harper & Row, 1954], p. 246). The *Old.* authors sympathize with both the needy and the parishioners, but are hostile to the government's bureaucratic handling of the problem.

5. housekeeping] in the sense of "hospitality" (*OED* 2).

6. even . . . writ] Mac. (p. 145) suggests 1 Peter, iv.9, as the text in question: "Use hospitality one to another without grudging."

10. cessed] taxed (Mal. [Steevens], p. 280).

1. [Sold.] It is a hard world the while.

Old man. If a poor man come to a door to ask for God's sake, they ask him for a licence, or a certificate from a justice.

2. [Sold.] Faith, we have none but what we bear upon our bodies--our maimed limbs, God help us.

4. [Sold.] And yet, lame as I am, I'll with the king into France. If I can crawl but a shipboard, I had rather be slain in France than starve in England.

Old man. Ha, were I but as lusty as I was at the Battle of Shrewsbury, I would not do as I do. But we are now come to the good Lord Cobham's, to the best man to the poor that is in all Kent.

4. [Sold.] God bless him, there be but few such.

Enter Lord Cobham with Harpool.

Cob. Thou peevish, froward man, what would'st thou have?

Harp. This pride, this pride brings all to beggary.

17-18. France . . . shipboard,] This ed.; France, . . . ship-board. Mal.; France, . . . ship-boorde, Q1.

---

12. the while] meanwhile (OED 2.a).

20. lusty] healthy (OED 5).

Battle of Shrewsbury] the battle of 1403 where Henry IV defeated the Percies, which the audience saw in 1 Henry IV. The Old. soldiers, then, are loyal subjects.

24. froward] perverse, hard to please (OED 1). Harpool perversely condemns his master for being self-indulgent and then over-generous.

I served your father, and your grandfather: show me such two men now. No, no, your backs, your backs, the devil and pride, has cut the throat of all good housekeeping. They were the best yeomen's masters that ever were in England.

Cob. Yea, except thou have a crew of seely knaves and sturdy rogues still feeding at my gate there is no hospitality with thee.

Harp. They may sit at the gate, well enough, but the devil of anything you give them, except they will eat stones.

Cob. 'Tis long then of such hungry knaves as you. (*Pointing to the beggars*) Yea, sir, here's your retinue; your guests be come. They know their hours, I warrant you.

Old man. God bless your honour, God save the good Lord Cobham and all his house--

26-29. I . . . England] *This ed*.; I . . . grandfather, / Shew . . . no, / Your . . . pride, / Has . . . housekeeping, / They . . . that / Ever . . . England *Q1*. 30-31. Yea . . . thee] *This ed*.; Yea . . . knaves, / And . . . gate, / There . . . thee *Q1*. 34-36. 'Tis . . . you] *This ed*.; Tis . . . you, / Yea . . . come, / They . . . you *Q1*.

26-29.] The cantankerous Harpool hearkens back to the good old days where aristocrats dealt generously with their servants, and contrasts this to Cobham's supposedly niggardly ways. Complaints about the decay in housekeeping were common; for example, Stow (*Survey*, p. 82) in similar spirit recalls the days when Thomas Cromwell fed over two hundred people a day.

27-28. your . . . housekeeping] Harpool accusingly points to Cobham's "fine" clothes, "your backs, your backs," as evidence that Cobham is spending money on himself rather than on "housekeeping."

30. seely] foolish (*OED* 6).

34. 'Tis long then] i.e., "It's because of" (*OED* "long" a2).

36. They . . . hours] i.e., "They know their meal times" (*OED* "hour" 5.a).

[A] Sold. Good your honour, bestow your blessed alms upon poor men.

Cob. Now, sir, here be your alms-knights. Now are you as safe as the emperor.

Harp. My alms-knights? Nay, th'are yours. It is a shame for you, and I'll stand to't, your foolish alms maintains more vagabonds than all the noblemen in Kent beside. Out, you rogues, you knaves, work for your livings. [Aside] Alas, poor men. O Lord, they may beg their hearts out, there's no more charity amongst men than amongst so many mastiff dogs. [To the beggars] What make you here, you needy knaves? Away, away, you villains.

2. Sold. I beseech you, sir, be good to us.

Cob. Nay, nay, they know thee well enough, I think that all the beggars in this land are thy acquaintance. Go bestow your alms. None will control you, sir.

Harp. What should I give them? You are grown so beggarly you have scarce a bit of bread to give at your door! You talk of your religion so long that you have banished charity from amongst you.

39. Good . . . men] Pope; Good . . . almes, / Upon . . . men Q1. 40-41. Now . . . emperor] This ed.; Now . . . knights. / Now . . . Emperour Q1. 42-48. My . . . villains] Mal.; My . . . yours, / It . . . too't, / Your . . . vagabonds, / Then . . . beside. / Out . . . livings, / Alas . . . out, / Theres . . . men, / Then . . . dogges, / What . . . knaves? / Away . . . villaines Q1. 45. S.D.] Mal.

---

40. alms-knights] continuing the conceit of Harpool's "retinue" (1.35).

40-41. as . . . emperor] Seems proverbial but Tilley does not mention it. No doubt the phrase means "very safe" and Cobham is using it ironically.

43-44. your . . . beside] The Puritan Earl of Bedford was accused by Elizabeth I of making all the beggars in the country by his charity (Conrad Russell, The Crisis of Parliaments: English History 1509-1660 [Oxford: Oxford Univ. Press, 1971], p. 171).

A man may make a flax shop in your kitchen chimneys, for any fire there is stirring.

Cob. If thou wilt give them nothing, send them hence. Let them not stand here starving in the cold.

Harp. Who, I drive them hence? If I drive poor men from your door, I'll be hanged. I know not what I may come to myself. Yea, God help you poor knaves, ye see the world, i'faith. [To Cob.] Well, you had a mother. Well, God be with thee, good lady, thy soul's at rest. She gave more in shirts and smocks to poor children than you spend in your house, and yet you live a beggar too.

Cob. Even the worst deed that e'er my mother did was in relieving such a fool as thou.

Harp. Yea, yea, I am a fool still. With all your wit you will die a beggar, go to.

Cob. Go, you old fool, give the poor people something. Go in, poor men, into the inner court, and take such alms as there is to be had.

[A] Sold. God bless your honour.

Harp. Hang you, rogues, hang you! There's nothing but misery amongst you. You fear no law, you. Exit.

Old man. God bless you, good Master Rafe, God save your life, you are

62. S.D.] Mal.

---

56. flax] linen (OED 6).

for] as regards (Abbott, #140).

68-69.] Harpool implies that it is not he who is the true fool.

good to the poor still. [Exeunt. *Manet Cobham*.]

Enter the Lord Powis disguised, and shroud himself.

Cob. What fellow's yonder comes along the grove?
Few passengers there be that know this way.
Methinks he stops as though he stayed for me,
And meant to shroud himself amongst the bushes.
I know the clergy hate me to the death,
And my religion gets me many foes;
And this may be some desperate rogue suborned
To work me mischief. As it pleaseth God,
If he come toward me, sure I'll stay his coming,
Be he but one man, whatsoe'er he be. *The Lord Powis comes on.*
I have been well acquainted with that face.

Pow. Well met, my honourable lord and friend.

Cob. You are welcome, sir, what e'er you be,
But of this sudden, sir, I do not know you.

Pow. I am one that wisheth well unto your honour.
My name is Powis, an old friend of yours.

Cob. My honourable lord and worthy friend,
What makes your lordship thus alone in Kent,

76. S.D.] *Mal. subst*. 83-86. And . . . be] *Mal*.; And . . . rogue, / Subornd . . . it / Pleaseth . . . sure / Ile . . . man, / What . . . be *Q1*.

---

76. still] always (*OED* 3).

76.1. *shroud himself*] hides (*OED* 4).

83. suborned] bribed (*OED* 1).

And thus disguisèd in this strange attire?
Pow. My lord, an unexpected accident
Hath at this time enforced me to these parts;
And thus it happed, not yet full five days since.
Now at the last assize at Hereford
It chanced that the Lord Herbert and myself,
'Mongst other things discoursing at the table,
To fall in speech about some certain points
Of Wycliffe's doctrine 'gainst the papacy
And the religion Catholic maintained
Through the most part of Europe at this day.
This wilful testy lord stuck not to say
That Wycliffe was a knave, a schismatic,
His doctrine devilish and heretical;
And whatsoe'er he was maintained the same,
Was traitor both to God and to his country.
Being movèd at his peremptory speech,
I told him some maintained those opinions,
Men, and truer subjects than Lord Herbert was.
And he replying in comparisons,

98. happed, not] Q1; hapt. Not Q2. since.] This ed.; since, Q1. 101. things] Q2; things, Q1.

---

106. stuck not] did not hesitate (OED 15).

107. schismatic] promoter of a break with the church (OED B).

111. peremptory] intolerant, dogmatic (OED 4).

114. comparisons] scoffing similitudes (OED 3.b).

Your name was urged, my lord, 'gainst his challenge,
To be a perfect favourer of the truth.
And to be short, from words we fell to blows,
Our servants and our tenants taking parts,
Many on both sides hurt. And for an hour
The broil by no means could be pacified,
Until the judges rising from the bench
Were in their persons forced to part the fray.

Cob. I hope no man was violently slain.

Pow. Faith, none, I trust, but the Lord Herbert's self,
Who is in truth so dangerously hurt
As it is doubted he can hardly 'scape.

Cob. I am sorry, my good lord, of these ill news.

Pow. This is the cause that drives me into Kent,
To shroud myself with you, so good a friend,
Until I hear how things do speed at home.

Cob. Your lordship is most welcome unto Cobham,
But I am very sorry, my good lord,
My name was brought in question in this matter,
Considering I have many enemies
That threaten malice and do lie in wait
To take advantage of the smallest thing.

---

130. speed] fare well or ill (OED 2.b).

131. Cobham] Hebel (V, 49) notes that the authors are not sure of where to locate their hero--at Cobham or Cooling. The latter is only referred to in scene vii, the first Cambridge scene.

But you are welcome, and repose your lordship,
And keep yourself here secret in my house,
Until we hear how the Lord Herbert speeds.
Here comes my man.

Enter Harpool.

Sirrah, what news?

Harp. Yonder's one Master Butler of the Privy Chamber, is sent unto you from the king.

Pow. I pray God the Lord Herbert be not dead, and the king, hearing whither I am gone, hath sent for me.

Cob. Comfort yourself, my lord, I warrant you.

Harp. Fellow, what ails thee? Dost thou quake? Dost thou shake? Dost thou tremble? Ha?

Cob. Peace, you old fool. Sirrah, convey this gentleman in the back way, and bring the other into the walk.

Harp. Come, sir, you are welcome if you love my lord.

Pow. God have mercy, gentle friend. Exeunt. [Manet Cobham.]

Cob. I thought as much, that it would not be long before I heard of something from the king about this matter.

Enter Harpool with Master Butler.

Harp. Sir, yonder my lord walks. You see him. I'll have your men into the cellar the while. [Exit.]

154-55. Sir . . . while] Mal.; Sir . . . him, / Ile . . . while Q1.

154-55. into the cellar] to drink, no doubt. Block, an equally unruly servant in the Admiral's Men play Look About You, takes a similar opportunity to drink with visiting officers.

<u>Cob</u>. Welcome, good Master Butler.

<u>But</u>. Thanks, my good lord. His majesty doth commend his love unto your lordship, and wills you to repair unto the court.

<u>Cob</u>. God bless his highness, and confound his enemies. I hope his majesty is well.

<u>But</u>. In health, my lord.

<u>Cob</u>. God long continue it. Methinks you look as though you were not well. What ails you, sir?

<u>But</u>. Faith, I have had a foolish old mischance that angers me. Coming over Shooters Hill, there came a fellow to me like a sailor, and asked me money. And whilst I stayed my horse to draw my purse, he takes th'advantage of a little bank and leaps behind me, whips my purse away, and with a sudden jerk I know not how, threw me at least three yards out of my saddle. I never was so robbed in all my life.

<u>Cob</u>. I am very sorry, sir, for your mischance. We will send our warrant forth to stay such suspicious persons as shall be found. Then, Master Butler, we will attend you.

---

158. repair] go (<u>OED</u> 1). The language Butler uses is courteous, not abrupt, and Cobham willingly goes. The authors have Butler acting for King Harry and coming before the summoner (unlike Foxe and the chronicles). This allows them to underline their thesis that Cobham is fundamentally loyal to the king.

165. Shooters Hill] a notorious place for robberies; located on the Dover Road 7 mi. ESE of London (Oliver Mason, <u>The Gazeteer of England</u> [Great Britain: Rowman & Littlefield, 1977]).

like a sailor] one of Sir John's Proteus-like disguises. No doubt contemporary thieves did the same thing and made the lot of needy soldiers all the more difficult.

But. I humbly thank your lordship, I will attend you. [*Exeunt*.]

[iv] *Enter the Sumner*.

Sum. I have the law to warrant what I do, and though the Lord Cobham be a nobleman, that dispenses not with law: I dare serve process were a five nobleman. Though we sumners make sometimes a mad slip in a corner with a pretty wench, a sumner must not go always by seeing: a man may be content to hide his eyes where he may feel his profit. Well, this is my Lord Cobham's house. If I can devise to speak with him--if not, I'll clap my citation upon's door, so my Lord of Rochester bid me. But methinks here comes one of his men.

Enter Harpool.

Harp. Welcome, good fellow, welcome. Who would'st thou speak with?

Sum. With my Lord Cobham I would speak, if thou be one of his men.

174. S.D.] *Mal*. Sc.iv.2. nobleman, . . . law:] *Mal*.; noble man, . . . law, *Q1*.

Sc.iv] The authors are not explicit here but it seems a night has passed between scenes iii and iv (see 1.105; vi.67-68).

1. warrant] guarantee immunity (*OED* 8).

2. process] See note for ii.143.

3. were a] were he (*OED* "a" 1).

6. devise] scheme (*OED* 7).

7-8. if . . . me] According to Foxe (11.74-85) this was done, on Archbishop Arundel's orders, *after* both a summoner and John Butler had gone to Cobham and failed to make him come to court.

7. citation] written summons for the spiritual court (*OED* 1. a,b).

Harp. Yes, I am one of his men, but thou canst not speak with my lord.

Sum. May I send to him then?

Harp. I'll tell thee that when I know thy errand.

Sum. I will not tell my errand to thee.

Harp. Then keep it to thyself and walk like a knave as thou camest.

Sum. I tell thee my lord keeps no knaves, sirrah.

Harp. Then thou servest him not, I believe. What lord is thy master?

Sum. My Lord of Rochester.

Harp. In good time! And what would'st thou have with my Lord Cobham?

Sum. I come by virtue of a process, to ascite him to appear before my lord in the court at Rochester.

Harp. (*Aside*) Well, God grant me patience, I could eat this conger. [*To Sumner*] My lord is not at home. Therefore it were good, Sumner, you carried your process back.

Sum. Why, if he will not be spoken withal, then will I leave it here, and see you that he take knowledge of it. [*Posts bill*.]

27. S.D.] *This ed*.; *Fixes a citation on the gate Mal*.

16.] Probably Harpool takes an immediate dislike to the Sumner not merely because Harpool is a perverse old servant but because the Sumner acts in the officious and pompous manner of the bureaucrat, and uses in patronizing fashion "thou" and "thee" when referring to Harpool.

20. In good time] an expression of amazement sometimes ironical (*OED* "time" 42.c).

21. ascite] summon (*OED*).

23. conger] a sea-eel (Mal., p. 287).

<u>Harp</u>. 'Swounds, you slave, do you set up your bills here? Go to, take it down again. Dost thou know what thou dost? Dost thee know on whom thou servest process?

<u>Sum</u>. Yes, marry, do I, Sir John Oldcastle, Lord Cobham.

<u>Harp</u>. I am glad thou knowest him yet. And sirrah, dost not thou know that the Lord Cobham is a brave lord that keeps good beef and beer in his house, and every day feeds a hundred poor people at's gate, and keeps a hundred tall fellows?

<u>Sum</u>. What's that to my process?

<u>Harp</u>. Marry this, sir. Is this process parchment?

<u>Sum</u>. Yes, marry.

<u>Harp</u>. And this seal wax?

<u>Sum</u>. It is so.

<u>Harp</u>. If this be parchment, and this wax, eat you this parchment, and this wax, or I will make parchment of your skin and beat your brains into wax! Sirrah Sumner, dispatch. Devour, sirrah, devour.

---

28. do . . . here] Archbishop Arundel (see note 11.7-8) had "letters citatory" put on gates of Rochester church; those who favoured Cobham took the bills down.

33. brave] "an indeterminate word, used to express the superabundance of any valuable quality in men and things" (<u>OED</u> 3--Johnson definition).

35. hundred tall fellows] A "tall fellow" is a stout fighting man (Mal., p. 288). The historical sources note that Cobham, in defending himself against his accusers, claimed that he had one hundred knights who would speak for him.

37. Marry] simply (<u>OED</u> a).

43. Devour, sirrah, devour] After the "letters citatory" had been taken down the Archbishop sent new letters but these "also were rent down and utterly consumed" (Foxe, 11.82-85).

Sum. I am my Lord of Rochester's sumner. I came to do my office, and thou shalt answer it!

Harp. Sirrah, no railing, but betake you to your teeth. Thou shalt eat no worse than thou bring'st with thee. Thou bring'st it for my lord, and wilt thou bring my lord worse than thou wilt eat thyself?

Sum. Sir, I brought it not my lord to eat.

Harp. O, do you "sir" me now? All's one for that, but I'll make you eat it for bringing it.

Sum. I cannot eat it.

Harp. Can you not? 'Sblood, I'll beat you until you have a stomach!

He beats him.

Sum. O hold, hold, good Master Serving-man, I will eat it.

Harp. Be champing, be chawing, sir, or I'll chaw you, you rogue. The purest of the honey.

---

46. betake you to your teeth] i.e., prepare to eat.

54. stomach] appetite (OED 5).

56. champing] chewing vigorously (OED).

chawing] chewing roughly (OED 1).

56-59. The . . . feed] Other emendations have been made which involve more radical changes to Q1. This does not seem necessary. In this edition, Harpool, who is forcing the Sumner to eat the seal, bullies the messenger into stating that the seal is even better than honey. The Sumner cries out for mercy, but Harpool is unbending and makes the Sumner continue eating.

Sum. Tough wax--is the purest of the honey. O lord, sir, oh, oh--

He eats.

Harp. Feed, feed. Wholesome, rogue, wholesome. Cannot you, like an honest sumner, walk with the devil your brother to fetch in your bailiff's rents, but you must come to a nobleman's house with process? 'Sblood, if thy seal were as broad as the lead that covers Rochester church, thou should'st eat it.

Sum. O, I am almost choked, I am almost choked!

Harp. Who's within there? Will you shame my lord? Is there no beer in the house? Butler, I say.

Enter Butler [with beer].

But. Here, here.

Harp. Give him beer. (Sumner drinks. [Exit Butler.]) There, tough old sheepskin's bare dry meat.

Sum. O sir, let me go no further, I'll eat my word.

Harp. Yea, marry sir, so I mean you shall eat more than your own word, for I'll make you eat all the words in the process. Why, you drab-monger, cannot the secrets of all the wenches in a shire serve

58. Sum. Tough . . . oh] conj. Mal. (Steevens); Sum. Tough . . . hony. Harp. O . . . oh Q1; Harp. . . . Tough . . . hony. Sum. O . . . oh conj.Mac.
68. Sumner] Mal.; he Q1. 69. sheepskin's] Mal.; sheepskins, Q1.

---

58. Tough wax] For beekeepers tough wax means the best honey.

62-63. as broad . . . church] a quaint localizing of such familiar phrases as "broad as a barn door" (Tilley, B93).

69. sheepskin's] A sheepskin could be used for parchment (OED 2).

73. drab-monger] an abusive term corresponding to "pimp." A "drab" was a prostitute (OED), and a "monger" was a disreputable dealer (OED 1).

your turn, but you must come hither with a citation, with a pox? I'll cite you. (*Sumner has then done* [*eating*]. [*To Butler within*]). A cup of sack for the sumner.

[*Re-enter Butler with sack.*]

But. Here, sir, here.

Harp. Here, slave, I drink to thee. [*Exit Butler.*]

Sum. I thank you, sir.

Harp. Now, if thou find'st thy stomach well, because thou shalt see my lord keeps meat in's house, if thou wilt go in thou shalt have a piece of beef to thy breakfast.

Sum. No, I am very well, good Master Serving-man. I thank you, very well, sir.

Harp. I am glad on't. Then be walking towards Rochester to keep your stomach warm. And Sumner, if I may know you disturb a good wench within this diocese, if I do not make thee eat her petticoat, if there were four yards of Kentish cloth in't, I am a villain.

Sum. God be with you, Master Serving-man. [*Exit.*]

Harp. Farewell, Sumner.

Enter Constable.

Con. God save you, Master Harpool.

Harp. Welcome, Constable, welcome, Constable, what news with thee?

75. S.D. *Sumner . . . done*] *This ed.*; *he has then done Q1*. 89. S.D.] *Q2*.

---

74. with a pox] an imprecation with sexual connotations.

76. sack] white wine (*OED* sb3.1).

Con. And't please you, Master Harpool, I am to make hue to cry for a fellow with one eye that has robbed two clothiers, and am to crave your hindrance for to search all suspected places-- and they say there was a woman in the company.

Harp. Hast thou been at the alehouse? Hast thou sought there?

Con. I durst not search, sir, in my Lord Cobham's liberty, except I had some of his servants, which are for my warrant.

Harp. An honest constable, an honest constable. Call forth him that keeps the alehouse there.

Con. Ho, who's within there?

[Enter Aleman.]

Aleman. Who calls there? Come near a God's name. Oh is't you, Master Constable and Master Harpool. You are welcome with all my heart. What make you here so early this morning?

Harp. Sirrah, what strangers do you lodge? There is a robbery done this morning, and we are to search for all suspected persons.

Aleman. God's bores, I am sorry for't. I'faith, sir, I lodge

102.1.] Mal.

---

93. hue to cry] a malapropism for "hue and cry"--the outcry calling for the pursuit of a felon (OED 1).

93-94. a fellow with one eye] another disguise of Sir John.

95. crave your hindrance] another malapropism.

98. liberty] a district within the limits of a county, but exempt from the jurisdiction of the sheriff (OED 7.c).

108. God's bores] an exclamation like "'Swounds." The "bores" are Christ's wounds (OED 1.c).

nobody but a good, honest, merry priest (they call him Sir John a Wrotham) and a handsome woman that is his niece that he says he has some suit in law for. And as they go up and down to London, sometimes they lie at my house.

Harp. What, is she here in thy house now?

Aleman. She is, sir. I promise you, sir, he is a quiet man, and because he will not trouble too many rooms, he makes the woman lie every night at his bed's feet.

Harp. Bring her forth, Constable, bring her forth. Let's see her, let's see her.

Aleman. Dorothy, you must come down to Master Constable.

Doll. [Within] Anon, forsooth.

She enters.

Harp. Welcome, sweet lass, welcome.

Doll. I thank you, good Master Serving-man, and Master Constable also.

Harp. A plump girl, by the mass, a plump girl. Ha, Doll, ha, wilt thou forsake the priest and go with me?

Con. Ah, well said, Master Harpool, you are a merry old man, i'faith. I'faith, you will never be old! Now, by the mack, a pretty wench indeed.

Harp. Ye old, mad, merry constable, art thou advised of that? Ha, well

113. she] Q2; he Q1. 114. S.H.] F3; Con. Q1. 119. S.H.] F3; Con. Q1.

---

126. by the mack] an unmeaning word suggested either by "by Mary" or "by the mass" (OED sb2).

128. advised] informed (OED 6). Harpool, using language appropriate for a constable, makes fun of the Constable's ogling of Doll.

said. Doll, fill some ale here.

Doll. (*Aside*) Oh, if I wist this old priest would not stick to me, by Jove, I would ingle this old serving-man.

[*Leaves and returns with ale*.]

Harp. Oh, you old mad colt, i'faith I'll feak you! Fill all the pots in the house there.

Con. Oh, well said, Master Harpool, you are heart of oak when all's done.

Harp. Ha, Doll, thou hast a sweet pair of lips, by the mass.

Doll. Truly you are a most sweet old man as ever I saw. By my troth, you have a face able to make any woman in love with you.

Harp. Fill, sweet Doll, I'll drink to thee. [*Doll does so*.]

Doll. I pledge you, sir, and thank you therefore, and I pray you let it come.

Harp. (*Embracing her*) Doll, canst thou love me? A mad merry lass--would to God I had never seen thee!

Doll. I warrant you, you will not out of my thoughts this twelve-

129. said.] *This ed.*; said *Q1*.

---

130. wist] knew (*OED*).

131. ingle] cajole (*OED* 2): either for fun or profit or both.

132. feak] beat (*OED* 1).

134. heart of oak] a stout, courageous spirit (*OED* 19.b). This expression is found in the 1598 *The Death of Robert Earl of Huntington* (I3v). Both antedate *OED*'s earliest listing of 1609.

140. pledge] to give assurance of friendship to someone in the act of drinking (*OED* 5).

month. Truly you are as full of favour as a man may be. Ah, these sweet grey locks, by my troth, they are most lovely.

Con. God's bores, Master Harpool, I will have one buss too!

Harp. No licking for you, Constable. Hand off, hand off!

Con. By'r lady, I love kissing as well as you.

Doll. Oh, you are an odd boy, you have a wanton eye of your own. Ah, you sweet sugar-lipped wanton, you will win as many women's hearts as come in your company.

Enter Sir John of Wrotham.

Sir John. Doll, come hither.

Harp. Priest, she shall not.

Doll. I'll come anon, sweet love.

Sir John. Hand off, old fornicator!

Harp. Vicar, I'll sit here in spite of thee. Is this fit stuff for a priest to carry up and down with him?

Sir John. Ah, sirrah, dost thou not know that a good-fellow parson may have a chapel of ease where his parish church is far off?

---

145. favour] beauty (*OED* 8).

147. buss] kiss (*OED* sb2).

150. odd boy] rare one, singular fellow (*OED* "odd" 6). Obviously Doll is teasing the Constable. One might emend "odd" to "old" ("od" in Q1) for "old boy" (*OED* "old" 8) was a common expression of familiarity.

151. sugar-lipped] i.e., flattering.

157. fit stuff] i.e., Doll. Harpool questions the propriety of Sir John's arrangement.

160. a chapel of ease] a chapel built for the convenience of parishioners (*OED* 3.a); lewdly applied to Doll.

Harp. You whoreson stoned vicar!

Sir John. You old stale ruffian, you lion of Cotswold!

Harp. 'Swounds, Vicar, I'll geld you! [Harpool] flies upon him.

Con. Keep the king's peace!

Doll. Murder, murder, murder!

Aleman. Hold, as you are men, hold! For God's sake be quiet! Put up your weapons, you draw not in my house.

Harp. You whoreson bawdy priest!

Sir John. You old mutton-monger!

Con. Hold, Sir John, hold!

Doll. (To Sir John) I pray thee, sweetheart, be quiet. I was but sitting to drink a pot of ale with him, even as kind a man as ever I met with.

Harp. Thou art a thief, I warrant thee.

Sir John. Then I am but as thou hast been in thy days. Let's not be ashamed of our trade, the king has been a thief himself.

Doll. [To Sir John] Come, be quiet. Hast thou sped?

Sir John. I have, wench, here be crowns, i'faith.

---

161. stoned] lascivious (OED 4.b--1st quote 1607).

162. stale] lacking vigour (OED 4). Harpool's jibe implies impotency.

lion of Cotswold] sheep (Mal. [Steevens], p. 293).

169. mutton-monger] whore-master, pimp. "Mutton" meant "prostitute" (Mal., p. 294).

176. the . . . himself] alluding to Prince Hal's legendary exploits and specifically to the robbery in 1 Henry IV which Sir John refers to later on (see x.77-83).

177. sped] fared well (OED 7).

Doll. Come, let's be all friends then.

Con. Well said, Mistress Dorothy, i'faith.

Harp. Thou art the madd'st priest that ever I met with.

Sir John. Give me thy hand. Thou art as good a fellow. I am a singer, a drinker, a bencher, a wencher; I can say a mass, and kiss a lass! Faith, I have a parsonage, and because I would not be at too much charges, this wench serves me for a sexton.

Harp. Well said, mad Priest. We'll in and be friends. Exeunt.

[v] Enter Sir Roger Acton, Master Bourne, Master Beverley, and William Murley the brewer of Dunstable.

Acton. Now, Master Murley, I am well assured
You know our errand, and do like the cause,
Being a man affected as we are?

Mur. Marry, God dild ye dainty my dear. No master--good Sir Roger Acton Knight,Master Bourne and Master Beverley, esquires, gentlemen, and justices of the peace--no master, I, but plain William Murley, the brewer of Dunstable, your honest neighbour,

---

183. bencher] habitué of tavern ale-benches (Mal., p. 294).

185. charges] expenses (OED 10.e).

sexton] church officer (OED). Sir John hints at Sir John's status as concubine; he does not pay for her services.

Sc. v.2. errand] "arrant" of Q1 is a spelling variation of "errand."

4. God dild ye dainty my dear] one of many catch phrases of Murley. His phrase means "God yield (reward OED 7) ye daintily" (handsomely OED 1).

and your friend, if ye be men of my profession.

Bev. Professèd friends to Wycliffe, foes to Rome.

Mur. Hold by me, lad, lean upon that staff, good Master Beverley.
All of a house, say your mind, say your mind.

Acton. You know our faction now is grown so great
Throughout the realm, that it begins to smoke
Into the clergy's eyes and the king's ears;
High time it is that we were drawn to head,
Our general and officers appointed.
And wars, ye wot, will ask great store of coin.
Able to strength our action with your purse,
You are elected for a colonel
Over a regiment of fifteen bands.

Mur. Phew, paltry paltry, in and out, to and fro, be it more or less, upon occasion, Lord have mercy upon us, what a world is this! Sir Roger Acton, I am but a Dunstable man, a plain brewer, ye know! Will lusty, cavaliering captains, gentlemen, come at my

---

8. profession] not in the sense of "occupation" but loosely in the sense of religious persuasion or point of view (see OED I.1).

11. house] family, ancestral line (OED 6); figuratively applied to the others and to Wycliffites in general.

17. wot] know (OED).

21. paltry] trifling (OED). Murley is probably both dumbfounded and ironical when replying to the honour being bestowed on him.

24. cavaliering] A "cavalier" was a "gentleman trained to arms" (OED 2). OED also notes that "cavalier" was used to refer to a swaggering fellow c. 1600. Murley is displaying his obsession with rank.

calling, go at my bidding? Dainty my dear, they'll do a dog of wax, a horse of cheese, a prick and a pudding. No, no, ye must appoint some lord or knight at least to that place.

Bourne. Why, Master Murley, you shall be a knight!
Were you not in election to be shrieve?
Have ye not passed all offices but that?
Have ye not wealth to make your wife a lady?
I warrant you, my lord, our general
Bestows that honour on you at first sight.

Mur. Marry, God dild ye dainty my dear! But tell me, who shall be our general? Where's the Lord Cobham, Sir John Oldcastle, that noble alms-giver, housekeeper, virtuous, religious gentleman? Come to me there, boys, come to me there.

Acton. Why, who but he shall be our general?

Mur. And shall he knight me, and make me colonel?

34-37. Marry . . . there] Mal.; Mary . . . deare: / But . . . Generall? / Wheres . . . Old-castle, / That . . . vertuous, / Religious . . . boies, / Come . . . there Q1.

25-26. they'll . . . pudding] obscure nonsense. Probably Murley means that they will do ridiculous things or, at least, anything they want to do.

28-33.] Bourne's speech seems entirely hypocritical and mocking. He sneers at Murley's obsession with rank, while using it to his advantage. The cunning "my lord" transports Murley to giddy heights. This chance for knighthood motivates Murley for the rest of the play. He is ready to kill a king so he can be knighted.

37. Come to me there] i.e., "Answer me that" (Brooke, p. 425).

Acton. My word for that, Sir William Murley Knight.

Mur. Fellow Sir Roger Acton Knight, all fellows, I mean in arms, how strong are we? How many partners? Our enemies beside the king are mighty. Be it more or less upon occasion, reckon our force.

Acton. There are of us, our friends, and followers,
Three thousand and three hundred at the least;
Of northern lads four thousand, beside horse;
From Kent there comes with Sir John Oldcastle
Seven thousand; then from London issue out
Of masters, servants, strangers, prentices,
Forty odd thousand into Ficket Field,
Where we appoint our special rendezvous.

Mur. Phew, paltry paltry, in and out, to and fro, Lord have mercy upon us, what a world is this! Where's that Ficket Field, Sir Roger?

Acton. Behind Saint Giles in the Field near Holborn.

40.] Acton's calling Murley "Sir William Murley Knight" is as good as knighting the brewer on the spot. The use of such sly tactics in this scene indicates to the audience that references to Cobham's support are to be given little credence.

45-52.] Probably taken from Hol. (11.47-51 "There had issued . . . time,").

56.] i.e., on the western edge of London.

Mur. Newgate, up Holborn, Saint Giles in the Field, and to Tyburn--and old saw. For the day, for the day?

Acton. On Friday next, the fourteenth day of January.

Mur. Tilly vally, trust me never if I have any liking of that day! Phew, paltry paltry, "Friday," quotha, dismal day. Childermas day this year was Friday.

Bev. Nay, Master Murley, if you observe such days
We make some question of your constancy;
All days are like to men resolved in right.

Mur. Say amen, and say no more. But say and hold, Master Beverley--Friday next, and Ficket Field, and William Murley and his merry

---

57-58. Newgate . . . saw] "At this hospital [St. Giles], the prisoners conveyed from the city of London towards Teyborne [Tyburn], there to be executed . . . , were presented a great bowl of ale, thereof to drink at their pleasure" (Survey, p. 393). Being a brewer Murley would be familiar with the "saw," but, presumably, be unaware of the irony of having the rebels take the familiar route of prisoners being led to execution.

57. Newgate] a famous London prison.

58. saw] proverb (OED sb2).

59. the fourteenth day of January] The chronicles mention January (except Hall who says December) but never as late as the fourteenth.

60. Tilly vally] an exclamation of dismay; and, as Mal. notes (p. 297) it is another example of Shakespearian borrowing for the Hostess in 2 Henry IV, II.iv.79, uses the same expression.

61-62. Childermas day] the festival of the Holy Innocents (28th of December) commemorating the slaughter of the children by Herod (OED 1). The rebels, then, should be meeting on the eleventh not the fourteenth. Hebel (V, 49) observes that both Childermas day and Fridays were considered unlucky and that Childermas fell on a Friday in 1599.

63. if . . . days] In Beverley's eyes (he was a preacher; see notes in Dramatis Personae) the practice of observing such days would be popish and not Wycliffite.

men shall be all one. I have half a score jades that draw my beer
carts: And every jade shall bear a knave,
And every knave shall wear a jack,
And every jack shall have a skull,
And every skull shall show a spear
And every spear shall kill a foe
At Ficket Field, at Ficket Field.
John and Tom, and Dick and Hodge, and
Rafe and Robin, William and George,
And all my knaves shall fight like men,
At Ficket Field on Friday next.

Bourne. What sum of money mean you to disburse?

Mur. It may be modestly, decently, soberly, and handsomely I may bring five hundred pound.

Acton. Five hundred, man? Five thousand's not enough.

69-78. And . . . next] Brooke subst.; as prose in Q1.

---

68. jades] cart-horses (OED 1.a).

70. jack] a coat of mail (Mal., p. 297).

71. skull] helmet (Mal., p. 297).

75-76.] The names of Murley's knaves are plain and short, underlining the lower class nature of the rebellion.

75. Hodge] nickname for Roger (E.G. Withycombe, The Oxford Dictionary of English Christian Names, 3rd ed. [Oxford: Clarendon Press, 1977], p. 244).

76. Rafe] common form of "Ralph" (Dict. Christian Names, p. 249).

A hundred thousand will not pay our men
Two months together. Either come prepared
Like a brave knight, and martial colonel,
In glittering gold and gallant furniture,
Bringing in coin a cart load at the least,
And all your followers mounted on good horse,
Or never come disgraceful to us all.

Bev. Perchance you may be chosen treasurer,
Ten thousand pound's the least that you can bring.

Mur. Paltry paltry, in and out, to and fro, upon occasion I have ten thousand pound to spend, and ten too. And rather than the bishop shall have his will of me for my conscience, it shall out all. Flame and flax, flame and flax, it was got with water and malt, and it shall fly with fire and gunpowder. Sir Roger, a cart load of money till the ax-tree crack, myself and my men in Ficket Field on Friday next. Remember my knighthood and my place. There's my hand I'll be there. Exit.

Acton. See what ambition may persuade men to:

83-84. A . . . together] War was incredibly expensive. In Elizabeth I's budget of 1600 the Ireland campaigns ate up 70% of the yearly expenditure and significantly contributed to that budget's overspending (Elton, pp. 46-47).

86. furniture] armour, weapons (OED 4.b).

91. Ten thousand] The numbers are fiction.

97. ax-tree] axle-tree of a wheel (OED 1).

100. ambition] capitalized in Q1. The vice is personified much like the tempters in morality plays.

In hope of honour he will spend himself.

Bourne. I never thought a brewer half so rich.

Bev. Was never bankrupt brewer yet but one,
With using too much malt, too little water.

Acton. That's no fault in brewers nowadays!
Come, away about our business. Exeunt.

[vi] Enter King Harry, Suffolk, Butler, and Cobham kneeling to the King.

King. 'Tis not enough, Lord Cobham, to submit;
You must forsake your gross opinion.
The bishops find themselves much injurèd,
And though for some good service you have done
We, for our part, are pleased to pardon you,
Yet they will not so soon be satisfied.

---

101. spend himself] i.e., exhaust his money (OED 5.d).

102-05.] The concluding joke on the greed of brewers and the wateriness of their beer comically concludes this scene of rebellion. The development of Murley's character in the play is a conscious effort by the authors to introduce comic touches in a drama that is potentially very serious indeed.

Sc. vi] In all versions of Cobham's meeting with the king, Henry V is ultimately displeased with Cobham and his replies; in Old. King Harry forgives Cobham completely. Only subsequent circumstantial evidence of Cobham's treason makes the king change his mind.

2. gross opinion] "opinion" is used pejoratively here, in that there cannot, in effect, be another opinion to that of the universal Church.

4. for . . . done] See notes for Cobham in Dramatis Personae.

Cob. My gracious lord, unto your majesty,
Next unto my God, I owe my life;
And what is mine, either by nature's gift
Or fortune's bounty, all is at your service.
But for obedience to the Pope of Rome,
I owe him none, nor shall his shaveling priests
That are in England alter my belief.
If out of Holy Scripture they can prove
That I am in an error, I will yield,
And gladly take instruction at their hands.
But otherwise, I do beseech your grace
My conscience may not be encroached upon.

King. We would be loath to press our subjects' bodies,
Much less their souls, the dear redeemèd part
Of Him that is the ruler of us all.
Yet let me counsel ye, that might command:
Do not presume to tempt them with ill words,
Nor suffer any meetings to be had
Within your house, but to the uttermost
Disperse the flocks of this new gathering sect.

---

12. shaveling] derogatory allusion to tonsured priests (Mal., [Percy], p. 728).

19-26.] King Harry anachronistically and unhistorically accepts Cobham's moderate (in terms of late 16th century England) Protestant stance. The king's particular concern is that this religion of individual faith not be transformed into a potentially treasonous force. His attitude reflects Elizabeth I's dealings with both Catholics and Puritans.

Cob. My liege, if any breathe that dares come forth
And say my life in any of these points
Deserves th'attainder of ignoble thoughts,
Here stand I, craving no remorse at all,
But even the utmost rigour may be shown.

King. Let it suffice we know your loyalty.
What have you there?

Cob. A deed of clemency,
Your highness pardon for Lord Powis life,
Which I did beg and you, my noble lord,
Of gracious favour did vouchsafe to grant.

King. But yet it is not signèd with our hand.

Cob. Not yet, my liege. *One ready with pen and ink.*

King. The fact, you say, was done
Not of prepensèd malice, but by chance.

Cob. Upon mine honour so, no otherwise.

King. There is his pardon. Bid him make amends. *[King] writes.*
And cleanse his soul to God for his offence;

---

29. th'attainder] accusation, stain of dishonour (*OED* 2.a, b).

30. remorse] mercy (Mal., p. 299).

38. fact] crime (*OED* 1.c).

39. prepensed] legal equivalent of intentional (*OED*).

41. There . . . pardon] This pardoning of Powis is unhistorical. One of the king's prerogatives that Sir Thomas Smith lists in *De Republica Anglorum*, a 16th century discussion of the law and the government (quoted in Elton, p. 19), is the right to pardon offenders--a right which Elizabeth I used extensively (Elton, p. 21).

What we remit is but the body's scourge.

Enter Bishop.

How now, Lord Bishop?

Bish. Justice, dread sovereign,
As thou art king, so grant I may have justice!

King. What means this exclamation? Let us know.

Bish. Ah, my good lord, the state's abused,
And our decrees most shamefully profaned.

King. How, or by whom?

Bish. Even by this heretic,
This Jew, this traitor to your majesty.

Cob. Prelate, thou liest, even in thy greasy maw,
Or whosoever twits me with the name
Of either traitor, or of heretic.

King. Forbear, I say, and Bishop, show the cause
From whence this late abuse hath been derived.

Bish. Thus, mighty king. By general consent
A messenger was sent to cite this lord

---

43. remit] pardon (Mal., p. 300).
body's scourge] corporal punishment (Mal., p. 300).

43.1.] The Bishop's late entry is unhistorical.

50. Jew] synonymous with "heretic" and "traitor."

51. greasy] used contemptuously to refer to anointed priests.
maw] voracious jaws or mouth (*OED* 3).

52. twits] censures (*OED* 1).

To make appearance in the consistory,
And coming to his house, a ruffian slave--
One of his daily followers--met the man,
Who knowing him to be a paritor
Assaults him first, and after in contempt
Of us and our proceedings, makes him eat
The written process--parchment, seal, and all!
Whereby his master neither was brought forth,
Nor we but scorned for our authority.

King. When was this done?

Bish. At six o'clock this morning.

King. And when came you to court?

Cob. Last night, my lord.

King. By this it seems he is not guilty of it.
And you have done him wrong t'accuse him so.

Bish. But it was done, my lord, by his appointment,
Or else his man durst ne'er have been so bold.

King. Or else you durst be bold to interrupt
And fill our ears with frivolous complaints.
Is this the duty you do bear to us?
Was't not sufficient we did pass our word

---

58. consistory] a bishop's court for ecclesiastical causes, and offences dealt with by ecclesiastical law (*OED* II.7).

61. paritor] summoner (Mal., p. 301); short form of "apparitor."

73-75.] King Harry's anger is fiction. Once again the authors have the king defend Cobham at the expense of the Bishop.

To send for him, but you, misdoubting it,
Or which is worse, intending to forestall
Our regal power, must likewise summon him?
This savours of ambition, not of zeal,
And rather proves you malice his estate
Than any way that he offends the law.
Go to, we like it not, and he your officer,
That was employed so much amiss herein,
Had his desert for being insolent!
So, Cobham, when you please you may depart.

Cob. I humbly bid farewell unto my liege. *Exit.*

King. Farewell.

Enter Huntington.

What's the news by Huntington?

Hunt. Sir Roger Acton and a crew, my lord,
Of bold seditious rebels are in arms,
Intending reformation of religion.
And with their army they intend to pitch
In Ficket Field, unless they be repulsed.

88. S.D.] *Simms*; *S.D. at 1.85 in Q1*; *S.D. bet. 11.87-88 Mal.*

---

81. malice] desire to injure (*OED* 1).

88. *Enter Huntington*] In Q1 Huntington's entry is placed earlier on because that is where the compositor found space for it. The effect of Cobham's quick exit and Huntington's entry demonstrates the melodramatic technique in *Old.* of constantly having the hero beset by new problems.

89. crew] armed force (*OED* 2); or, insultingly, "mob" (*OED* 3).

King. So near our presence? Dare they be so bold?
And will proud war, and eager thirst of blood,
Whom we had thought to entertain far off,
Press forth upon us in our native bounds?
Must we be forced to handsel our sharp blades
In England here, which we prepared for France?
Well, a God's name be it. What's their number, say,
Or who's the chief commander of this rout?
Hunt. Their number is not known as yet, my lord,
But 'tis reported Sir John Oldcastle
Is the chief man, on whom they do depend.
King. How, the Lord Cobham?
Hunt. Yes, my gracious lord.
Bish. I could have told your majesty as much
Before he went, but that I saw your grace
Was too much blinded by his flattery.
Suff. Send post, my lord, to fetch him back again.
But. Traitor unto his country, how he smoothed,
And seemed as innocent as truth itself!
King. I cannot think it yet he would be false,
But if he be, no matter, let him go.

100. number, say] *Rowe*; number? say *Q1*.

---

98. handsel] inaugurate (*OED* 3).

101. rout] rabble (*OED* 7).

110. smoothed] flattered (*OED* 5).

We'll meet both him and them unto their woe.

Exeunt. Manet Bishop.

Bish. This falls out well, and at the last I hope
To see this heretic die in a rope. Exit.

[vii] Enter Earl of Cambridge, Lord Scroop, [Sir Thomas] Gray, and [Monsieur de] Chartres the French factor.

Scroop. Once more, my Lord of Cambridge, make rehearsal
How you do stand entitled to the crown.
The deeper shall we print it in our minds,
And every man the better be resolved
When he perceives his quarrel to be just.

Camb. Then thus, Lord Scroop, Sir Thomas Gray, and you,
Monsieur de Chartres, agent for the French:
This Lionel, Duke of Clarence, as I said,
Third son of Edward (England's King) the Third,

114. 1.] Mal. subst.; Exeunt at end of 1.115 in Q1. 116. S.D.] Mal.; not in Q1. Sc.vii.0.1. Sir Thomas] Mal.

116.] A heretic was usually burnt, but "burnt" does not rhyme with "hope."

Sc.vii.02. Chartres] The name does not come from the chronicles, though French agents are mentioned.

factor] agent (OED).

1. make rehearsal] recount (OED).

2. stand entitled] The emphasis is on Cambridge's rightful claim.

Had issue Philip, his sole daughter and heir,
Which Philip afterward was given in marriage
To Edmund Mortimer, the Earl of March,
And by him had a son called Roger Mortimer,
Which Roger likewise had of his descent
Edmund, Roger, Anne, and Eleanor--
Two daughters and two sons. But those three
Died without issue. Anne that did survive,
And now was left her father's only heir,
My fortune was to marry, being too,
By my grandfather, of King Edward's line.
So of his surname I am called, you know,
Richard Plantagenet. My father was
Edward the Duke of York, and son and heir
To Edmund Langley, Edward the Third's fifth son.

Scroop. So that it seems your claim comes by your wife
As lawful heir to Roger Mortimer,
The son of Edmund, which did marry Philip,
Daughter and heir to Lionel, Duke of Clarence.

Camb. True. For this Harry, and his father both,
Harry the Fifth, as plainly doth appear,

24. fifth] *Mal*.; first *Q1*. 30. Fifth] *Hebel*; first *Q1*.

---

10. Philip] variant of Philippa.

30. Fifth] The phrase "Harry the Fifth" is in apposition to the "Harry" in the line above and is preferable to the obscure Q1 original, "Harry the first." At 1.24 above the compositor also set "first" for "fifth"--an obvious historical error--so the workman apparently misread the MS version of "fifth" consistently.

Are false intruders, and usurp the crown.
For when young Richard was at Pomfret slain,
In him the title of Prince Edward died,
That was the eldest of King Edward's sons.
William of Hatfield, and their second brother,
Death in his nonage had before bereft.
So that my wife, derived from Lionel,
Third son unto King Edward, ought proceed
And take possession of the diadem
Before this Harry or his father king,
Who fetched their title but from Lancaster,
Fourth of that royal line. And being thus,
What reason is't but she should have her right?

Scroop. I am resolved our enterprise is just.

Gray. Harry shall die, or else resign his crown.

Chart. Perform but that, and Charles, the King of France,
Shall aid you lords not only with his men
But send you money to maintain your wars.
Five hundred thousand crowns he bade me proffer,
If you can stop but Harry's voyage for France.

---

36. nonage] period of legal minority (OED 1).

49. Five hundred thousand] The particular amount is not mentioned in the chronicles. The mention of money after the elucidation of Cambridge's claim to the crown has the cynical effect of making an audience doubt the "honour" behind Cambridge's claim.

bade] command (OED IV. 10).

proffer] present (OED 1).

Scroop. We never had a fitter time than now,
The realm in such division as it is.

Camb. Besides, you must persuade ye there is due
Vengeance for Richard's murder, which although
It be deferred, yet will it fall at last,
And now as likely as another time.
Sin hath had many years to ripen in,
And now the harvest cannot be far off
Wherein the weeds of usurpation
Are to be cropped, and cast into the fire.

Scroop. No more, Earl Cambridge. Here I plight my faith
To set up thee, and thy renownèd wife.

Gray. Gray will perform the same, as he is knight.

Chart. And to assist ye, as I said before,
Chartres doth gage the honour of his king.

Scroop. We lack but now Lord Cobham's fellowship,
And then our plot were absolute indeed.

Camb. Doubt not of him, my lord, his life's pursued
By th'incensèd clergy, and of late
Brought in displeasure with the king, assures
He may be quickly won unto our faction.

---

61. plight] pledge (_OED_ 2.b).

65. gage] pledge (_OED_ 2).

67. absolute] perfect (_OED_ II.4).

Who hath the articles were drawn at large
Of our whole purpose?

Gray. That have I, my lord.

Camb. We should not now be far off from his house;
Our serious conference hath beguiled the way.
See where his castle stands. Give me the writing.
When we are come unto the speech of him,
Because we will not stand to make recount
Of that which hath been said, here he shall read
Our minds at large, and what we crave of him.

Enter Cobham.

Scroop. A ready way! Here comes the man himself
Booted and spurred. It seems he hath been riding.

Camb. Well met, Lord Cobham.

Cob. My Lord of Cambridge?
Your honour is most welcome into Kent.
And all the rest of this fair company.
I am new come from London, gentle lords.
But will ye not take Cooling for your host,

80.1.] *Q2*; *enter Cob. at end of l.79 in Q1.*

---

72. articles] indictment (*OED* 5).

80. at large] in both senses of "at liberty" and "in full" (*OED* II.5.a; 5.c).

81. ready way] referring both to this direct method of telling Cobham and to Cobham's quick entrance.

87. Cooling] Lord Cobham's seat in Kent (Mal., p. 306) and not to be confused with the town Cobham.

And see what entertainment it affords?
Camb. We were intended to have been your guests,
But now this lucky meeting shall suffice
To end our business, and defer that kindness.
Cob. Business, my lord? What business should you have
But to be merry? We have no delicates,
But this I'll promise you: a piece of venison,
A cup of wine, and so forth--hunter's fare.
And if you please, we'll strike the stag ourselves
Shall fill our dishes with his well-fed flesh.
Scroop. That is indeed the thing we all desire.
Cob. My lords, and you shall have your choice with me.
Camb. Nay, but the stag which we desire to strike
Lives not in Cooling. If you will consent
And go with us, we'll bring you to a forest
Where runs a lusty herd. Amongst the which
There is a stag superior to the rest,
A stately beast, that when his fellows run
He leads the race and beats the sullen earth
As though he scorned it with his trampling hoofs.
Aloft he bears his head, and with his breast

---

93. delicates] delicacies (*OED* 2).

96. strike] to kill or wound deer (*OED* 33.b).

103. lusty] both "vigorous" (*OED* 5) and "insolent" (*OED* 6).

106. sullen] both "stubborn" (*OED* 1) and "dull-sounding" (*OED* 3.b).

Like a huge bulwark counter-checks the wind.
And when he standeth still, he stretcheth forth
His proud ambitious neck, as if he meant
To wound the firmament with forkèd horns.

Cob. 'Tis pity such a goodly beast should die.

Camb. Not so, Sir John, for he is tyrannous,
And gores the other deer, and will not keep
Within the limits are appointed him.
Of late he's broke into a several
Which doth belong to me, and there he spoils
Both corn and pasture. Two of his wild race,
Alike for stealth and covetous encroaching,
Already are removed; if he were dead,
I should not only be secure from hurt
But with his body make a royal feast.

Scroop. How say you then, will you first hunt with us?

Cob. Faith, lords, I like the pastime. Where's the place?

Camb. Peruse this writing. It will show you all,

---

109. bulwark] rampart (OED 1).

117. several] enclosed pasture land (Mal. [Percy], p. 728).

119-21. Two . . . removed] Mac. (p. 148) supposes this to mean Henry IV and Roger Mortimer, who was heir designate to Richard II, while Hebel (V, 49) thinks this refers to Edward II and Richard II. Of the four choices Henry IV is the only one to make complete sense because he alone "covetously encroached" a throne that was not his. Roger Mortimer, because he is dead and was heir designate, is a possible candidate. No other candidates are appropriate.

120. encroaching] insidious usurping (OED 1).

And what occasion we have for the sport.

[*Gives writing to Cobham*.] *He reads*.

Cob. Call ye this hunting, my lords? Is this the stag
You fain would chase, Harry, our dread king?
So we may make a banquet for the devil,
And in the stead of wholesome meat prepare
A dish of poison to confound ourselves!

Camb. Why so, Lord Cobham? See you not our claim?
And how imperiously he holds the crown?

Scroop. Besides, you know yourself is in disgrace,
Held as a recreant, and pursued to death.
This will defend you from your enemies
And 'stablish your religion through the land.

Cob. (*Aside*) Notorious treason! Yet I will conceal
My secret thoughts, to sound the depth of it.
[*To Camb*.] My Lord of Cambridge, I do see your claim,
And what good may redound unto the land
By prosecuting of this enterprise.
But where are men? Where's power and furniture
To order such an action? We are weak;
Harry you know's a mighty potentate.

Camb. Tut, we are strong enough. You are beloved,

127.1. *Gives* . . . *Cobham*] *This ed*.; *Presents a paper Mal*.

---

129. fain] gladly (*OED*).

142. redound] result in some advantage (*OED* 6).

And many will be glad to follow you;
We are the light, and some will follow us.
Besides, there is hope from France. Here's an ambassador
That promiseth both men and money too.
The commons likewise, as we hear, pretend
A sudden tumult. We will join with them.

Cob. Some likelihood, I must confess, to speed.
But how shall I believe this is plain truth?
You are, my lords, such men as live in court,
And highly have been favoured of the king,
Especially Lord Scroop, whom oftentimes
He maketh choice of for his bedfellow.
And you, Lord Gray, are of his Privy Council.
Is not this a train to entrap my life?

149. the light] *Q1*; the like *F3*.

---

149. the light] one eminent in virtue (*OED* 8.a). Probably the audience is supposed to pick up Cambridge's *biblical* allusion. Here 1 John, i.5, "This then is the message which we have heard of him, and declare unto you, that God is light," is the basis for the Earl's blasphemous analogy.

152. pretend] intend (Mal., p. 308).

153. We . . . them] They do not (see xi.15-16). This is another example of the loose ends caused by collaborative work.

154. likelihood] indication (*OED* 3).

160. Lord Gray] only referred to as Sir Thomas Gray in the chronicles.

Privy Council] a Tudor anachronism. Gray was on the General or King's Council. The authors are not only updating their sources but are also making Gray's position and treason that much greater.

161. train] animal trap (*OED* 2); continuing the hunting conceit.

Camb. Then perish may my soul! What, think you so?
Scroop. We'll swear to you.
Gray. Or take the sacrament.
Cob. Nay, you are noble men, and I imagine,
As you are honourable by birth and blood,
So you will be in heart, in thought, in word.
I crave no other testimony but this:
That you would all subscribe, and set your hands
Unto this writing which you gave to me.
Camb. With all our hearts. Who hath any pen and ink?
Scroop. My pocket should have one. Yea, here it is.
Camb. Give it me, Lord Scroop. There is my name.
Scroop. And there is my name.
Gray. And mine.
Cob. Sir, let me crave
That you would likewise write your name with theirs,
For confirmation of your master's word,
The King of France.
Chart. That will I, noble lord.
Cob. So now this action is well-knit together,
And I am for you. Where's our meeting, lords?
Camb. Here, if you please, the tenth of July next.
Cob. In Kent? Agreed. Now let us in to supper.
I hope your honours will not away tonight.

---

168. subscribe] write one's signature in token of assent (OED 6).

Camb. Yes, presently, for I have far to ride
About soliciting of other friends.

Scroop. And we would not be absent from the court,
Lest thereby grow suspicion in the king.

Cob. Yet taste a cup of wine before ye go.

Camb. Not now, my lord, we thank you. So, farewell.

Cob. Farewell, my noble lords. [*Exeunt. Manet Cobham.*] My noble
lords?
My noble villains, base conspirators!
How can they look his highness in the face,
Whom they so closely study to betray?
But I'll not sleep until I make it known.
This head shall not be burdened with such thoughts,
Nor in this heart will I conceal a deed
Of such impiety against my king.

Enter Lady Cobham, Lord Powis, Lady Powis, and Harpool.

Madam, how now?

La. Cob. You are welcome home, my lord.

188. S.D.] *This ed.*; *Exeunt all but* Cobham. *bet.* ll.187 *and* 188 *Rowe*.
195.1.] *Rowe*; *Enter Harpoole and the rest. Q1*.

---

183. soliciting] both appealing for aid (*OED* 11) and inciting rebellion (*OED* 3). Like a morality vice figure Cambridge often uses such self-condemning language.

191. study] endeavour (*OED* 4.a).

195.1. Lady Powis] Her presence is unexplained and unprepared for. She is never mentioned in the chronicles and is obviously the invention of one of the collaborators.

Why seem ye so disquiet in your looks?
What hath befallen you that disquiets your mind?

La. Pow. Bad news, I am afraid, touching my husband.

Cob. Madam, not so. There is your husband's pardon.
Long may ye live, each joy unto the other.

Pow. So great a kindness as I know not how
To make reply; my sense is quite confounded.

Cob. Let that alone. And madam, stay me not,
For I must back unto the court again
With all the speed I can. Harpool, my horse.

La. Cob. So soon, my lord? What, will you ride all night?

Cob. All night or day, it must be so, sweet wife.
Urge me not why, or what my business is,
But get you in. Lord Powis, bear with me,
And madam, think your welcome ne'er the worse,
My house is at your use. Harpool, away.

Harp. Shall I attend your lordship to the court?

Cob. Yea, sir. Your gelding mount you presently. *Exit.*

La. Cob. I prithee, Harpool, look unto thy lord,
I do not like this sudden posting back. *Exit Harpool.*

202-03. So . . . confounded] *Mal.*; *as prose in Q1*. 214. S.D.] *Q2*; *exe. Q1*. 216. S.D.] *Mal.*; *not in Q1*.

---

197. disquiet] restless, disturbed (*OED*); a cue to Cobham.

216. posting] hasty riding.

Pow. Some earnest business is afoot belike.
What e'er it be, pray God be his good guide.

La. Pow. Amen, that hath so highly us bestead.

La. Cob. Come, madam, and my lord, we'll hope the best.
You shall not into Wales till he return.

Pow. Though great occasion be we should depart,
Yet, madam, will we stay to be resolved
Of this unlooked-for doubtful accident. *Exeunt.*

[viii] *Enter Murley and his men,* [*Dick and Tom,*] *prepared in some filthy order for war.*

Mur. Come, my hearts of flint, modestly, decently, soberly, and handsomely, no man afore his leader. Follow your master, your captain, your knight that shall be, for the honour of mealmen,

222-24. Though . . . accident] *Rowe*; *as prose in Q1*.

217-18.] Cobham's reluctance to speak of the Cambridge rebellion and Powis' ignorance of this affair may be an important issue in the context of *1&2 Old*. As the Ficket Field affair takes place soon after, and as Powis is the man who eventually brings Cobham to trial, Powis' motivation for such a disloyal act may be rationalized by putting two and two together: the "earnest business" and the rebellion. This is making mountains of molehills, but it does lend this anti-climactic conclusion to scene vii a dramatic *raison d'être*.

217. belike] probably (*OED*).

219. bestead] assisted (*OED* 1).

sc. viii.1. hearts of flint] echoes Constable's "heart of oak" (iv.134).

millers and maltmen. Dun is the mouse. Dick and Tom, for the credit of Dunstable, ding down the enemy tomorrow. Ye shall not come into the field like beggars. Where be Leonard and Laurence, my two loaders? Lord have mercy upon us, what a world is this! I would give a couple of shillings for a dozen of good feathers for ye, and forty pence for as many scarves to set ye out withal. Frost and snow, a man has no heart to fight till he be brave.

Dick. Master, I hope we be no babes. For our manhood, our bucklers and our town footballs can bear witness! And this light 'parel we have shall off, and we'll fight naked afore we run away.

Tom. Nay, I am of Laurence mind for that, for he means to leave his life behind him. He and Leonard, your two loaders, are making their wills because they have wives. Now we bachelors bid our friends scramble for our goods if we die. But master, pray ye let me ride upon Cut.

---

4. dun is the mouse] proverbial (Tilley, D644). It is the cry for sallying forth. "Dun" is the grayish-brown colour of a mouse (OED 1).

5. ding down] knock down, demolish (OED 4).

7. loaders] presumably those men who arranged Murley's wheat on a wagon during harvesting (see OED 1.a).

10. brave] punning on "finely-dressed" and "valiant" (Mal. [Percy], p. 729).

11. bucklers] shields (OED 1).

12. our town footballs] "after dinner, all the youths go into the field to play at the ball" (Survey, p. 84).

18. Cut] "a familiar expression for a common or labouring horse" (OED VI. 28--Nares definition).

Mur. Meal and salt, wheat and malt, fire and tow, frost and snow, why Tom, thou shalt. Let me see, here are you, William and George are with my cart, and Robin and Hodge holding my own two horses--proper men, handsome men, tall men, true men.

Dick. But master, master, methinks you are a mad man to hazard your own person and a cart load of money too.

Tom. Yea, and master, there's a worse matter in't. If it be as I heard say, we go to fight against all the learned bishops that should give us their blessing, and if they curse us we shall speed ne'er the better.

Dick. Nay, by'r lady, some say the king takes their part, and master, dare you fight against the king?

Mur. Fie, paltry paltry, in and out, to and fro, upon occasion, if the king be so unwise to come there, we'll fight with him too.

Tom. What if ye should kill the king?

Mur. Then we'll make another.

Dick. Is that all? Do ye not speak treason?

Mur. If we do, who dare trip us? We come to fight for our conscience and for honour. Little know you what is in my bosom; look here, mad knaves, a pair of gilt spurs.

Tom. A pair of golden spurs? Why do you not put them on your heels? Your bosom's no place for spurs.

---

19. tow] the fibre of flax (*OED* 2).

36-37. We . . . honour] Murley is being unconsciously ironic and so misuses and misapplies these terms to justify his treason. Murley's and Cobham's contrasting conceptions of honour and conscience are clearly counterpointed in the play.

Mur. Be't more or less upon occasion, Lord have mercy upon us, Tom th'art a fool, and thou speakest treason to knighthood. Dare any wear golden or silver spurs till he be a knight? No, I shall be knighted tomorrow, and then they shall on. Sirs, was it ever read in the church book of Dunstable that ever maltman was made knight?

Tom. No, but you are more. You are mealman, maltman, miller, cornmaster and all.

Dick. Yea, and half a brewer too, and the devil and all for wealth. You bring more money with you than all the rest.

Mur. The more's my honour; I shall be a knight tomorrow. Let me 'spose my men: Tom upon Cut, Dick upon Hob, Hodge upon Ball, Rafe upon Sorell, and Robin upon the fore-horse.

Enter Acton, Bourne, and Beverley.

Tom. Stand, who comes there?

Acton. All friends, good fellow.

Mur. Friends and fellows indeed, Sir Roger.

Acton. Why, thus you show yourself a gentleman,

41. mercy upon us] *Q2*; mercy us *Q1*.

---

45. church book] a parish register (*OED* c).

46. cornmaster] grain seller (*OED* 1). Murley has a stranglehold on all aspects of the brewing industry.

50. 'spose] i.e., dispose (Hopk., p. 45).

51. Hob] a small or middle-sized horse (*OED* 1).

Ball] a white-faced horse (*OED* 3.2).

52. Sorell] a name for a chestnut-coloured horse (*OED* B.1).

fore-horse] the leader (*OED*).

To keep your day and come so well prepared.
Your cart stands yonder, guarded by your men,
Who tell me it is loaden well with coin.
What sum is there?

Mur. Ten thousand pound, Sir Roger. And modestly, decently, soberly, and handsomely, see what I have here against I be knighted.

Acton. Gilt spurs? 'Tis well.

Mur. But where's our army, sir?

Acton. Dispersed in sundry villages about:
Some here with us in Highgate; some at Finchley,
Tot'nam, Enfield, Edmonton, Newington,
Islington, Hoxton, Pancras, Kensington;
Some nearer Thames, Ratcliffe, Blackwall and Bow.

---

66. Highgate] 4 miles NNW of Charing Cross in central London (Mason, *The Gazeteer of England*).

66-68. some . . . Kensington] The forces have, in effect, surrounded London: Finchley 7 miles NW; Tot'nam (Tottenham) 4 miles NE; Edmonton 7 miles N; Newington (either Newington Butts south of the Thames River, or Stoke Newington near Highgate--Mac., pp. 148-49); Islington 2 miles NW; Hoxton ½ mile NE; Kensington 2 miles SW (Frank Smith, *A Genealogical Gazeteer of England* [Baltimore: Genealogical Publishing Co., Inc., 1968]).

68. Pancras] "Pancredge" in Q1; it was probably pronounced as it was spelt. Mac. (p. 149) notes that Pancras is S point of triangle with Islington and Hoxton.

69. Ratcliffe] "A good mile from the Tower [of London]" (*Survey*, p. 375); in SE area of London.

Blackwall] street right by the Thames (Lilian and Ashmore Russan, *Historical Streets of London* [New York: Thomas Y. Crowell Co., 1927] p. 32); in S area of London.

Bow] There was a Bow Lane that "branched off south to Upper Thames Street" (Eilert Ekwall, *Street-Names of the City of London* [Oxford: Clarendon Press, 1953], p. 149); in S area of London.

But our chief strength must be the Londoners,
Which ere the sun tomorrow shine
Will be near fifty thousand in the field.

Mur. Marry, God dild ye dainty my dear! But upon occasion, Sir Roger Acton, doth not the king know of it, and gather his power against us?

Acton. No, he's secure at Eltham.

Mur. What do the clergy?

Acton. Fear extremely, yet prepare no force.

Mur. In and out, to and fro, bully my bodkin, we shall carry the world afore us! I vow, by my worship, when I am knighted we'll take the king napping, if he stand on their part.

Acton. This night we few in Highgate will repose.
With the first cock we'll rise and arm ourselves
To be in Ficket Field by break of day,
And there expect our general.

Mur. Sir John Oldcastle. What if he come not?

Bourne. Yet our action stands.
Sir Roger Acton may supply his place.

Mur. True, Master Bourne, but who shall make me knight?

Bev. He that hath power to be our general.

Acton. Talk not of trifles. Come, let's away.
Our friends of London long till it be day. *Exeunt.*

---

78. bully] a term of endearment (OED I.1).

bodkin] dagger (OED 1).

Enter Sir John of Wrotham and Doll.

Doll. By my troth, thou art as jealous a man as lives.

Sir John. Canst thou blame me, Doll? Thou art my lands, my goods, my jewels, my wealth, my purse. None walks within forty miles of London but a plies thee as truly as the parish does the poor man's box.

Doll. I am as true to thee as the stone is in the wall, and thou knowest well enough, Sir John, I was in as good doing when I came to thee as any wench need to be! And therefore thou hast tried me, that thou hast! By God's body, I will not be kept as I have been, that I will not.

Sir John. Doll, if this blade hold there's not a pedlar walks with a pack but thou shalt as boldly choose of his wares as with thy ready money in a merchant's shop. We'll have as good silver as the king coins any.

Doll. What, is all the gold spent you took the last day from the courtier?

Sc. ix.4.] a plies i.e., he solicits (OED 1).

4-5. poor man's box] poor box (OED). Sir John means that there are as many poor supported by the poor box of the parish, or as many people dipping into the poor box, as there are Doll's "suitors."

6-10.] Doll claims she is loyal and that the only stain on her honour comes from association with Sir John. However, the use of "kept" in the sense of being a concubine is a double entendre that undercuts Doll's claim.

15-16. the courtier] i.e., Butler.

Sir John. 'Tis gone, Doll, 'tis flown. Merrily come, merrily gone. He comes a horseback that must pay for all. We'll have as good meat as money can get, and as good gowns as can be bought for gold. Be merry, wench, the maltman comes on Monday.

Doll. You might have left me at Cobham until you had been better provided for.

Sir John. No, sweet Doll, no, I do not like that. Yond old ruffian is not for the priest. I do not like a new clerk should come in the old belfry.

Doll. Ah, thou art a mad priest, i'faith.

Sir John. Come, Doll, I'll see thee safe at some alehouse here at Cray, and the next sheep that comes shall leave his fleece.

Exeunt.

---

17. merrily] Sir John puns on "merrily" and "merely" meaning "entirely" (*OED* 2).

20. the . . . Monday] Tilley (M599). The phrase means "do not worry about money."

24-25. I . . . belfry] Sir John is alluding to non-ecclesiastical affairs.

28. Cray] "the name of a group of Kentish villages about halfway from Rochester to London" (Hebel, V, 50). They are moving along the Watling Road, which went through London, and on to St. Albans where Sir John and Doll later spend a night.

Enter the king [disguised], Suffolk, and Butler.

King. (In great haste) My Lord of Suffolk, post away for life,
And let our forces of such horse and foot
As can be gathered up by any means
Make speedy rendezvous in Tothill Fields.
It must be done this evening, my lord,
This night the rebels mean to draw to head
Near Islington, which if your speed prevent not,
If once they should unite their several forces
Their power is almost thought invincible.
Away, my lord, I will be with you soon.
Suff. I go, my sovereign, will all happy speed. Exit.
King. Make haste, my Lord of Suffolk, as you love us.
Butler, post you to London with all speed.
Command the mayor and shrieves on their allegiance
The city gates be presently shut up

0.1. disguised] Mal.

Scene x] All the chronicles agree that the king was at his estates in Eltham when he received news of the rebellion (scene vi in Old.). He is still in that area (in Kent 8½ miles SE of London--Smith, A Genealogical Gazeteer) though nothing specific is mentioned in this scene. Specific information as to the king's whereabouts is supplied in scene xi.101, but see note 1.33.1 below.

0.1. disguised] See 1.32.

4. Tothill Fields] in present-day Westminster (Russan, Historical Streets, p. 205) and where the king, himself, is heading.

And guarded with a strong sufficient watch,
And not a man be sufferèd to pass
Without a special warrant from ourself.
Command the postern by the Tower be kept,
And proclamation on the pain of death
That not a citizen stir from his doors
Except such as the mayor and shrieves shall choose
For their own guard and safety of their persons.
Butler, away, have care unto my charge.

But. I go, my sovereign.

King. Butler.

But. My lord?

King. Go down by Greenwich and command a boat.
At the Friar's Bridge attend my coming down.

But. I will, my lord. *Exit.*

King. It's time, I think, to look unto rebellion
When Acton doth expect unto his aid
No less than fifty thousand Londoners.
Well, I'll to Westminster in this disguise

---

16. watch] guards, patrol (OED 11).

19.] "the gate next the Tower of London, now commonly called the Postern" (Survey, p. 27).

26. by Greenwich] in Kent 6 miles SE of London (Smith, A Genealogical Gazeteer).

27. Friar's Bridge] a fixed or floating landing-stage or pier (OED "bridge" 3.b).

attend] wait (OED III.13).

To hear what news is stirring in these brawls.

Enter Sir John.

Sir John. Stand, trueman, says a thief.

King. Stand, thief, says a trueman. How if a thief?

Sir John. Stand, thief, too.

King. Then, thief or trueman, I see I must stand. I see howsoever the world wags the trade of thieving yet will never down. What art thou?

Sir John. A good fellow.

King. So am I too. I see thou dost know me.

Sir John. If thou be a good fellow play the good fellow's part: deliver thy purse without more ado.

King. I have no money.

33.1.] *Q1*; *Enter Sir John and Doll Mal.*

33.1.] Malone's emendations here and at 1.114 are based on two pieces of evidence: at 1.106 Sir John supposedly directly speaks to Doll and at xi.102 King Harry recalls the incident of scene x and says a woman was there. I find neither piece of evidence compelling. As Hebel (V, 50) contends, in the first case it is not required that Doll be on stage when Sir John calls her name as she neither speaks nor is referred to in the rest of the speech. There are also other places in *Old.* where characters apostrophize others not present. In the second case King Harry describes his own reaction to the robbery in scene xi in terms not applicable to the scene x events. Finally, I base my retention of Q1's reading on these other points: Doll is not alluded to in scene x when Sir John and King Harry are on stage together; 11.27-28 in scene ix indicate that Doll will be in an alehouse in Cray at the time of the robbery. I concur with Hebel that different writers are responsible for scenes x and xi.

37-38. howsoever . . . wags] i.e., "how affairs are going" (*OED* "wags" 7.c).

38. will never down] i.e., will never be in low spirits (*OED* 18)

40. good fellow] both "roisterer" (see note ii.160) and "thief" (*OED* 2).

Sir John. I must make you find some before we part. If you have no money you shall have ware, as many sound dry blows as your skin can carry.

King. Is that the plain truth?

Sir John. Sirrah, no more ado. Come, come, give me the money you have. Dispatch, I cannot stand all day.

King. Well, if thou wilt needs have it, there 'tis. [Aside] Just the proverb: one thief robs another. Where the devil are all my old thieves that were wont to keep this walk? Falstaff the villain is so fat he cannot get on's horse, but methinks Poins and Peto should be stirring hereabouts.

Sir John. How much is there on't, of thy word?

King. A hundred pound in angels, on my word. The time has been I would have done as much for thee, if thou hadst passed this way as I have now.

Sir John. Sirrah, what art thou? Thou seem'st a gentleman?

King. I am no less, yet a poor one now, for thou hast all my money.

Sir John. From whence cam'st thou?

King. From the court at Eltham.

57-59. A . . . now] This ed.; A . . . word, / The . . . much / For . . . now Q1.

---

46. ware] goods; usually used in apposition to "money" (OED sb3.4).

dry blows] those which bruise but do not draw blood (OED 12).

53-54. Falstaff . . . horse] the first overt reference to the "pampered glutton" alluded to in the Prologue.

54. Poins and Peto] other companions of Prince Hal in 1&2 Henry IV.

Sir John. Art thou one of the king's servants?

King. Yes, that I am, and one of his chamber.

Sir John. I am glad thou art no worse, thou mayst the better spare thy money. And think'st thou thou might'st get a poor thief his pardon if he should have need?

King. Yes, that I can.

Sir John. Wilt thou do so much for me when I shall have occasion?

King. Yes, faith, will I, so it be for no murder.

Sir John. Nay, I am a pitiful thief. All the hurt I do a man, I take but his purse. I'll kill no man.

King. Then of my word I'll do it.

Sir John. Give me thy hand of the same.

King. There 'tis.

Sir John. Methinks the king should be good to thieves, because he has been a thief himself, though I think now he be turned trueman.

King. Faith, I have heard indeed he has had an ill name that way in his youth, but how canst thou tell he has been a thief?

Sir John. How? Because he once robbed me before I fell to the trade myself, when that foul villainous guts that led him to all that roguery was in's company there--that Falstaff.

King. (*Aside*) Well, if he did rob thee then, thou art but even with him now, I'll be sworn. [*To Sir John*] Thou knowest not the king now, I think, if thou sawest him?

Sir John. Not I, i'faith.

---

72. pitiful] merciful (Mal., p. 319).

King. (*Aside*) So it should seem.

Sir John. Well, if old King Henry had lived, this king that is now had made thieving the best trade in England.

King. Why so?

Sir John. Because he was the chief warden of our company. It's pity that e'er he should have been a king, he was so brave a thief. But sirrah, wilt remember my pardon if need be?

King. Yes, faith, will I.

Sir John. Wilt thou? Well then, because thou shalt go safe, for thou mayest hap (being so early) be met with again before thou come to Southwark, if any man when he should bid thee good morrow bid thee stand, say thou but "Sir John" and he will let thee pass.

King. Is that the word? Well then let me alone.

Sir John. Nay, sirrah, because I think indeed I shall have some occasion to use thee, and as thou com'st oft this way I may light on thee another time not knowing thee, here, I'll break this angel. Take thou half of it. This is a token betwixt thee and me.

King. God have mercy, farewell. *Exit*.

Sir John. Oh, my fine golden slaves! Here's for thee, wench, i'faith.

---

92. chief . . . company] i.e., head of the guild of thieves.

97. hap] come about by chance (*OED* 1).

98. Southwark] near London on the south side of the Thames (Smith, *A Genealogical Gazeteer*).

106. slaves] i.e., coins. This figurative sense of "slaves" is not recorded in the *OED*.

Now Doll, we will revel in our bever. This is a tithe pig of my vicarage. God have mercy, neighbour Shooters Hill, you paid your tithe honestly. Well, I hear there is a company of rebels up against the king got together in Ficket Field near Holborn, and as it is thought here in Kent, the king will be there tonight in's own person. Well, I'll to the king's camp, and it shall go hard, but if there be any doings I'll make some good boot amongst them. *Exit*.

[xi] *Enter King Harry, Suffolk, Huntington,* [*all in disguise*], *and two with lights*.

King. My Lords of Suffolk and of Huntington,
Who scouts it now? Or who stands sentinels?
What men of worth? What lords do walk the round?

107. bever] *Q1*; bower *conj. Mal*. 114. S.D.] *Q1*; *Exeunt Sir John and Doll Mal*. Sc. xi.01. *all in disguise*] *This ed*.; *Enter King Henry disguised Mal*.

---

107. bever] mid-afternoon snack (*OED* 3). Mal. (p. 321) points out the almost identical phrase later on in *Old*., " . . . we'll to Saint Albans and revel in our bower" (xvii.39), and emends "bever" to "bower."

tithe-pig] a pig taken as "tithe"--a tenth part of annual produce given to the church (*OED*).

113. doings] action (*OED* 8).

make some good boot] plunder (*OED* b).

Sc. xi.01. *All in disguise*] See 11.29-30.

3. round] night walk of the watch (*OED* 14).

<u>Suff</u>. May it please your highness--

<u>King</u>. Peace, no more of that,
The king's asleep. Wake not his majesty
With terms nor titles, he's at rest in bed.
Kings do not use to watch themselves, they sleep,
And let rebellion and conspiracy
Revel and havoc in the commonwealth.
Is London looked unto?

<u>Hunt</u>. It is, my lord.
Your noble uncle Exeter is there,
Your brother Gloucester, and my Lord of Warwick,
Who with the mayor and the aldermen
Do guard the gates and keep good rule within.
The Earl of Cambridge and Sir Thomas Gray
Do walk the round, Lord Scroop and Butler scout;
So though it please your majesty to jest,
Were you in bed, well might you take your rest.

<u>King</u>. I thank ye, lords, but you do know of old
That I have been a perfect night-walker,
London, you say, is safely looked unto.
Alas, poor rebels, there your aid must fail.

---

7. do not use] i.e., are not accustomed (<u>OED</u> 20).

15-16.] The mention of the other conspirators is unhistorical and another example of the dramatists' heavy reliance on dramatic irony.

And the Lord Cobham, Sir John Oldcastle,
He's quiet in Kent. Acton, ye are deceived;
Reckon again, you count without your host.
Tomorrow you shall give account to us;
Till when, my friends, this long cold winter's night
How can we spend? King Harry is asleep,
And all his lords, these garments tell us so,
All friends at football, fellows all in field--
Harry, and Dick, and George. Bring us a drum,
Give us square dice. We'll keep this court of guard
For all good fellows' companies that come.
Where's that mad priest ye told me was in arms
To fight as well as pray, if need required?

<u>Suff</u>. He's in the camp, and if he knew of this
I undertake he would not be long hence.

<u>King</u>. Trip Dick, trip George. <u>They trip</u>.

<u>Hunt</u>. I must have the dice.

23-24. And . . . Kent] The audience does not know how Harry got this information, but the fact that the audience knows that Cobham is unconnected with the whole affair allows them to accept the statement at face value.

29-30. these . . . field] i.e., dressed as soldiers. No one, because of his rank, is distinguished from the others. This is necessary because Sir John is shortly to be duped by Harry, Dick and George.

31. Dick, and George] As Hebel (V, 50) observes, the names are unhistorical (see notes for Suffolk and Huntington in <u>Dramatis Personae</u>).

drum] to be used as the dicing-table (Mal., p. 322).

38. Trip] throw the dice in a nimble fashion (<u>OED</u> 4).

What do we play at? *They play at dice*.

Suff. Passage, if ye please.

Hunt. Set round then. So, at all. [*They play*.]

King. George, you are out.

Give me the dice. I pass for twenty pound.

Here's to our lucky passage into France. [*They play*.]

Hunt. Harry, you pass indeed, for you sweep all.

Suff. A sign King Harry shall sweep all in France.

Enter Sir John.

Sir John. Edge ye, good fellows, take a fresh gamester in.

King. Master Parson? We play nothing but gold.

Sir John. And fellow, I tell thee that the priest hath gold. Gold?
'Sblood, ye are but beggarly soldiers to me, I think I have more
gold than all you three.

Hunt. It may be so, but we believe it not.

King. Set, Priest, set, I pass for all that gold. [*They play*.]

Sir John. Ye pass indeed.

39. S.D. *They*] *Brooke*; *the Q1*.

---

39. Passage] "a game at dice to be played at but by two, and it is performed with three dice. The Caster throws continually till he hath thrown Dubblets under ten, and then he is out and loseth. Or Dubblets above ten, and then he passeth and wins" (*OED* IV.5--*Compleat Gamester* definition). In *Old*. the game seems to be played like the modern "craps" where the thrower plays against all the bettors.

40. Set] wager (*OED* 14).

out] See note for 1.39.

41. pass] See note for 1.39.

King. Priest, hast thou any more?

Sir John. Zounds, what a question's that? I tell thee I have more than all you three--at these ten angels.

King. I wonder how thou com'st by all this gold. How many benefices hast thou, Priest?

Sir John. I'faith, but one. Dost wonder how I come by gold? I wonder rather how poor soldiers should have gold. For I'll tell thee, good fellow, we have every day tithes, offerings, christ'nings, weddings, burials; and you poor snakes come seldom to a booty. I'll speak a proud word: I have but one parsonage--Wrotham. 'Tis better than the bishopric of Rochester. There's ne'er a hill, heath, nor down in all Kent but 'tis in my parish. Barham Down, Cobham Down, Gadshill, Wrotham Hill, Blackheath, Cox-heath, Birchen Wood--all pay me tithe. Gold, quotha? Ye pass not for that. [_They play_.]

Suff. Harry, ye are out. Now, Parson, shake the dice.

Sir John. Set, set. I'll cover ye. At all. [_They play_.] A plague on't, I am out. The devil, and dice, and a wench--who will trust them?

53-54. Zounds . . . angels] _This ed._; Zounds . . . that? / I . . . three, / At . . . Angells _Q1_.

---

56. benefices] ecclesiastical livings (_OED_ 6).

60. poor snakes] drudges (_OED_ 3).

down] treeless pasture land (_OED_ 1, 2).

63-65. Barham . . . Birchen Wood] Sir John lists all the best places in Kent to rob people. Mac. (p. 149) conjectures that Birchen Wood is the "'Birch-wood' on the road from Rochester to Greenwich by way of Shooters Hill."

Suff. Say'st thou so, Priest? Set fair. At all for once. [*They play*.]

King. Out, sir, pay all.

Sir John. 'Sblood, pay me angel gold.
I'll none of your cracked French crowns nor pistolets.
Pay me fair angel gold, as I pay you.

King. No cracked French crowns? I hope to see more cracked French crowns ere long.

Sir John. Thou meanest of Frenchmen's crowns, when the king is in France.

Hunt. Set round, at all. [*They play*.]

Sir John. Pay all! This is some luck.

King. Give me the dice. 'Tis I must shred the priest.
At all, Sir John.

Sir John. The devil and all is yours! At that. [*They play*.] 'Sdeath, what casting is this?

Suff. Well thrown, Harry, i'faith.

King. I'll cast better yet.

Sir John. Then I'll be hanged. Sirrah, hast thou not given thy soul to the devil for casting?

King. I pass for all.

---

72. French crowns] The French crown was in common usage in Elizabethan times.
pistolets] foreign gold coins in value of about six shillings (*OED*).

76-77.] King Harry's pun in 11.74-75 is explained by Sir John to what, presumably, were the dimmer wits of the audience.

79. shred] fleece (*OED* 1.b).

82. casting] throwing the dice (*OED* I.3).

Sir John. Thou passest all that e'er I played withal!

Sirrah, dost thou not cog, nor foist, nor slur?

King. Set, Parson, set, the dice die in my hand!

When, Parson, when? What, can ye find no more?

Already dry? Was't you bragged of your store?

Sir John. All's gone but that.

Hunt. What, half a broken angel?

Sir John. Why sir, 'tis gold.

King. Yea, and I'll cover it.

Sir John. The devil do ye good on't--I am blind, ye have blown me

up. [Going.]

King. Nay, tarry, Priest, ye shall not leave us yet.

Do not these pieces fit each other well?

Sir John. What if they do?

King. Thereby begins a tale.

There was a thief, in face much like Sir John

---

87. passest] punning on "pass" meaning "playing and winning at Passage" and "conjuring money from one place to another" (OED 25).

88. cog . . . slur] i.e., either cheat by palming good dice for false dice (OED "cog" v3; OED "foist" 1) or cheat by throwing the dice out of the box so that they do not turn (OED "slur" v2).

92. broken angel] the other half of the "token" Sir John gave to King Harry in scene x.

93. cover] place a coin of equal value upon another (OED 7.a--1st quote given is from 1857).

94-95. blown me up] i.e., ruined me (OED 25) or "exposed me" (OED 27).

99-113.] See note for x.33.1.

(But 'twas not he--that thief was all in green),
Met me last day on Blackheath near the park,
With him a woman. I was all alone
And weaponless, my boy had all my tools
And was before, providing me a boat.
Short tale to make, Sir John, the thief I mean,
Took a just hundred pound in gold from me.
I stormed at it and swore to be revenged
If e'er we met. He, like a lusty thief,
Brake with his teeth this angel just in two,
To be a token at our meeting next,
Provided I should charge no officer
To apprehend him, but at weapon's point
Recover that and what he had beside.
Well met, Sir John, betake ye to your tools
By torchlight. For, Master Parson, you are he
That had my gold.

Sir John. Zounds, I won't in play, in fair square play of the keeper of Eltham Park, and that I will maintain with this poor whinyard.

---

101. near the park] There were three parks near Eltham, which was in the hundred of Blackheath, Horne Park being one of them (William Lambarde, *A Perambulation of Kent* [1576] pp. 48, 386).

103. tools] sword, weapons of war (*OED* 1.b).

117. won't] i.e., won it.

fair square] honest (*OED*).

118. whinyard] short sword (*OED*).

Be you two honest men to stand and look upon's, and let's alone, and take neither part.

King. Agreed. I charge ye do not budge a foot.
Sir John, have at ye.

Sir John. Soldier, 'ware your sconce.

Here, as they are ready to strike, enter Butler and draws his weapon and steps betwixt them.

But. Hold, villain, hold! My lords, what do ye mean
To see a traitor draw against the king?

Sir John. The king! God's will, I am in a proper pickle.

King. Butler, what news? Why dost thou trouble us?

But. Please it, your highness, it is break of day,
And as I scouted near to Islington
The gray-eyed morning gave me glimmering
Of armèd men coming down Highgate Hill,
Who by their course are coasting hitherward.

King. Let us withdraw, my lords. Prepare our troops

123. villain] *Q2*; villaines *Q1*.

---

122. 'ware your sconce] i.e., "look out for your skull" (Mac., p. 150). Another meaning of "sconce" is "lantern" (*OED* 1.1); Sir John, then, could be warning one of the "two with lights" (see S.D. at 0.2).

129. The gray-eyed morning] a dollop of poetry probably lifted, as Mal. (p. 326) indicates, from Shakespeare's use of the phrase in *Romeo and Juliet*, II.iii.1.

131. coasting] approaching hostilely (*OED* 9).

To charge the rebels, if there be such cause.
For this lewd priest, this devilish hypocrite,
That is a thief, a gamester, and what not,
Let him be hanged up for example sake.

Sir John. Not so, my gracious sovereign. I confess I am a frail man, flesh and blood as other are. But set my imperfections aside, by this light ye have not a taller man nor a truer subject to the crown and state than Sir John of Wrotham.

King. Will a true subject rob his king?

Sir John. Alas, 'twas ignorance and want, my gracious liege.

King. 'Twas want of grace! Why, you should be as salt
To season others with good document;
Your lives as lamps to give the people light;
As shepherds, not as wolves to spoil the flock.
Go hang him, Butler.

But. Didst thou not rob me?

Sir John. I must confess I saw some of your gold. But, my dread lord, I am in no humour for death; therefore, save my life. God will that sinners live, do not you cause me die. Once in their lives

---

133. if . . . cause] one more example of King Harry's prudence. Certainly this Harry does not display the passion of Henry V at Harfleur and Agincourt in Henry V.

143-46. Why . . . flock] This outburst of similes consists of conventional sayings highly popular in homiletic literature. Harry is ironically using the language of churchmen to condemn the hypocritical priest, Sir John.

144. document] instruction (OED 1).

147. Didst . . . me] See iii.164-70.

the best may go astray, and if the world say true yourself, my liege, have been a thief.

King. I confess I have.

But I repent and have reclaimed myself.

Sir John. So will I do if you will give me time.

King. Wilt thou? My lords, will you be his sureties?

Hunt. That when he robs again he shall be hanged.

Sir John. I ask no more.

King. And we will grant thee that.

Live and repent, and prove an honest man,
Which when I hear, and safe return from France,
I'll give thee living. Till when, take thy gold,
But spend it better than at cards or wine,
For better virtues fit that coat of thine.

Sir John. *Vivat rex et currat lex.* My liege, if ye have cause of battle, ye shall see Sir John of Wrotham bestir himself in your quarrel. *Exeunt.*

[xii] *After an alarum, enter Harry, Suffolk, Huntington, Sir John, bringing forth Acton, Beverley, and Murley, prisoners.*

157.] This is possibly an important statement for 2 Old. as Sir John is probably executed in this play for robbing and breaking his word to King Harry and the lords.

164. *Vivat . . . lex*] "May the king live and the law run (i.e., work, reign)."

Sc. xii.0.1. *alarum*] a warning peal rung on an alarm bell (*OED* 5). This indicates a battle taking place off stage.

<u>King</u>. Bring in those traitors whose aspiring minds
Thought to have triumphed in our overthrow.
But now ye see, base villains, what success
Attends ill actions wrongfully attempted.
Sir Roger Acton, thou retain'st the name
Of knight, and shouldst be more discreetly tempered
Than join with peasants. Gentry is divine,
But thou hast made it more than popular.

<u>Acton</u>. Pardon, my lord, my conscience urged me to it.

<u>King</u>. Thy conscience? Then thy conscience is corrupt,
For in thy conscience thou art bound to us,
And in thy conscience thou shouldst love thy country;
Else what's the difference 'twixt a Christian
And the uncivil manners of the Turk?

<u>Bev</u>. We meant no hurt unto your majesty,
But reformation of religion.

<u>King</u>. Reform religion? Was it that ye sought?
I pray, who gave you that authority?
Belike then we do hold the sceptre up
And sit within the throne but for a cipher.
Time was good subjects would make known their grief

---

7. divine] in the secular sense of "excellent" (<u>OED</u> 5).

8. popular] vulgar (Mal., p. 328).

13-14.] In effect, rebels are not merely politically misguided but, most fundamentally, ungodly.

And pray amendment, not enforce the same,
Unless their king were tyrant, which I hope
You cannot justly say that Harry is.
What is that other?

Suff. A maltman, my lord,
And dwelling in Dunstable, as he says.

King. Sirrah, what made you leave your barley broth
To come in armour thus against your king?

Mur. Fie, paltry paltry, to and fro, in and out upon occasion, what a world's this! Knighthood, my liege, 'twas knighthood brought me hither. They told me I had wealth enough to make my wife a lady.

King. And so you brought those horses which we saw,
Trapped all in costly furniture, and meant
To wear these spurs when you were knighted once.

Mur. In and out upon occasion, I did.

King. In and out upon occasion, therefore
You shall be hanged. And in the stead of wearing
These spurs upon your heels, about your neck
They shall bewray your folly to the world.

Sir John. In and out upon occasion, that goes hard.

Mur. Fie, paltry paltry, to and fro, good my liege, a pardon, I am sorry for my fault.

King. That comes too late. But tell me, went there none

36-39. In . . . world] _Mal_.; _as prose Q1_.

---

39. bewray] declare (_OED_ 4).

Beside Sir Roger Acton upon whom
You did depend to be your governor?

Mur. None, none, my lord, but Sir John Oldcastle.

King. Bears he part in this conspiracy?

Acton. We looked, my lord, that he would meet us here.

King. But did he promise you that he would come?

Acton. Such letters we receivèd forth of Kent.

Enter Bishop.

Bish. Where is my lord the king? Health to your grace.
Examining, my lord, some of these caitiff rebels,
It is a general voice amongst them all
That they had never come unto this place
But to have met their valiant general,
The good Lord Cobham, as they title him.
Whereby, my lord, your grace may now perceive
His treason is apparent, which before
He sought to colour by his flattery.

King. Now by my royalty I would have sworn,
But for his conscience which I bear withal,
There had not lived a more true-hearted subject.

Bish. It is but counterfeit, my gracious lords.
And therefore may it please your majesty

50.1.] *Mal.*; *at end of 1.47 Q1*.

---

52. caitiff] vile (*OED* 3).

To set your hand unto this precept here,
By which we'll cause him forthwith to appear
And answer this by order of the law.

King. Bishop, not only that, but take commission
To search, attach, imprison, and condemn
This most notorious traitor as you please.

Bish. It shall be done, my lord, without delay.
[*Aside*] So now I hold, Lord Cobham, in my hand
That which shall finish thy disdainèd life. [*Exit*.]

King. I think the iron age begins but now
(Which learnèd poets have so often taught),
Wherein there is no credit to be given
To either words, or looks, or solemn oaths.
For if there were, how often hath he sworn,
How gently tuned the music of his tongue,
And with what amiable face beheld he me,
When all, God knows, was but hypocrisy.

Enter Cobham.

Cob. Long life and prosperous reign unto my lord.

72. S.D.] *Mal*.

---

65. precept] warrant (*OED* 3).

68. commission] delegated authority to carry out an investigation (*OED* 1.2).

69. attach] to arrest by authority of a writ (*OED* 1.1).

74. iron age] last age (after golden, silver, brazen) of world in Greek and Roman mythology; a period of wickedness (*OED*).

<u>King</u>. Ah, villain, canst thou wish prosperity,
Whose heart includeth naught but treachery?
I do arrest thee here myself, false knight,
Of treason capital against the state.

<u>Cob</u>. Of treason, mighty prince? Your grace mistakes.
I hope it is but in the way of mirth.

<u>King</u>. Thy neck shall feel it is in earnest shortly.
Dar'st thou intrude into our presence knowing
How heinously thou hast offended us?
But this is thy accustomèd deceit.
Now thou perceiv'st thy purpose is in vain,
With some excuse or other thou wilt come
To clear thyself of this rebellion.

<u>Cob</u>. Rebellion! Good my lord, I know of none.

<u>King</u>. If you deny it, here is evidence.
See you these men? You never counsellèd
Nor offered them assistance in their wars?

<u>Cob</u>. Speak, sirs, not one but all. I crave no favour.
Have ever I been conversant with you,
Or written letters to encourage you,
Or kindled but the least or smallest part
Of this your late unnatural rebellion?

85-86.] On the battlefield the king had such power that his word was law (Sir Thomas Smith, <u>De Republica Anglorum</u>, quoted in Elton, p. 19).

96.] Cobham <u>does</u> know of another conspiracy but the authors avoid further complications.

Speak, for I dare the uttermost you can.

Mur. In and out upon occasion, I know you not.

King. No? Didst not say that Sir John Oldcastle
Was one with whom you purposed to have met?

Mur. True, I did say so, but in what respect?
Because I heard it was reported so.

King. Was there no other argument but that?

Acton. To clear my conscience ere I die, my lord,
I must confess we have no other ground
But only rumour to accuse this lord,
Which now I see was merely fabulous.

King. The more pernicious you to taint him then,
Whom you knew not was faulty, yea or no.

Cob. Let this, my lord, which I present your grace,
Speak for my loyalty. Read these articles
And then give sentence of my life or death.

King. Earl Cambridge, Scroop, and Gray corrupted
With bribes from Charles of France either to win
My crown from me or secretly contrive
My death by treason! Is this possible?

Cob. There is the platform and their hands, my lord,
Each severally subscribèd to the same.

114.] A commonplace idea but the *Old.* dramatists are always borrowing from Shakespeare--so see Rumour's opening speech in *2 Henry IV*.

125. platform] written outline (*OED* II.3.b).

King. Oh, never heard of base ingratitude!
Even those I hug within my bosom most
Are readiest evermore to sting my heart.
Pardon me, Cobham, I have done thee wrong;
Hereafter I will live to make amends.
Is then their time of meeting so near hand?
We'll meet with them, but little for their ease
If God permit. [To Hunt.] Go, take these rebels hence;
Let them have martial law. [To Cob.] But as for thee,
Friend to thy king and country, still be free.

Exeunt. [Manet Huntington and prisoners.]

Mur. Be it more or less, what a world is this! Would I had continued still of the order of knaves and never sought knighthood, since it costs so dear. Sir Roger, I may thank you for all.

Acton. Now 'tis too late to have it remedied,
I prithee, Murley, do not urge me with it.

Hunt. Will you away, and make no more to do?

Mur. Fie, paltry paltry, to and fro, as occasion serves. If you be so hasty take my place.

Hunt. No, good Sir Knight, you shall begin in your hand.

137-39. Be . . . all] This ed.; Be . . . this? / Would . . . knaves, / And . . . costes / So . . . all Q1. 143-44. Fie . . . place] This ed.; Fy . . . serves, / If . . . place Q1.

---

135. martial law] No formal trial, then, would be needed to punish the rebels.

145. in your hand] The meaning is obscure. Probably Huntington is being ironic and is telling "Sir Knight" that he (Murley) may leave at his discretion or in his own custody (see OED "hand" 29.d).

Mur. I could be glad to give my betters place. *Exeunt.*

[xiii] *Enter Bishop, Lord Warden, Cromer the shrieve, Lady Cobham and attendants.*

Bish. I tell ye, lady, it's not possible
But you should know where he conveys himself,
And you have hid him in some secret place.

La. Cob. My lord, believe me. As I have a soul,
I know not where my lord my husband is.

Bish. Go to, go to. Ye are an heretic
And will be forced by torture to confess
If fair means will not serve to make ye tell.

La. Cob. My husband is a noble gentleman,
And need not hide himself for any fact
That e'er I heard of. Therefore wrong him not.

Bish. Your husband is a dangerous schismatic--
Traitor to God, the king, and commonwealth.

Sc. xiii.01. Lord Warden] At the time that *Old.* was written the 11th Lord Cobham was Lord Warden of the Cinque Ports (seven seaports on the Kentish coast), having succeeded his father in this appointment despite the Earl of Essex's intense lobbying for one of his own candidates (J.E. Neale, *The Elizabethan House of Commons*, [1963; rpt. Glasgow: Fontana/Collins, 1976] pp. 205-6). The fact that a Cobham was Lord Warden explains why the *Old.* dramatists make the character sympathetic to the *Old.* Cobham, and why *he* is present in the scene at all.

Cromer the shrieve] See notes in *Dramatis Personae*. Neale, in *Elizabethan House of Commons* (p. 207) writes that in the election of 1571 in Hythe (one of the Cinque Ports) Lord Cobham (the 10th) got one of his nominees elected, a William Cromer of Kent.

And therefore, Master Cromer shrieve of Kent,
I charge you take her to your custody
And seize the goods of Sir John Oldcastle
To the king's use. Let her go in no more
To fetch so much as her apparel out.
There is your warrant from his majesty.

L. Ward. Good my Lord Bishop, pacify your wrath
Against the lady.

Bish. Then let her confess
Where Oldcastle her husband is concealed.

L. Ward. I dare engage mine honour and my life,
Poor gentlewoman, she is ignorant
And innocent of all his practices,
If any evil by him be practiced.

Bish. "If," my Lord Warden? Nay then, I charge you
That all the Cinque Ports, whereof you are chief,
Be laid forthwith, that he escape us not.
Show him his highness warrant, Master Shrieve.

L. Ward. I am sorry for the noble gentleman.

Enter Cobham and Harpool.

Bish. Peace, he comes here. Now do your office.

27-29.] The Lord Warden was, in effect, sheriff of the Cinque Ports, and had broad legal and administrative powers there (Neale, Elizabethan House of Commons, p. 204).

29. laid] posted with soldiers (OED 20) with added sense of being "set for ambush" (OED 18).

Cob. Harpool, what business have we here in hand?
What makes the bishop and the sheriff here?
I fear my coming home is dangerous.
I would I had not made such haste to Cobham.

Harp. Be of good cheer, my lord. If they be foes we'll scramble shrewdly with them; if they be friends they are welcome. One of them, my Lord Warden, is your friend. But methinks my lady weeps. I like not that.

Crom. Sir John Oldcastle, Lord Cobham, in the king's majesty's name I arrest ye of high treason.

Cob. Treason, Master Cromer?

Harp. Treason, Master Shrieve? 'Sblood, what treason?

Cob. Harpool, I charge thee stir not but be quiet still.
Do ye arrest me, Master Shrieve, for treason?

Bish. Yea, of high treason, traitor, heretic.

Cob. Defiance in his face that calls me so!
I am as true a loyal gentleman
Unto his highness as my proudest enemy.
The king shall witness my late faithful service
For safety of his sacred majesty.

Bish. What thou art, the king's hand shall testify.
Show't him, Lord Warden.

43. Cromer] F3; Croomes Q1.

---

37. scramble] struggle (OED 2).

38-39. One . . . friend] See note above, 1.0.1.

Cob. Jesu defend me!
Is't possible your cunning could so temper
The princely disposition of his mind
To sign the damage of a royal subject?
Well, the best is, it bears an antedate,
Procurèd by my absence and your malice.
But I, since that, have showed myself as true
As any churchman that dare challenge me.
Let me be brought before his majesty;
If he acquit me not, then do your worst.

Bish. We are not bound to do kind offices
For any traitor, schismatic, nor heretic.
The king's hand is our warrant for our work,
Who is departed on his way for France
And at Southampton doth repose this night.

Harp. (*Aside*) O, that it were the blessed will of God that thou and I were within twenty mile of it, on Salisbury plain! I would lose my head if ever thou brought'st thy head hither again.

Cob. My Lord Warden o'th' Cinque Ports, and my Lord Rochester, ye are joint commissioners. Favour me so much, on my expense, to

57. royal] *Q1*; Loyal *Rowe*. 73. much, on] *F3*; much, / On *Q1*.

58-59.] Either the audience is supposed to assume that the Bishop had put an earlier date on the warrant than that called for (for Cobham saw King Harry but one speech after the Bishop left with warrant in hand), or the audience is not supposed to care for such small details.

73. joint commissioners] with respect to the warrant, that is.

bring me to the king.

Bish. What, to Southampton?

Cob. Thither, my good lord.

And if he do not clear me of all guilt
And all suspicion of conspiracy,
Pawning his princely warrant for my truth,
I ask no favour but extremest torture.
Bring me or send me to him, good my lord.
Good my Lord Warden, Master Shrieve, entreat.

Here the Lord Warden and Cromer uncover to the Bishop, and secretly whispers with him.

[*To La. Cob.*] Come hither, lady. Nay, sweet wife, forbear
To heap one sorrow on another's neck.
'Tis grief enough falsely to be accused
And not permitted to acquit myself.
Do not thou with thy kind respective tears
Torment thy husband's heart that bleeds for thee,
But be of comfort. God hath help in store
For those that put assurèd trust in him.
Dear wife, if they commit me to the Tower,
Come up to London to your sister's house,

78.] Cobham means that King Harry will believe him and annul the warrant.

81.1.] *uncover*] remove their hats (*OED* 4). They do so, presumably, to mask themselves from the sight of the audience so that they do not distract the audience from the Cobham-Lady Cobham scene.

86. respective] heedful (*OED* 2).

That being near me you may comfort me.
One solace find I settled in my soul:
That I am free from treason's very thought.
Only my conscience for the gospel's sake
Is cause of all the troubles I sustain.

La. Cob. O, my dear lord, what shall betide of us?
You to the Tower, and I turned out of doors,
Our substance seized unto his highness use,
Even to the garments 'longing to our backs.

Harp. Patience, good madam, things at worst will mend,
And if they do not, yet our lives may end.

Bish. [To L. Ward. and Crom.] Urge it no more; for if an angel spake,
I swear, by sweet Saint Peter's blessèd keys,
First goes he to the Tower, then to the stake.

Crom. But by your leave, this warrant doth not stretch
To imprison her.

Bish. No. Turn her out of doors

Lord Warden and Cobham whisper.

Even as she is, and lead him to the Tower
With guard enough for fear of rescuing.

---

104. sweet . . . keys] This Catholic oath alluding to the power, "keys," conferred by Christ on St. Peter emphasizes the Inquisition-like harshness of the Bishop's actions.

107.1.] Possibly Cobham is asking the Lord Warden to allow Harpool to come with him, and sometime between then and Cromer's next speech the Lord Warden similarly whispers to Cromer what Cobham whispered to him.

La. Cob. O, God requite thee, thou blood-thirsty man!

Cob. May it not be, my Lord of Rochester?
Wherein have I incurred your hate so far
That my appeal unto the king's denied?

Bish. No hate of mine, but power of holy church
Forbids all favour to false heretics.

Cob. Your private malice more than public power
Strikes most at me, but with my life it ends.

Harp. (Aside) O, that I had the bishop in that fear
That once I had his sumner by ourselves!

Crom. My lord, yet grant one suit unto us all:
That this same ancient serving-man may wait
Upon my lord his master in the Tower.

Bish. This old iniquity, this heretic,
That in contempt of our church discipline,
Compelled my sumner to devour this process?
Old ruffian past-grace, upstart schismatic,
Had not the king prayed us to pardon ye,
Ye had fried for it, ye grizzled heretic.

---

123. old iniquity] alluding to one of the comic vices in the morality plays (Mal. [Steevens], p. 337).

126. past-grace] The phrase is not recorded in OED. It means "beyond blessing" or "beyond hope."

Harp. 'Sblood, my Lord Bishop, ye do me wrong. I am neither heretic nor Puritan, but of the old church. I'll swear, drink ale, kiss a wench, go to mass, eat fish all Lent, and fast Fridays with cakes and wine, fruit and spicery, shrive me of my old sins afore Easter, and begin new afore Whitsuntide.

Crom. A merry, mad, conceited knave, my lord.

Harp. That knave was simply put upon the bishop.

Bish. Well, God forgive him, and I pardon him.
Let him attend his master in the Tower,
For I in charity wish his soul no hurt.

Cob. God bless my soul from such cold charity!

Bish. To th'Tower with him. And when my leisure serves
I will examine him of articles.
Look, my Lord Warden, as you have in charge,
The shrieve perform his office.

L. Ward. Yes, my lord.

129-30. I . . . church] an obvious anachronism. The fact that Harpool is comparing heretics and Puritans reflects upon the unsettled position of Puritans in late Elizabethan England.

130-33. I'll . . . Whitsuntide] Harpool is humorously and conventionally anti-clerical. Whitsuntide is the season of Whit Sunday, the seventh Sunday after Easter.

134. conceited] clever (OED 1.c).

135. simply] foolishly (OED 5).

put upon] imposed as a burden (OED 23.a).

140-41. And . . . articles] See following scene. Historically, this examination took place before the Ficket Field rebellion.

Enter the Sumner with books.

Bish. What bring'st thou there? What, books of heresy?

Sum. Yea, my lord, here's not a Latin book; no, not so much as our Lady's Psalter. Here's the Bible, the Testament, the Psalms in metre, The Sickman's Salve, The Treasure of Gladness and all in English, not so much but the almanac's English.

Bish. Away with them! To th'fire with them, Clun!
Now, fie upon these upstart heretics!
All English! Burn them, burn them quickly, Clun!

Harp. But do not, Sumner, as you'll answer it. For I have there English books, my lord, that I'll not part with for your bishopric: Bevis of Hampton, Owlglass, The Friar and the Boy, Eleanor Rumming, Robin Hood, and other such godly stories, which if ye

145-48. Yea . . . English] Mal.; Yea . . . booke, / No . . . Psalter, / Heres . . . meter, / The . . . gladnesse, / And . . . English Q1.
154. Eleanor] Mal.; Ellen of Q1.

144-57.] It would seem that the Old. dramatists were cleverly mixing historical facts with contemporary events when they have the Bishop give the order for the burning of books. This is probably an ironic allusion to the Bishop of London's June 1, 1599, order for the burning of satirical books. Certainly there is nothing of a seditious nature in any of the secular books named, and so the Old. authors are wryly criticizing such extreme forms of censorship.

147. The Sickman's . . . Gladness] The former, a series of model dialogues for death-bed situations, was first published in 1561. Compiled by Thomas Becon it was declared heretical in Mary's reign. The anonymous Treasure of Gladness (1562) was a collection of prayers (Hebel, V, 50).

154-55. Bevis . . . Hood] These were popular works throughout the 16th century. The metrical romances Bevis of Hampton and Robin Hood had been well-known since the medieval era. Owlglass, a comical adventure, was "the name of a popular German tale (Tyll Eulenspiegel) translated into English at the end of the sixteenth century" (Mac., p. 151). The Friar and the Boy "is a fabliau in tail-rhyme verse, first known in Wynken de Worde's edition, burn, by this flesh I'll make ye drink their ashes in Saint Marg'et's ale. Exeunt.

[xiv] Enter the Bishop of Rochester with his [Serving-]men in livery coats.

1. Serv. Is it your honour's pleasure we shall stay,
Or come back in the afternoon to fetch you?
Bish. Now you have brought me here into the Tower,
You may go back unto the porter's lodge
And send for drink or such things as you want,
Where if I have occasion to employ you
I'll send some officer to call you to me.
Into the city go not, I command you.
Perhaps I may have present need to use you.
2. [Serv.] We will attend your worship here without.
Bish. Do so, I pray you.
3. [Serv.] [To 1. and 2. Serv.] Come, we may have a quart of wine

10, 12, 15, 16. Serv.] Rowe.

---

and twice reprinted for E. Allde (nd and 1617)" (Hebel, V, 50). The Tunning of Eleanor Rumming was a typically irreverent work of John Skelton written in 1518 and subsequently published c. 1521 and included in Skelton's collected works, Certayne Bokes (c. 1545), and later 16th century editions of it (John Skelton, Poems, Robert C. Kinsman, ed. [Oxford: Clarendon Press, 1969], p. 152).

156-57. Saint Marg'et's ale] i.e., water (Mal. p. 341).

at the Rose at Barking, I warrant you, and come back an hour before he be ready to go.

1. [Serv.] We must hie us then.

3. [Serv.] Let's away. Exeunt. [Manet Bishop.]

Bish. Ho, Master Lieutenant.

Lieu. [Within] Who calls there?

Bish. A friend of yours.

[Enter Lieutenant of Tower.]

Lieu. My Lord of Rochester, your honour's welcome.

Bish. Sir, here's my warrant from the council
For conference with Sir John Oldcastle
Upon some matter of great consequence.

Lieu. Ho, Sir John.

Harp. [Within] Who calls there?

Lieu. Harpool, tell Sir John that my Lord of Rochester comes from the council to confer with him.

Harp. [Within] I will, Sir.

Lieu. I think you may as safe without suspicion
As any man in England, as I hear,
For it was you most laboured his commitment.

18. S.D.] Hopk. 19.1.] Hopk.; bet. 11.17 and 18 Mal. 25. S.D.] Mal.

---

13. the Rose at Barking] "Barking is a district of London lying to the north-east of the Tower" (Mac., p. 151). The Rose Tavern was on Great Tower Street (Hebel, V, 51). Oliver in The London Prodigal (1605) mentions another (?) Rose Tavern located at Temple Bar (C2r).

15. hie] hasten (OED 2).

Bish. I did, sir, and nothing repent it. I assure you.

Enter Lord Cobham [and Harpool].

Master Lieutenant, I pray you give us leave,
I must confer here with Sir John a little.

Lieu. With all my heart, my lord. [Exit.]

Harp. (Aside [to Cob.]) My lord, be ruled by me. Take this occasion while 'tis offered, and on my life your lordship shall escape.

Cob. No more, I say. Peace, lest he should suspect it.

Bish. Sir John, I am come unto you from the lords of his highness most honourable council to know if yet you do recant your errors, conforming you unto the holy church.

Cob. My Lord of Rochester, on good advice
I see my error. But yet understand me,
I mean not error in the faith I hold,
But error in submitting to your pleasure.
Therefore your lordship, without more to do.
Must be a means to help me to escape.

Bish. What means? [Harp. and Cob. set upon the Bish.] Thou heretic!
Dar'st thou but lift thy hand against my calling?

Cob. No, not to hurt you for a thousand pound.

Harp. Nothing but to borrow your upper garments a little. Not a word more, for if you do, you die. Peace, for waking the children. [To

32.1. and Harpool] Rowe. 35. S.D.] Rowe.

---

52. Peace . . . children] Harpool is being threateningly ironic and probably has gagged the Bishop by this time. Cobham then proceeds to put on the Bishop's outer garments.

Cob.] There, put them on. Dispatch, my lord. The window that goes out into the leads is sure enough--I told you that before. There, make you ready. I'll convey him after and bind him surely in the inner room. [*Exit with Bishop.*]

Cob. This is well begun. God sent us happy speed.
Hard shift you see men make in time of need.
Harpool!

[*Enter Harpool.*]

Harp. Here, my lord. Come, come away. [*Exeunt.*]

[xv] *Enter* [*Bishop's*] *Serving-men again.*

1. [*Serv.*] I marvel that my lord should stay so long.

2. [*Serv.*] He hath sent to seek us, I dare lay my life.

3. [*Serv.*] We come in good time, see where he is coming.

58-59. need. / Harpool] *Brooke*; need: Harpoole *Q1*. Sc. xv. 1, 2, 3, 21, 22, 23, 27, 45, 48. *Serv.*] *Rowe*.

---

54. leads] meaning either "lead roof" (*OED* 1.7.a) or "paths" (*OED* 2.3.c).

56. inner room] i.e., through the entrance into the tiring house whence Harpool and Cobham originally came.

60. *Exeunt.*] It is possible that Harpool and Cobham do not exit. In this case the serving-men would enter to Harpool and Cobham and only spy the latter after they had spoken.

Sc. xv.3. see . . . coming] As I interpret the action the prisoners have left the stage before the serving-men enter; when they re-enter the prisoners have left the prison-area proper, by way of the "leads," and meet the serving-men near the entrance of the Tower (see 11.24-25).

[*Enter Cobham and Harpool*.]

Harp. I beseech you, good my Lord of Rochester, be favourable to my lord and master.

Cob. The inner rooms be very hot and close.
I do not like this air here in the Tower.

Harp. His case is hard, my lord. [*Aside to Cob*.] You shall safely get out of the Tower, but I will down upon them, in which time get you away.

Cob. Fellow, thou troublest me.

Harp. Hear me, my lord. [*Aside to Cob*.] Hard under Islington wait you my coming. I will bring my lady ready, with horses to convey you hence.

Cob. Fellow, go back again unto thy lord and counsel him.

Harp. Nay, my good Lord of Rochester. [*Aside to Cob*.] I'll bring you to Saint Albans through the woods, I warrant you.

Cob. Villain, away.

Harp. Nay, since I am past the Tower's liberty, thou part'st not so.

He draws [*his sword*].

Cob. Clubs, clubs, clubs!

1. [*Serv*.] Murder, murder, murder!

8. S.D.] *Mal. subst*. 20. S.H.] *Rowe; Bish. Q1*.

6-7.] Indicating, I believe, that the two have come from the inside.

12. Hard] close (*OED* 6).

19. Tower's liberty] i.e., beyond its jurisdiction. A more specific meaning would be the limits outside a prison within which prisoners were allowed to reside (*OED* 7.c).

2. [Serv.] Down with him! They fight.

3. [Serv.] A villain traitor!

Harp. You cowardly rogues! Cobham escapes.

Enter Lieutenant and his men.

Lieu. Who is so bold as dare to draw a sword
So near unto the entrance of the Tower?

1. [Serv.] This ruffian servant to Sir John Oldcastle was like to have slain my lord.

Lieu. Lay hold on him.

Harp. Stand off, if you love your puddings.

Bish. (Calls within) Help, help, help! Master Lieutenant, help!

Lieu. Who's that within? Some treason in the Tower upon my life. [To one of his men] Look in. [Exit Lieutenant's man.] Who's that which calls?

Enter Bishop bound [and Lieutenant's man].

Without your cloak, my Lord of Rochester?

Harp. [Aside] There, now it works. Then let me speed, for now is the fittest time for me to 'scape away. Exit.

Lieu. Why do you look so ghastly and affrighted?

Bish. Oldcastle that traitor and his man, when you had left me to confer with him, took, bound, and stripped me as you see, and left me

33. Exit . . . man] Mal. subst. 34.1. and . . . man] Mal. subst. 39-41. Oldcastle . . . departed] This ed.; Old-castle . . . man, / When . . . him, / Tooke . . . see, / And . . . chamber, / And . . . departed Q1.

---

30. puddings] guts (OED 2).

lying in his inner chamber and so departed.

1. Serv. And I--

Lieu. And you! Ne'er say that the Lord Cobham's man
Did here set upon you like to murder you?

1. [Serv.] And so he did.

Bish. It was upon his master then he did,
That in the brawl the traitor might escape.

Lieu. Where is this Harpool?

2. [Serv.] Here he was even now.

Lieu. Where, can you tell? They are both escaped.
Since it so happens that he is escaped,
I am glad you are a witness of the same;
It might have else been laid unto my charge
That I had been consenting to the fact.

Bish. Come,
Search shall be made for him with expedition,
The havens laid that he shall not escape,
And hue and cry continue thorough England
To find this damnèd, dangerous heretic. Exeunt.

41-42. departed. / 1. Serv. And I--] Mal.; departed, and I Q1. 54-59. Come . . . heretic] Rowe; as prose Q1.

---

42. 1. Serv.] a sensible Malone emendation. It would be very odd indeed for the Lieutenant to interrupt the Bishop so curtly and then proceed to speak to 1. Serv. as occurs in Q1.

50-53.] See note for Lieutenant in Dramatis Personae.

52. laid . . . charge] imputed (OED "charge" 16.b).

57. thorough] throughout (OED 3).

Enter Cambridge, Scroop, and Gray as in a chamber, and set down at a table, consulting about their treason. King Harry and Suffolk list'ning at the door.

Camb. In mine opinion Scroop hath well advised.
Poison will be the only aptest mean,
And fittest for our purpose to dispatch him.
Gray. But yet there may be doubt in their delivery.
Harry is wise. Therefore, Earl of Cambridge,
I judge that way not so convenient.
Scroop. What think ye then of this? I am his bedfellow,
And unsuspected nightly sleep with him.
What if I venture in those silent hours,
When sleep hath sealèd up all mortal eyes,
To murder him in bed? How like ye that?
Camb. Herein consists no safety for yourself,
And you disclosed, what shall become of us?
But this day (as ye know) he will aboard,
The wind so fair, and set away for France.
If as he goes or ent'ring in the ship
It might be done, then it were excellent.
Gray. Why, any of these. Or, if you will,

Sc. xvi.0.2. set] seated (_OED_ 143.1.b).

3. dispatch] kill (_OED_ 4). The conspirators continue to use the same fine language to gloss their treacherous acts.

I'll cause a present sitting of the council,
Wherein I will pretend some matter of such weight
As needs must have his royal company,
And to dispatch him in the council-chamber.

Camb. Tush, yet I hear not anything to purpose.
I wonder that Lord Cobham stays so long;
His counsel in this case would much avail us.

They rise from the table and the King steps in to them with his lords.

Scroop. What, shall we rise thus and determine nothing?

King. That were a shame, indeed. No, sit again,
And you shall have my counsel in this case. [_They sit_.]
If you can find no way to kill this king,
Then you shall see how I can further ye.
Scroop's way by poison was indifferent,
But yet being bedfellow unto the king
And unsuspected sleeping in his bosom,
In mine opinion, that's the likelier way;
For such false friends are able to do much,
And silent night is treason's fittest friend.
Now, Cambridge, in his setting hence for France,
Or by the way, or as he goes aboard,
To do the deed, that was indifferent too;

22. to] _Q1_; so _conj. MSR_.

---

23. Tush] exclamation of impatience (_OED_).

Yet somewhat doubtful, might I speak my mind,
For many reasons needless now to urge.
Marry, Lord Gray came something near the point:
To have the king at council and there murder him,
As Caesar was amongst his dearest friends!
None like to that, if all were of his mind.
Tell me, oh, tell me, you bright honour's stains,
For which of all my kindnesses to you
Are ye become thus traitors to your king?
And France must have the spoil of Harry's life?

All. Oh, pardon us, dread lord. *All kneeling*.

King. How, pardon ye? That were a sin indeed!
Drag them to death, which justly they deserve.

The lords lead the conspirators away.

And France shall dearly buy this villainy,
So soon as we set footing on her breast.
God have the praise for our deliverance,
And next, our thanks, Lord Cobham, is to thee,

46. honour's] *F3*; honors *Q1*. 52.1.] *This ed*.; *they leade them away Q1*.

---

40. doubtful] See note for Prologue 1.1.

44.] *Julius Caesar* was performed at the new Globe theatre on September 21, 1599 (E.K. Chambers, *The Elizabethan Stage*, II, 364-66). I wonder whether King Harry's conventional horror at Caesar's death is a passing jibe of the *Old*. authors at Shakespeare's "sympathetic" treatment of the assassination.

45. None . . . that] i.e., "No better plan than that."

56. Lord Cobham] King Harry is apostrophizing the absent Cobham (Brooke, p. 425).

True perfect mirror of nobility. *Exeunt*.

[xvii] *Enter Sir John and Doll*.

Sir John. Come, Doll, come; be merry, wench. Farewell Kent, we are not for thee. Be lusty, my lass, come for Lancashire. We must nip the bung for these crowns.

Doll. Why, is all the gold spent already that you had the other day?

Sir John. Gone, Doll; gone, flown, spent, vanished. The devil, drink, and the dice has devoured all.

Doll. You might have left me in Kent, that you might, until you had been better provided. I could have stayed at Cobham.

Sir John. No, Doll, no, I'll none of that. Kent's too hot, Doll,

Sc. xvii] *See explanatory note*. 1-3. Come . . . crowns] *Mal*.; Come . . . wench, / Farewell . . . thee, / Be . . . Lancashire, / We . . . crownes *Q1*.

Sc. xvii] This scene begins on page I3r in Q1; what follows scene xvi on pages I1r-I3r is scenes xx-xxiv. This blunder was probably caused by MS pages being mixed up. A different kind of printing error occurred in the Simmes 1600 printing of *2 Henry IV*. A 108-line cancel was inserted into a second issue of the play when, apparently, an MS leaf of *2 Henry IV* was temporarily lost (Charlton Hinman, "Shakespeare's Text--Then, Now and Tomorrow," *Shakespeare Survey*, 18 [1965],26-27).

1-19.] This section of the scene is little more than a slight variation on scene ix. It is conceivable, if over-generous, to consider the repetition of phrases to be deliberately comic. Thus the audience would recognize the authors' attempt, through repetition, to convey the quarrelsome domesticity of the couple and, instead of being irritated at the paucity of the authors' imagination, would knowingly nod at the familar nature of the conversation.

2-3. nip the bung] i.e., "cut a purse" (Mal., [Steevens], p. 347).

Kent's too hot. The weathercock of Wrotham will crow no longer. We have plucked him; he has lost his feathers; I have pruned him bare, left him thrice. Is moulted, is moulted, wench.

Doll. Faith, Sir John, I might have gone to service again. Old Master Harpool told me he would provide me a mistress.

Sir John. Peace, Doll, peace. Come, mad wench, I'll make thee an honest woman. We'll into Lancashire to our friends. The troth is, I'll marry thee. We want but a little money to buy us a horse and to spend by the way. The next sheep that comes shall lose his fleece. We'll have these crowns, wench, I warrant thee.

Enter the Irishman with his master slain.

Stay, who comes here? Some Irish villain methinks that has slain a man and draws him out of the way to rifle him. Stand close, Doll, we'll see the end.

The Irishman falls to rifle his master.

[Irish.] Alas, po'mester, Sir Rishard Lee, be Saint Patrick I's rob and cut thy t'roat for dee shain, and dy money, and dee gold ring. Be me truly, I's love thee well, but now dow be kill, thee bee-shitten kanave.

19.1.] Brooke; after methinks that Q1. 23. S.H.] Q2. 25. kill, thee Brooke; kil thee, Q1.

10-12. The . . . thrice] Geese are plucked twice a year; thus a weathercock "pruned" three times would indeed be "bare" (Mal. [Steevens], p. 347).

13. gone to service] become a servant (OED 1).

14. provide me a mistress] a double entendre playing upon the audience's understanding of Harpool as a dirty old man.

23-26.] Irish dialect in Q1 is indicated in this speech and other speeches

Sir John. Stand, sirrah. What art thou?

Irish. Be Saint Patrick, mester, I's poor Irishman, I's a leufter.

Sir John. Sirrah, sirrah, you are a damned rogue. You have killed a man here and rifled him of all that he has. 'Sblood, you rogue, deliver, or I'll not leave you so much as an Irish hair above your shoulders, you whoreson Irish dog. Sirrah, untruss presently. Come off and dispatch, or by this cross I'll fetch your head off as clean as a bark.

Irish. Wee's me, Saint Patrick, I's kill me mester for chain and his ring, and nows be rob of all, me's undo. *Sir John robs him*.

Sir John. Avant, you rascal. Go, sirrah, be walking. [*Exit Irish*.] Come, Doll, the devil laughs when one thief robs another. Come, mad wench, we'll to Saint Albans and revel in our bower. Hey, my brave girl!

Doll. O, thou art old Sir John when all's done, i'faith. [*Exeunt*.]

41. S.D.] *Rowe*.

---

of the Irishman primarily through the change of "th" to "d" (though this is not consistent) and a haphazard tinkering with an occasional vowel or pronoun. In scene xxi the Irishman uses "v" for "wh." I normalize every dialect "is" in Q1 to the more recognizable "I's", i.e. "I is."

28. leufter] This may be an Irish corruption of "lifter"--a thief (Brooke, p. 425).

31-32. Irish . . . shoulders] The Irish were known for their long hair. The authors sympathize with Sir John's virulent anti-Irish feelings and this attitude would undoubtedly be endorsed by an audience embittered by the recent fiascos in Ireland. Generally speaking the *Old*. authors' attitude to anyone other than the English is patronizing at best and racist at worst.

35. Wee's me] a corruption of "woe's me."

Enter the Host of the Bell with the Irishman.

Irish. Be me tro', mester, I's poor Irisman, I's want ludging, I's have no money, I's starve and cold. Good mester, give her some meat, I's famise and tie.

Host. I'faith, my fellow, I have no lodging but what I keep for my guests that I may not disappoint. As for meat, thou shalt have such as there is. And if thou wilt lie in the barn there's fair straw and room enough.

Irish. I's thank my mester heartily, de straw is good bed for me.

Host. Ho, Robin.

[*Enter Robin*.]

Rob. Who calls?

Host. Show this poor Irishman into the barn. Go, sirrah. [*Exeunt*.]

[xix] *Enter* [*Club the*] *carrier and Kate*.

Club. Ho, who's within here? Who looks to the horses? God's hat, here's fine work, the hens in the manger and the hogs in the litter.

Sc. xviii.9.1.] *Mal*. 11. S.D.] *Simms*. Sc. xix.1. horses? God's] *Mal*.; horses? / Gods *Q1*.

Sc. xviii.0. the Bell] This reference to the Bell would seem to be purely literary for no one in the play refers to the inn by its name, but it is possible that the reference indicates that a tavern sign was set on stage.

3. famise and tie] i.e., "famish and die."

Sc. xix.2. litter] straw (*OED* 3).

A bots 'found you all, here's a house well looked to, i'vaith.

Kate. Mass, goff Club, Ise very cawd.

Club. Get in Kate. Get in to fire and warm thee. [*Exit Kate.*] Ho, John Ostler.

Enter Ostler.

Ostler. What gaffer Club, welcome to Saint Albans. How does all our friends in Lancashire?

Club. Well, God have mercy, John. How does Tom? Where's he?

Ostler. O, Tom is gone from hence. He's at the Three Horse-Loaves at Stony Stratford. How does old Dick Dun?

Club. God's hat, old Dun has been moyered in a slough in Brickhill

6.1.] *Simms.* 7-8. What . . . Lancashire] *This ed.*; What . . . Albons, / How . . . Lancashire *Q1*.

---

3. A bots . . . i'vaith] Club is being sarcastic; he thinks everything is in disorder. Country dialect is indicated in the couple's speeches in Q1 through spellings that point to variant pronounciation. Club does consistently use the form "i'vaith" and also uses certain other quaint phrases.

A bots] an expression of contempt (*OED* 2).

'found] short for "confound."

4. goff] Mac. (p. 152) says this is an equivalent for "gaffer"--a country term for an old man (*OED* 2).

9. Tom] either another ostler or a horse.

10. Three Horse-Loaves] a name for an inn (Brooke, pp. 425-26). A "horse-loaf" is bread made of bran or beans for the food of horses (*OED* "horse-bread").

11. Stony Stratford] in Buckinghamshire along the road (Watling Street) heading northwest from London, north of Dunstable (Mac., p. 152). St. Albans is roughly halfway between London and Stony Stratford.

Dick Dun] a horse (Hebel, V, 51).

12. moyered] sunk in mire (*OED* II.3). The proverbial phrase "Dun is in the

Lane. A plague 'found it, yonder is such abomination weather as never was seen.

Ostler. God's hat, thief, have one half peck of peas and oats more for that. As I am John Ostler, he has been ever as good a jade as ever travelled.

Club. Faith, well said, old Jack, thou art the old lad still.

Ostler. Come, gaffer Club, unload, unload and get to supper, and I'll rub Dun the while. Come. Exeunt.

[xx] Enter the Host, Lord Cobham, [Lady Cobham,] and Harpool.

Host. Sir, you are welcome to this house, to such as here is with all my heart. But by the mass, I fear your lodging will be the worst.

---

mire" means "things are at a standstill" (OED "dun" 5).

12-13. Brickhill Lane] "part of Watling Street which crosses Brickhill, 9 miles south of Stony Stratford" (Hebel, V, 51).

13-14. yonder . . . seen] F.G. Fleay (A Chronicle History of the London Stage, 1549-1642 [New York: G.E. Stechert & Co., 1909], p. 163--extracting from Stow's Survey) notes that there were significant rain and floods in June 1599.

20. rub Dun] punning on the name "Dun" and the phrase "rub down."

Sc. xx.0.1. Lady Cobham] Her presence is not required in this scene but it would be curious for both the Host and Cobham to refer to her if she were not present. Furthermore, she is supposed to be with her husband (see xv. 12-14) and she does appear with her husband leaving the inn in disguise in scene xxiii. The whole scene echoes the nativity plays of the medieval cycles, and particularly the scene in the Coventry Cycle (see Samuel B. Hemingway, English Nativity Plays [1909; rpt. New York: Russell and Russell Inc., 1964], pp. 103-05) where Joseph speaks to the citizen of his wife's weariness. In this scene Mary is present, obviously, which is perhaps another reason for having Lady Cobham here.

I have but two beds and they are both in a chamber; and the carrier and his daughter lies in the one, and you and your wife must lie in the other.

Cob. In faith, sir, for myself I do not greatly pass. My wife is weary and would be at rest, for we have travelled very far today. We must be content with such as you have.

Host. But I cannot tell how to do with your man.

Harp. What, hast thou never an empty room in thy house for me?

Host. Not a bed, by my troth. There came a poor Irishman and I lodged him in the barn where he has fair straw, though he have nothing else.

Harp. Well, mine Host, I pray thee help me to a pair of fair sheets and I'll go lodge with him.

Host. By the mass, that thou shalt. A good pair of hempen sheets, were never lain in. Come. Exeunt.

[xxi] Enter [the Saint Albans] Constable, Mayor, and Watch.

Mayor. What, have you searched the town?

Con. All the town, sir. We have not left a house unsearched that uses to lodge.

6-8. In . . . have] This ed.; In . . . passe, / My . . . rest, / For . . . day, / We . . . have Q1.

---

6. pass] care (OED 23).

Mayor. Surely my Lord of Rochester was then deceived or ill-informed of Sir John Oldcastle. Or, if he come this way, he's past the town; he could not else have 'scaped you in the search.

Con. The privy watch hath been abroad all night, and not a stranger lodgeth in the town but he is known; only a lusty priest we found in bed with a pretty wench, that says she is his wife, yonder at the Shears. But we have charged the host with his forthcoming tomorrow morning.

Mayor. What think you best to do?

Con. Faith, Master Mayor, here's a few straggling houses beyond the bridge and a little inn where carriers use to lodge, though I think surely he would ne'er lodge there. But we'll go search, and the rather, because there came notice to the town the last night of an Irishman that had done a murder, whom we are to make search for.

Mayor. Come, I pray you, and be circumspect.

Con. First, beset the house before you begin the search.

Officer [of Watch.] Content, every man takes a several place. *Exeunt*.

4-6. Surely . . . search] *This ed.*; Surely . . . deceivde, / Or . . . Oldcastle, / Or . . . towne, / He . . . search Q1. 7-11. The . . . morning] *This ed.*; The . . . night, / And . . . towne / But . . . priest / We . . . wench, / That . . . sheeres: / But . . . comming / To . . . morning *Q1*. 21. S.D.] *This ed.*; *at end of 1.19. Q1*.

Sc. xxi.10. the Shears] the name of an inn (Mac., p. 151).

16. the rather] the more readily (*OED* 2.b).

20. beset] surround (*OED* 2.b).

21. *Exeunt*.] Q1's placement of the stage direction at the end of 1.19 seems

Here is heard a great noise within.

[Within] Keep, keep! Strike him down there! Down with him!

[Re-]enter Constable [,Mayor, and Watch] with the Irishman in Harpool's apparel.

Con. Come, you villainous heretic, confess where your master is!

Irish. Vat mester?

Mayor. "Vat mester?" You counterfeit rebel, this shall not serve your turn.

Irish. Be Sent Patrick, I ha' no mester!

Con. Where is the Lord Cobham, Sir John Oldcastle, that lately is escaped out of the Tower?

Irish. Vat Lort Cobham?

Mayor. You counterfeit, this shall not serve you. We'll torture you, we'll make you to confess where that arch-heretic Lord Cobham is. [To Watch] Come, bind him fast.

Irish. Ahone, ahone, ahone, a cree!

Con. Ahone, you crafty rascal? Exeunt.

---

to me another example of the compositor's habit of placing a stage direction where it will fit in the text.

22.1-2.] One could call this a new scene as the stage was cleared; I however have decided not to because no new venue is indicated, and no more time than the actual playing time is indicated to have elapsed. The situation recalls that in scene xii except that the interval between scenes xi and xii is unrealistically (but conventionally) meant to represent a battle of sorts--something, of course, that would take longer than the actual stage time.

34. ahone, a cree] The Gaelic O hone a rie means "alas for the prince, or chief" (OED "ohone").

<u>Lord Cobham comes out in his gown stealing</u>.

<u>Cob</u>. Harpool, Harpool, I hear a marvelous noise about the house. God warrant us, I fear we are pursued. What, Harpool!

<u>Harp</u>. (<u>Within</u>) Who calls there?

<u>Cob</u>. 'Tis I. Dost thou not hear a noise about the house?

<u>Harp</u>. [<u>Within</u>] Yes, marry, do I. 'Swounds, I cannot find my hose! This Irish rascal, that was lodged with me all night, hath stolen my apparel and has left me nothing but a lousy mantle and a pair of brogues. Get up, get up. And if the carrier and his wench be asleep, change you with them as he hath done with me, and see if we can escape. [<u>Exit Cobham</u>.]

[xxiii] <u>A noise again heard about the house a pretty while, then enter the Constable</u> [,<u>Mayor, and Watch</u>] <u>meeting Harpool in the Irishman's apparel</u>.

10. S.D.] <u>Mal</u>. Sc. xxiii.0.2. <u>Mayor, and Watch</u>] <u>Mal</u>. subst.

Sc. xxii.0.1. stealing] creeping secretly (<u>OED</u> 10).

5. within] It is possible that either at the beginning of the speech or sometime during it (a likely break being after "brogues") Harpool is actually seen. If this is so, then I would think that Harpool's "Get up, get up" might mean something more than "wake up" or "get moving" and might literally mean "get upstairs;" in that case it would seem logical and dramatically convenient if Harpool said his lines from above.

7. mantle] a loose sleeveless cloak (<u>OED</u> 1) or "long cloak" (Mal., p. 353), or "a blanket or plaid" (<u>OED</u> 1.b).

8. brogues] hose or trousers (<u>OED</u> 2--1st quote 1615); or, less likely, "a crude Irish shoe" (<u>OED</u> 1).

Con. Stand close. Here comes the Irishman that did the murder. By all tokens this is he.

Mayor. And, perceiving the house beset, would get away. Stand, sirrah.

Harp. What art thou that bidd'st me stand?

Con. I am the officer, and am come to search for an Irishman, such a villain as thyself, that hast murdered a man this last night by the highway.

Harp. 'Sblood, Constable, art thou mad? Am I an Irishman?

Mayor. Sirrah, we'll find you an Irishman before we part. [_To Watch_] Lay hold upon him.

Con. Make him fast. O, thou bloody rogue!

Enter Lord Cobham and his Lady in the carrier and wench's apparel.

Cob. What, will these ostlers sleep all day? [_To Con. and others_] Good morrow, good morrow. [_To La. Cob._] Come, wench, come. Saddle, saddle. Now afore God, too ford-days, ha?

Con. Who comes there?

Mayor. Oh, 'tis Lancashire carrier. Let him pass.

Cob. What, will nobody open the gates here? Come, let's int' stable to look to our capons. [_Exeunt._]

12-14. What . . . ha] _Mal._; What . . . day? / Good . . . come, / Saddle . . . ha _Q1_. 17-18. What . . . capons] _Mal._; What . . . here? / Come . . . capons _Q1_. 18. S.D.] _This ed._; _Exeunt lord and lady Cobham Mal._

---

14. ford-days] a dialectal pronunciation of the expression meaning "too late in the day" (_OED_ "forth" 4.b).

18. _Exeunt._] Obviously the two Cobhams leave the stage; I also think that the Mayor et al. leave as it makes their reaction to the Host (at xxiv.12)

Enter Club above.

Club. (Calling) Host! Why, Ostler! Zwooks, here's such abomination company of boys! A pox of this pigsty at the house end, it fills all the house full of fleas. Ostler, ostler!

[Enter Ostler.]

Ostler. Who calls there? What would you have?

Club. Zwooks, do you rob your guests? Do you lodge rogues, and slaves and scoundrels, ha? They ha' stolen our clothes here! Why, Ostler?

Ostler. A murrain choke you, what a bawling you keep!

[Enter Host.]

Host. How now, what would the carrier have? Look up there.

Ostler. They say that the man and woman that lay by them have stolen their clothes.

Host. What, are the strange folks up yet that came in yesternight?

[Enter Constable, Mayor, Watch, and Harpool.]

Con. What, mine Host, up so early?

0.1] This ed.; The carrier calling Q1. 1. Calling] Q1; Within Mal. (and at 1.5). 3.1.] Mal. 7.1.] Mal.

---

more realistic. Moreover, if the latter group were present on stage, it would be odd for them not to react to what Club is screaming at xxiv.1. ff.

0.1. above] See 1.8.

1. Zwooks] a dialectal variation of "zooks" which is short for "gadzooks" (OED).

2. boys] knaves (OED 4).

7. murrain] plague (OED 1).

Host. What, Master Mayor and Master Constable!

Mayor. We are come to seek for some suspected persons, and such as here we found, have apprehended.

Enter Club and Kate in Lord Cobham and Lady's apparel.

Con. Who comes here?

Club. Who comes here? "A plague 'found o'me, you bawl," quotha. Od's hat, I'll forzwear your house. You lodged a fellow and his wife by us that ha' run away with our 'parel and left us such gew-gaws here. Come, Kate, come to me, Thou's dizened, i'faith.

Mayor. Mine Host, know you this man?

Host. Yes, Master Mayor, I'll give my word for him. Why, neighbour Club, how comes this gear about?

Kate. Now, a foul on't, I cannot make this gew-gaw stand on my head. Now the lads and the lasses won flout me too too.

Con. How came this man and woman thus attired?

---

20. gew-gaws] trifles, vanities (OED 1.b).

dizened] gaudily dressed (Mal., p. 355).

23. gear] probably refers generally to the brouhaha--("goings on" OED III. 11.b) or, perhaps, to the new clothes Club and Kate wear--("attire" OED I. 1.a).

24. a foul on't] an oath like "a pox on't."

I . . . head] The country Kate is having difficulties with the new fashions in headdresses that Lady Cobham appeared in. Probably she is trying to put on a French hood, a headdress "having the front band depressed over the forehead and raised in folds or loops over the temples" (OED "head" 1.b). Henslowe paid out 10s. for a "frenche hoode" on April 11, 1599 (Diary, p. 107).

25. won] probably a dialectal variation of "will."

flout] mock (OED 1).

Host. Here came a man and woman hither this last night, which I did take for substantial people and lodged all in one chamber by these folks, methinks have been so bold to change apparel and gone away this morning ere they rose.

Mayor. That was that villain traitor Oldcastle that thus escaped us. [*To Con. and Watch*] Make out hue and cry yet after him. Keep fast that traiterous rebel his servant there. Farewell, mine Host. [*Exeunt Mayor, Constable, Watch, and Harpool*.]

Club. Come, Kate Owdham, thou and Ise trimly dizened.

Kate. I'faith, neam Club, Ise wot ne'er what to do, Ise be so flouted and so shouted at. But by th' mess, Ise cry. *Exeunt*.

[xxv] *Enter Lord Cobham and his Lady disguised*.

Cob. Come, madam, happily escaped, here let us sit.
This place is far remote from any path,
And here awhile our weary limbs may rest
To take refreshing, free from the pursuit
Of envious Rochester.

La. Cob. But where, my lord,
Shall we find rest for our disquiet minds?
There dwell untamèd thoughts that hardly stoop
To such abasement of disdainèd rags.

5. Rochester] *Q2*; Winchester *Q1*.

---

36. neam] uncle (*OED*).

We were not wont to travel thus by night,
Especially on foot.

Cob. No matter, love,
Extremities admit no better choice.
And were it not for thee, say froward time
Imposed a greater task, I would esteem it
As lightly as the wind that blows upon us,
But in thy sufferance I am doubly tasked.
Thou wast not wont to have the earth thy stool,
Nor the moist dewy grass thy pillow, nor
Thy chamber to be the wide horizon.

La. Cob. How can it seem a trouble, having you
A partner with me in the worst I feel?
No, gentle lord, your presence would give ease
To death itself, should he now seize upon me.
Behold what my foresight hath underta'en

Here's bread, and cheese, and a bottle.

For fear we faint. They are but homely cates,
Yet sauced with hunger they may seem as sweet
As greater dainties we were wont to taste.

Cob. Praise be to Him whose plenty sends both this
And all things else our mortal bodies need.
Nor scorn we this poor feeding, nor the state
We now are in. For what is it on earth--

---

24. cates] food (*OED* 1).

Nay, under heaven--continues at a stay?
Ebbs not the sea when it hath overflown?
Flows not darkness when the day is gone?
And see we not sometime the eye of heaven
Dimmed with overflying clouds? There's not that work
Of careful nature or of cunning art
(How strong, how beauteous, or how rich it be),
But falls in time to ruin. Here, gentle madam,
In this one draught I wash my sorrow down. *Drinks.*

La. Cob. And I, encouraged with your cheerful speech,
Will do the like.

Cob. Pray God poor Harpool come.
If he should fall into the bishop's hands
Or not remember where we bade him meet us,
It were the thing of all things else that now
Could breed revolt in this new peace of mind.

La. Cob. Fear not, my lord. He's witty to devise
And strong to execute a present shift.

Cob. That power be still his guide hath guided us,
My drowsy eyes wax heavy. Early rising,

33. Flows] *Q1*; Followes *Q2*.

---

31. stay] standstill (*OED* 7).

36. careful] concerned (*OED* 3).
cunning] expert (*OED* 2).

47. shift] ingenious device (*OED* III.3).

Together with the travel we have had,
Make me that I could gladly take a nap,
Were I persuaded we might be secure.

La. Cob. Let that depend on me. Whilst you do sleep
I'll watch that no misfortune happen us.
Lay then your head upon my lap, sweet lord,
And boldly take your rest.

Cob. I shall, dear wife
Be too much trouble to thee.

La. Cob. Urge not that;
My duty binds me and your love commands.
I would I had the skill with tunèd voice
To draw on sleep with some sweet melody.
But imperfection and unaptness too
Are both repugnant; fear inserts the one,
The other nature hath denied me use.
But what talk I of means to purchase that
Is freely happened? Sleep with gentle hand
Hath shut his eyelids. Oh, victorious labour,
How soon thy power can charm the body's sense!
And now thou likewise climb'st unto my brain,

61-63.] In these lines the dramatists are attempting to write complex, allusive poetry in the style of Spenser and Shakespeare. In effect the authors wish to say that fear inserts or gives rise to imperfection in Lady Cobham and that nature has denied her the ability or aptness (*not* inaptness) to sing. MSR (p. ix) suggests "infects" as an emendation for "inserts."

Making my heavy temples stoop to thee.
Great God of heaven, from danger keep us free. *Both sleeps*.

Enter Sir Richard Lee and his men.

Lee. A murder closely done and in my ground?
Search carefully. If anywhere it were,
This obscure thicket is the likeliest place.

[*1.*] *Serv*. Sir, I have found the body stiff with cold
And mangled cruelly with many wounds.

Lee. Look if thou knowest him. Turn his body up.
Alack, it is my son; my son and heir
Whom two years since I sent to Ireland
To practise there the discipline of war.
And coming home (for so he wrote to me),
Some savage heart, some bloody devilish hand,
Either in hate or thirsting for his coin,
Hath here sluiced out his blood. Unhappy hour,
Accursèd place, but most inconstant fate,
That hadst reserved him from the bullet's fire

85. bullet's] *Mal*.; bullets *Q1*.

---

71. closely] secretly (*OED* 3).

78.] referring to contemporary events. In May 1597 Lord Burgh became the new English deputy in Ireland and reinforcements, under the command of Sir John Norris, went with him (G.R. Elton, *England Under the Tudors* [London: Methuen and Co. Ltd., 1974], p. 391). Perhaps Lee's son is meant to be one of those soldiers who returned from Ireland with the Earl of Essex in September 1599.

And suffered him to 'scape the wood-kern's fury,
Didst here ordain the treasure of his life
(Even here within the arms of tender peace
And where security gat greatest hope)
To be consumed by treason's wasteful hand!
And what is most afflicting to my soul,
That this his death and murder should be wrought
Without the knowledge by whose means 'twas done.

2. Serv. Not so, sir, I have found the authors of it.
See where they sit, and in their bloody fists
The fatal instruments of death and sin.

Lee. Just judgement of that power, whose gracious eye,
Loathing the sight of such a heinous fact,
Dazzled their senses with benumbing sleep
Till their unhallowed treachery were known.
Awake, ye monsters! Murderers, awake!
Tremble for horror. Blush, you cannot choose,
Beholding this inhuman deed of yours.

Cob. What mean you, sir, to trouble weary souls
And interrupt us of our quiet sleep?

Lee. Oh, devilish! Can you boast unto yourselves

86. wood-kern's] Hopk.; wood-kerns' Mal.; wood-karnes Q1.

---

86. wood-kern's] A "kern" was an Irish foot-soldier (Mal., p. 359); a "wood-kern" was an Irish outlaw (OED). Whatever meaning Lee has in mind, his attitude is contemptuous.

89. gat] past tense of "get." This seems to be a deliberate archaism.

Of quiet sleep, having within your hearts
The guilt of murder waking, that with cries
Deafs the loud thunder and solicits heaven
With more than mandrakes' shrieks for your offence?

La. Cob. What murder? You upbraid us wrongfully.

Lee. Can you deny the fact? See you not here
The body of my son by you misdone?
Look on his wounds, look on his purple hue.
Do we not find you where the deed was done?
Were not your knives fast-closèd in your hands?
Is not this cloth an argument beside,
Thus stained and spotted with his innocent blood?
These speaking characters, were nothing else
To plead against ye, would convict you both.
Bring them away--bereavers of my joy.
At Hertford, where the 'sizes now are kept,

---

110. mandrakes' shrieks] The forked root of the mandrake plant was "thought to resemble the human form, and was fabled to utter a deadly shriek when plucked up from the ground" (OED 1).

117-18.] The cloth is bloody because Lord Cobham had a nosebleed (see sc. xxvii.75-76). Presumably Cobham would have entered scene xxv attending to his nosebleed.

119. characters] either "symbols" (OED 6) or "means of evidence" (OED II.8).

122. Hertford] Old. began in the assize city of Hereford in the Welsh-English area of Herefordshire where we met a mayor and two judges, and will end in the assize city Hertford in the shire of Hertfordshire just north-west of London where we will meet a mayor, a judge, and two justices. Conceivably, this superficial neatness of the plot was the result of a plotter's work.

Their lives shall answer for my son's lost life.

Cob. As we are innocent, so may we speed.

Lee. As I am wronged, so may the law proceed. *Exeunt*

[xxvi] *Enter Bishop of Rochester, Constable of Saint Albans, with Sir John of Wrotham, Doll his wench, and the Irishman in Harpool's apparel.*

Bish. What intricate confusion have we here?
Not two hours since we apprehended one
In habit Irish, but in speech not so.
And now you bring another that in speech
Is altogether Irish, but in habit
Seems to be English: yea, and more than so,
The servant of that heretic Lord Cobham.

Sc. xxvi] The writers of this scene do not indicate where it takes place, except that it is not in Hertford or London. We are, I suspect, to suppose that we are somewhere in the environs of St. Albans and that the Bishop has followed the chase of Cobham from the Tower to St. Albans.

1-7.] Of course the Irishman was caught before Harpool, and logically, he should have been the one dealt with "two hours since." Moreover, Sir John and Doll were caught before either the Irishman or Harpool was and it is odd, but unusually convenient, for them to appear before the Bishop at the same time as the Irishman as they alone know that he is the murderer of Lee's son. Also, while there would be reasons to bring the supposed "Harpool" to the Bishop, it is difficult to see why either the one "in habit Irish" or Sir John and Doll would have been brought to an ecclesiastical authority. Plainly the *Old*. collaborators are determined to tie up all the threads of the plot and are each aware of what the others are writing, but the details between different authors' scenes do not exactly mesh.

Irish. Fait', me be no servant of the Lord Cobham's, me be MacShane
of Ulster.

Bish. Otherwise called Harpool of Kent. Go to, sir,
You cannot blind us with your broken Irish.

Sir John. Trust me, my Lord Bishop, whether Irish
Or English, Harpool or not Harpool, that
I leave to be decided by the trial.
But sure I am this man by face and speech
Is he that murdered young Sir Richard Lee--
I met him presently upon the fact--
And that he slew his master for that gold,
These jewels, and that chain I took from him.

Bish. Well, our affairs do call us back to London
So that we cannot prosecute the cause
As we desire to do. [*To Con*.] Therefore we leave
The charge with you, to see they be conveyed
To Hertford 'size: both this counterfeit
And you, Sir John of Wrotham, and your wench,
For you are culpable as well as they,

8-9. Fait' . . . Ulster] *Mal*.; Fait . . . Cobhams, / Me . . . Ulster *Q1*.
22. S.D.] *Mal*.

---

8. MacShane]In Ulster the MacShanes were a branch of the O'Neills (Edward MacLysaght, *The Surnames of Ireland*, [Shannon: Irish Univ. Press, 1969], p. 196). The name is used because it is typically Irish, though it could bring to mind the Irish rebel Shane O'Neill, who fought Elizabeth I's deputies in the early part of her reign (see *Annals*, p. 1127).

21-22. So . . . do] Of course the Bishop could not prosecute a common law case.

Though not for murder yet for felony.
But since you are the means to bring to light
This graceless murder, you shall bear with you
Our letters to the judges of the bench,
To be your friends in what they lawful may.

Sir John. I thank your lordship.

Bish. So, away with them. *Exeunt*.

[xxvii] *Enter Jailer and his man bringing forth Cobham*.

Jail. [*To his man*] Bring forth the prisoners. See the court prepared.
The justices are coming to the bench.
So, let him stand. Away, and fetch the rest. *Exeunt*. [*Manet Cob*.]

Cob. Oh give me patience to endure this scourge,
Thou that art fountain of that virtuous stream.
And though contempt, false witness, and reproach
Hang on these iron gyves to press my life
As low as earth, yet strengthen me with faith,
That I may mount in spirit above the clouds.

Enter Jailer bringing in Lady Cobham and Harpool.

Here comes my lady. Sorrow, 'tis for her
Thy wound is grievous, else I scoff at thee.
What, and poor Harpool! Art thou i'th' briars too?

Sc. xxvii.7. iron gyves] shackle, chains--usually on the leg (*OED*).

12. briars] difficulties (*OED* 4).

Harp. I'faith, my lord, I am in, get out how I can. [*Exit Jailer*.]

La. Cob. Say, gentle lord, for now we are alone
And may confer, shall we confess in brief
Of whence and what we are, and so prevent
The accusation is commenced against us?

Cob. What will that help us? Being known, sweet love,
We shall for heresy be put to death,
For so they term the religion we profess.
No, if it be ordainèd we must die,
And at this instant, this our comfort be:
That of the guilt imposed our souls are free.

Harp. Yea, yea, my lord, Harpool is so resolved.
I reck of death the less in that I die
Not by the sentence of that envious priest
The Bishop of Rochester. Oh, were it he,
Or by his means that I should suffer here,
It would be double torment to my soul.

La. Cob. Well, be it then according as heaven please.

Enter Lord Judge, two Justices, [Attendants,] Mayor of Saint Albans, Lord Powis and his Lady, and old Sir Richard Lee. The Judge and Justices take their places.

Judge. Now, Master Mayor, what gentleman is that
You bring with you before us and the bench?

---

25. I reck of] i.e., "I am troubled by" or "concerned by" (*OED* 4).

Mayor. The Lord Powis, if it like your honour,
And this his Lady, travelling toward Wales,
Who, for they lodged last night within my house
And my Lord Bishop did lay search for such,
Were very willing to come on with me,
Lest for their sakes suspicion we might wrong.

Judge. We cry your honour mercy, good my lord.
Wilt please ye take your place. Madam, your ladyship
May here or where you will repose yourself
Until this business now in hand be passed.

La. Pow. I will withdraw into some other room
So that your lordship and the rest be pleased.

Judge. With all our hearts. Attend the lady there.

Pow. Wife, I have eyed yond prisoners all this while,
And my conceit doth tell me 'tis our friend
The noble Cobham and his virtuous lady.

La. Pow. I think no less. Are they suspected, trow ye,
For doing of this murder?

Pow. What it means
I cannot tell, but we shall know anon.

33-38.] The Mayor's explanation is tortuous given the fact he has the task of accounting for the palpably unrealistic appearance of the Powises in the courtroom. Powis has his pardon so there is really no need for him to fear the Bishop's wrath even if the Bishop "did lay search for such." The last line of the speech is confusing: it seems to mean that the Powises have come out into the open to make everything clear and aboveboard in order that no one judge the Mayor's hospitality in anything but the most favourable light.

49. trow ye] i.e., "believe ye" (_OED_ 4).

Mean space, as you pass by them ask the question.
But do it secretly you be not seen,
And make some sign that I may know your mind.

La. Pow. (*As she passeth over the stage by them*) My lord Cobham?
Madam?

Cob. No "Cobham" now nor "madam," as you love us,
But John of Lancashire and Joan his wife.

La. Pow. Oh, tell what is it that our love can do
To pleasure you, for we are bound to you.

Cob. Nothing but this: that you conceal our names.
So, gentle lady, pass for being spied.

La. Pow. [*Gives sign*] My heart I leave to bear part of your grief.
Exit.

Judge. Call the prisoners to the bar. Sir Richard Lee,
What evidence can you bring against these people
To prove them guilty of the murder done?

Lee. This bloody towel and these naked knives.
Beside, we found them sitting by the place
Where the dead body lay within a bush.

Judge. What answer you why law should not proceed,
According to this evidence given in,
To tax ye with the penalty of death?

54. S.D.] *This ed*.; *at end of 1.55 in Q1*.

---

54. *As* . . . *them*] i.e., crosses the stage.

Cob. That we are free from murder's very thought,
And know not how the gentleman was slain.

1. Just. How came this linen cloth so bloody then?

La. Cob. My husband hot with travelling, my lord,
His nose gushed out a bleeding. That was it.

2. Just. But wherefore were your sharp-edged knives unsheathed?

La. Cob. To cut such simple victual as we had.

Judge. Say we admit this answer to those articles,
What made ye in so private a dark nook,
So far remote from any common path,
As was the thick where the dead corpse was thrown?

Cob. Journ'ying, my lord, from London from the term
Down into Lancashire where we do dwell,
And what with age and travel being faint,
We gladly sought a place where we might rest
Free from resort of other passengers,
And so we strayed into that secret corner.

Judge. These are but ambages to drive off time
And linger justice from her purposed end.

Enter the Constable [*of Saint Albans*] *bringing in the Irishman, Sir John of Wrotham, and Doll.*

But who are these?

90.1-2.] *Mal.*; *bet. ll.91 and 92 Q1.*

---

82. thick] dense wood (*OED* 1).

89. ambages] evasions (Simms, p. 114).

<u>Con</u>. Stay judgement and release those innocents,
For here is he whose hand hath done the deed
For which they stand indicted at the bar.
This savage villain, this rude Irish slave,
His tongue already hath confessed the fact,
And here is witness to confirm as much.

<u>Sir John</u>. Yes, my good lords. No sooner had he slain
His loving master for the wealth he had,
But I upon the instant met with him;
And what he purchased with the loss of blood
With strokes I presently bereaved him of,
Some of the which is spent. The rest remaining
I willingly surrender to the hands
Of old Sir Richard Lee as being his.
Beside, my Lord Judge, I greet your honour
With letters from my Lord of Rochester. <u>Delivers a letter</u>.

<u>Lee</u>. Is this the wolf whose thirsty throat did drink
My dear son's blood? Art thou the snake
He cherished, yet with envious piercing sting
Assailed'st him mortally? Foul stigmatic,
Thou venom of the country where thou lived'st,
And pestilence of this! Were it not that law
Stands ready to revenge thy cruelty,

107, 137. Rochester] <u>Q2</u>; Winchester <u>Q1</u>.

---

111. stigmatic] criminal, villain (<u>OED</u> B.1).

Traitor to God, thy master, and to me,
These hands should be thy executioner.

Judge. Patience, Sir Richard Lee, you shall have justice,
And he the guerdon of his base desert.
The fact is odious, therefore take him hence;
And being hanged until the wretch be dead,
His body after shall be hanged in chains
Near to the place where he did act the murder.

Irish. Prethee, Lord Shudge, let me have mine own clothes, my strouces there, and let me be hanged in a with after my cuntry, the Irish, fashion. *Exit* [*attended*.]

Judge. Go to, away with him. And now, Sir John,
Although by you this murder came to light
And therein you have well deserved, yet upright law
So will not have you be excused and quit,
For you did rob the Irishman, by which

---

118. guerdon] reward (*OED*).

123-124. let . . . there] i.e., the clothes that Harpool is wearing. According to xxii.7-8. the Irishman (and then Harpool) wore a "mantle" and a "pair of brogues."

123. strouces] "Trouses" were Irish close-fitting pants worn to above the knee (*OED* 2.1).

124. with] a halter usually made from willow branches (*OED* 2). As Mal. (p. 367) and Hebel (V, 51) point out, Francis Bacon in his essay "Of Custom and Education" discusses an Irishman who, in the early years of Elizabeth I's reign, also desired to be hung in a with. Bacon writes: " . . . an *Irish Rebell* Condemned, put vp a petition to the Deputie, that he might be hanged in a With, and not in a Halter, because it had been so vsed, with former rebels" (*The Essays*, [1625; rpt. Great Britain: Scolar Press, 1971], p. 233).

You stand attainted here of felony.
Beside, you have been lewd, and many years
Led a lascivious unbeseeming life.

Sir John. Oh, but my lord, he repents. Sir John repents and he will mend.

Judge. In hope thereof, together with the favour
My Lord of Rochester entreats for you,
We are content you shall be proved.

Sir John. I thank your good lordship.

Judge. These other falsely here accused and brought
In peril wrongfully, we in like sort
Do set at liberty, paying their fees.

Pow. That office, if it please ye, I will do
For country's sake, because I know them well.
They are my neighbours, therefore of my cost
Their charges shall be paid.

Lee. And for amends,
Touching the wrong unwittingly I have done,
There are a few crowns more for them to drink. *Gives them a purse*.

Judge. Your kindness merits praise, Sir Richard Lee.
So let us hence. *Exeunt all but Lord Powis and Cobham*.

Pow. But Powis still must stay.

131. attainted] *Q2*; attained *Q1*.

138.] i.e., "We are content that a trial shall be made of your sincerity" (Mal., p. 367). Sir John, like Cobham, has once more barely escaped punishment.

There yet remains a part of that true love
He owes his noble friend unsatisfied
And unperformed; which first of all doth bind me
To gratulate your lordship's safe delivery,
And then entreat that since unlooked for thus
We here are met, your honour would vouchsafe
To ride with me to Wales, where though my power
Though not to quittance those great benefits
I have received of you, yet both my house,
My purse, my servants, and what else I have
Are all at your command. Deny me not.
I know the bishop's hate pursues ye so
As there's no safety in abiding here.

Cob. 'Tis true, my lord, and God forgive him for it.

Pow. Then let us hence. You shall be straight provided
Of lusty geldings, and once entered Wales,
Well may the bishop hunt, but spite his face,
He never more shall have the game in chase. *Exeunt.*

F I N I S.

---

154. gratulate] hail (*OED* 1).

158. quittance] cancel (*OED* 2).

157-59. where . . . you] It is impossible to tease syntactic sense out of these lines. If a compositor is not to blame for the problem, perhaps the author's simple inability to sort out his own intricate sentence is the culprit.

168. in chase] in a hunting ground, an enclosed area (*OED* 3). The analogy is reminiscent of that used in Cambridge's "hunting" speech in scene vii.

Appendices

I. Press Variants and Running-titles of Q1

Press Variants

I have collated the following copies of Q1 for press variants:

BM.: British Museum - C. 34 1.2, London

Bodl. 768: Bodleian Library - Malone 768, Oxford University

Bodl. 817: Bodleian Library - Malone 817, Oxford University

Bodmer.: Bibliotheca Bodmeriana, 1223 Cologny-Genève

Folger: The Folger Shakespeare Library, Washington, D.C.

Clark: Clark Library, University of California

Hunt.: The Huntington Library, San Marino, California

The first three copies were studied in the original and the last four on microfilm. The following is a list of press corrections found in Q1. The reading inside the bracket is that of the corrected copies.

Sheet B (inner forme)

Corrected: BM, Bodl. 768, Folger, Clark, Hunt.

Uncorrected: Bodl. 817, Bodmer.

Sig. B1v

ii.47. France:] France,

53. Lords of the cleargie do] Lords the cleargie doth

Sig. B2r

68. refuse] refuse,

76. begin] begin,

84. Cobham, in] Cobham in (+ Folger)

90. apparant] aparant

Sig. B3v

169. gold,] gold

Sig. B4r

iii.25. pride, this] pride this

27. backes, your] backes your

Sheet C (inner forme)

Corrected: BM, Bodl. 768, Folger, Clark, Hunt.

Uncorrected: Bodl. 817, Bodmer.

Sig. C1v

iii.127. newes] newus

Sig. C2r

iv.3. Sum-/ners] Sum-/mers

4. not goe] not no goe

5. manne] man

6. profit:] profit,

Sig. C3v

74. citation] citatoin

82. break fast] break_fast

86. warme:] warme,

86. Sumner,] Sumner

87. peticote] peticoate

88. there were four] the were foure

92. thee?] thee. (watermark blot in Bodl. 817 blots "the")

93. crie, for] crie for,

97. Alehouse] Alehous

99. seruants,] seruants

103. <u>Ale</u> <u>man</u>] <u>Aleman</u>

Sig. C4r

110-11. saies he has] saies has

111. sute] suite

111. &] and

117. forth] foth

126. old:] old

131. ingle] ijngle

132. Ile feak] I fleak

132. fil] fill

Sheet F (outer forme)

Corrected: Bodl. 768, Bodl. 817, Bodmer., Clark, Hunt.

Uncorrected: BM, Folger

Sig. F1r

viii.85. Sir Iohn Old-castle, what if he come not?] Sir Old-castle, what if he come not Iohn?

87. supply] suppie

ix.3. none walks within xl.] no walks within forty

9. me, that] me that

11. theres] thers

Sig. F2v

x.73. kill no man] kill man

85. sworne:] sworne,

87. yfaith.] yfaith,

Sig. F3r

100. me alone] me a alone

107. beuer, this] beuer this

110. Ficket] Fickle

111. Kent] Kenr

Sig. F4v

xi.76. mens crownes,] mens, crownes

Sheet G (outer forme)

Corrected: BM, Bodl. 817, Bodmer., Clark, Hunt.

Uncorrected: Bodl. 768, Folger

Sig. G1r

xi.104. boate:] boate,

113. beside.] beside,

Sig. G2v

xii.51. King?] King,

61. conscience,] conscience

Sig. G3r

82. vnto] ynto

85. selfe, false] selfe false

87. prince, your grace mistakes,] prince your grace mistakes.

99. warres] warres.

104. rebellion?] rebellion,

Sig. G4v

xiii.32. Peace, he] Peace he

35. I feare] feare

36. I would] would

43. Croomes?] Croomes.

51. late] late,

53. art, the] art the

Sheet I (outer forme)

Corrected: BM, Bodl. 768, Bodl. 817, Bodmer., Folger, Hunt.

Uncorrected: Clark

Sig. I2v

xxiv.17. heere] here (+ BM)

20. dizeard] dizeand

28. chamber] chamber:

29. folkes:] folkes,

35. <u>Carier</u>] <u>Carrier</u>

35. dizard] disand

Sig. I3r

xvii.10. hot] ho

25-26. bee shit-] dee shit-

Sig. I4v

xxv.40. incoragde] in courage

Sheet K

Corrected: BM, Bodl. 768, Bodl. 817, Bodmer., Clark, Hunt.

Uncorrected: Folger

Sig. K1r

xxv.81. hart] heart

Sig. K1v

89. security] secuerity

100. knowne:] knowne,

103. yours.] yours,

Sig. K4r

xxvii.113. law] law,

128. deseru'd] deserud

132. Beside,] Beside

133. Led] Lead

Sig. K4v

140. accusde, and brought] accusde and brought,

141. sort] sort,

142. liberty,] liberty

150. <u>all but</u>] <u>but</u>

155. intreat,] intreat

163. here.] here,

165. shall] shalt

167. face,] face.

The evidence above indicates that normal press correction has taken place in five of the six sheets (B, C, F, G, I). That is, one forme or side of a sheet was corrected during the press run leaving us with corrected and uncorrected states of that forme, while the other forme or side of that sheet is in the corrected state only and so was corrected before the press run. There are two small anomalies to this conventional pattern. On B2r (ii.84) the Folger copy of Q1, which is in the corrected state elsewhere, is in the uncorrected state. There seem to be two reasonable explanations for this: either the corrected comma did not print onto the Folger sheet or the corrected comma was only inserted after the original press corrections were made and after the otherwise corrected Folger copy was printed. The latter printing scenario would also explain why the corrected BM copy displays the uncorrected variant on I2v (xxiv.17).

The press variants found in sheet K are of a different order than those found in the other press-corrected sheets, for press correction in sheet K does not follow the familiar pattern of either the inner or outer forme being in the variant and the other forme being in the invariant state. In sheet K, then, the press corrector possibly changed his method of press correction, perhaps because of a change in printing procedure. Thus, both inner and outer formes of sheet K would have been corrected during their press runs, but press correction was restricted to one half of each forme.

Almost all the press variants in Q1 are straightforward and indicate that press corrections were made by one of the Simmes workmen who checked his printed copy against the MS. Oddities are the I2v "dizeand" and "disand" changed to the less appropriate "dizeard" and "dizard" and the K1r "heart" changed to "hart" since the "heart" spelling is the one usually preferred by Compositor A. Such exceptions, however, certainly do not point to an authorial source for Q1's press corrections, nor do they outweigh the evidence in favour of simple compositorial proof-reading.

Running-titles

Investigation of the running-titles shows that two skeletons were used to print Q1. The running-title for Q1 (modern spelling) is "The first part of / Sir John Oldcastle.". Now one can readily identify the running-titles in each forme. Of the four "The first part of" running-titles, two (b and f -- see below) spell "first" with a normal "s" and two (a and g) with a long "s". Further, one can differentiate the two in the former pair by the length of the "f" in "first"; while the two in the latter pair can be differentiated by the faintness or clarity of the "e" in "The". Of the four "Sir John Oldcastle" running-titles, two (e and h) spell "John" with a "J" and two (c and d) with an "I". One can differentiate the former pair by the length of the "s" in "Sir" and the latter pair by the presence or absence of a period after "Oldcastle". The following is a list of the running-title variants arranged according to this schematic pattern:

	outer forme		inner forme	
	4v	1r	3v	2r
	3r	2v	4r	1v
Sheet A				
	b	--	a	--
	--	--	c	--
Sheet B				
	a	d	b	e

c	f	h	g

Sheet C

a	d	b	e
c	f	h	g

Sheet D

b	e	a	d
h	g	c	f

Sheet E

a	d	b	e
c	f	h	g

Sheet F

b	e	a	d
h	g	c	f

Sheet G

b	e	a	d
h	g	c	f

Sheet H

g	e	f	c
h	b	d	a

Sheet I

f	e	a	d
h	b	c	g

Sheet K

a	c	f	h
d	g	e	b

A clear pattern is discernible from sheet B through sheet G. Sheets B and C were printed in identical fashion; then the skeletons were exchanged for sheet D so that the skeleton in which the inner forme of B and C was set now becomes the skeleton in which the outer forme of D is set. However, the period which had been in place on C3r becomes dislodged in its new position on D4r. For sheet E the skeletons (and, of course, the running-titles) are back in their original positions. The skeletons are again exchanged for the printing of sheet G.

Something slightly different, however, occurred before the printing of sheet H. The formes are neither reversed nor printed exactly as in sheet G. For the printing of sheet H the evidence indicates that the inner forme skeleton was turned, and that in the outer forme, b and g running-titles exchanged places. Something odder still, though, occurred before the printing of sheet I. One section of one running-title from each forme (H3v and H4v) was exchanged. This definite change in procedure might have been caused by any number of print-shop problems, for instance, a significant delay in the printing of Q1 after sheet H had been run off. Whatever the reason, the fact that something peculiar happened before the printing of sheet I may perhaps explain the dreadful mix-up in sheet I where scenes xx-xxiv (I1r-I3r) are printed before scenes xvii-xix (I3r-I4r). That is, a problem or delay in printing Q1 could account for a mix-up in the MS copy. This may also explain those anomalies, noted above (p.   ), in press correction for the last formes of Q1.

For the printing of sheet I the inner forme skeleton was turned (as happened for the printing of sheet H), while the outer forme one remained in place. For sheet K the skeletons were exchanged, as with sheets D, E, and F.

In the outer forme running-titles c and d, and in the inner forme running-titles e and h, exchanged places.

II. Raphael Holinshed, Chronicles[1]

Also in this first yeere of this kings reigne, sir John Oldcastell, which by his wife was called lord Cobham, a valiant capteine and a hardie gentleman, was accused to the archbishop of Canturburie of certeine points of heresie, who knowing him to be highlie in the kings favour, declared to his highnesse the whole accusation. The king first having compassion of the noble man, required the prelats, that if he were a straied sheepe, rather by gentlenes than by rigor to reduce him to the fold. And after this, he himselfe sent for him, and right earnestlie exhorted him, and lovinglie admonished him to reconcile himselfe to God and to his lawes. The lord Cobham not onelie thanked him for his most favourable clemencie, but also declared first to him by mouth, and afterwards by writing, the foundation of his faith, and the ground of his beliefe, affirming his grace to be his supreme head and competent judge, and none other person, offering an hundred knights and esquiers to come to his purgation, or else to fight in open lists in defence of his just cause.

The king understanding and persuaded by his councell, that by order of the lawes of his realme, such accusations touching matters of faith ought to be tried by his spirituall prelats, sent him to the Tower of London, there to abide the determination of the clergie, according to the statutes in that case provided, after which time a solemne session was appointed in the cathedrall church of saint Paule, upon the three and twentith day of September, and an other the five and twentith daie of the same moneth, in the hall of the Blacke friers at London, in which places the said lord was examined, apposed, and fullie heard, and in conclusion by the archbishop of Canturburie denounced an heretike, and remitted againe to the Tower of London, from which place, either by helpe of freends, or favour of keepers, he privilie escaped and came into Wales, where he remained for a season.

After this, the king keeping his Christmasse at his manor of Eltham, was advertised, that sir Roger Acton knight, a man of great wit and possessions, John Browne esquier, John Beverlie priest, and a great number of other were assembled in armour against the king, his brethren, the clergie and realme. These news came to this king, on the twelfth daie in Christmasse, whereupon understanding that they were in a place called Ficket field beside London, on the backe side of saint Giles, he streight got him to his palace at Westminster, in as secret wise as he might, and there calling to him certeine bands of armed men, he repaired unto saint Giles fields, neere to the said place (where he understood they should fullie meet about midnight) and so handled the matter, that he tooke some, and slue some, even as stood with his pleasure. The capteins of them afore mentioned, being apprehended, were brought to the kings presence, and to him declared the causes of their commotion and rising,

---

[1] From Raphael Holinshed, Holinshed's Chronicles. Eds. R.S.Wallace and Alma Hansen (Oxford: Clarendon Press, 1923), pp. 4-6, 10-11, 14, 18-20, 21, 56-57, 60-61.

accusing a great number of their complices.

The king used one policie, which much served to the discomfiting of the adversaries (as Thom. Walsingham saith) which was this: he gave order, that all the gates of London should be streictlie kept and garded so as none should come in or out, but such as were knowen to go to the king. Hereby came it to passe, that the chiefest succour appointed to come to the capteins of the rebels, was by that meanes cut off, where otherwise suerlie (had it not beene thus prevented and staied) there had issued foorth of London to have joined with them, to the number (as it was thought) of fiftie thousand persons, one and other, servants, prentises, and citizens, confederate with them that were thus assembled in Ficket field. Diverse also that came from sundrie parts of the realme, hasting towards the place, to be there at their appointed time, chanced to light among the kings men, who being taken and demanded whither they went with such speed, answered, they came to meet with their capteine the lord Cobham.

But whether he came thither at all, or made shift for himselfe to get awaie, it dooth not appeare; for he could not be heard of at that time (as Thomas Walsingham confesseth) although the king by proclamation promised a thousand marks to him that could bring him foorth, with great liberties to the cities or townes that would discover where he was. By this it maie appeare, how greatlie he was beloved, that there could not one be found, that for so great a reward would bring him to light. Among other that were taken was one William Murlie, who dwelt in Dunstable, a man of great wealth, and by his occupation a brewer, an earnest mainteiner of the lord Cobhams opinions, and (as the brute ran) in hope to be highlie advanced by him if their purposed devise had taken place, apparant by this: that he had two horses trapped with guilt harnesse led after him, and in his bosome a paire of gilt spurs (as it was deemed) prepared for himselfe to weare, looking to be made knight by the lord Cobhams hands at that present time. But when he saw how their purpose quailed, he withdrew into the citie with great feare to hide himselfe; howbeit he was perceived, taken, and finallie executed among others.

To conclude, so manie persons hereupon were apprehended, that all the prisons in and about London were full, the chiefe of them were condemned by the cleargie of heresie, and atteinted of high treason in the Guildhall of London, and adjudged for that offense to be drawen and hanged, and for heresie to be consumed with fire, gallowes and all, which judgement was executed the same moneth, on the said sir Roger Acton, and eight and twentie others....

And to the intent his loving chapleins and obedient subjects of the spiritualtie might shew themselves willing and desirous to aid his majestie, for the recoverie of his ancient right and true inheritance, the archbishop declared that in their spirituall convocation, they had granted to his highnesse such a summe of monie, as never by no spirituall persons was to any prince before those daies given or advanced....

Diverse other things were concluded at that present: for the king had caused not onelie the lords of the spiritualtie, but also of the temporaltie to assemble here at London the same time, to treat speciallie of his journie that he purposed to make shortlie into France: and hereupon meanes was made for the gathering of monie; which was granted with so good a will both of the spiritualtie and temporaltie, that there was levied the summe of three hundred thousand markes English....

But see the hap, the night before the daie appointed for their departure, he was crediblie informed, that Richard earle of Cambridge brother to Edward duke of Yorke, and Henrie lord Scroope of Masham lord treasuror, with Thomas Graie a knight of Northumberland, being confederat togither, had conspired his death: wherefore he caused them to be apprehended. The said lord Scroope was in such favour with the king, that he admitted him sometime to be his bed-fellow, in whose fidelitie the king reposed such trust, that when anie privat or publike councell was in hand, this lord had much in the determination of it. For he presented so great gravitie in his countenance, such modestie in behaviour, and so vertuous zeale to all godlinesse in his talke, that what-soever he said was thought for the most part necessarie to be doone and fol-lowed. Also the said sir Thomas Graie (as some write) was of the kings privie councell.

These prisoners upon their examination, confessed, that for a great summe of monie which they had received of the French king, they intended verelie either to have delivered the king alive into the hands of his enimies, or else to have murthered him before he should arrive in the duchie of Normandie. When king Henrie had heard all things opened, which he desired to know, he caused all his nobilitie to come before his presence, before whome he caused to be brought the offendors also, and to them said. 'Having thus conspired the death and destruction of me, which am the head of the realme and governour of the people, it maie be (no doubt) but that you likewise have sworne the confusion of all that are here with me, and also the desolation of your owne countrie. To what horror (O lord) for any true English hart to consider, that such an execrable iniquitie should ever so bewray you, as for pleasing of a forren enimie to imbrue your hands in your bloud, and to ruine your owne native soile. Revenge herein touching my person, though I seeke not; yet for the safeguard of you, my deere freends, and for due perservation of all sorts, I am by office to cause example to be shewed. Get ye hence therefore ye poore miserable wretches to the receiving of your just reward, wherein Gods majestie give you grace of his mercie and repentance of your heinous offenses.' And so immediatlie they were had to execution.

This doone, the king calling his lords againe afore him, said in words few and with good grace. Of his enterprises he recounted the honor and glorie, whereof they with him were to be partakers, the great confidence he had in their noble minds, which could not but remember them of the famous feats that their ancestors aforetime in France had atchived, whereof the due report for ever recorded remained yet in register. The great mercie of God that had so gratiously revealed unto him the treason at hand, whereby the true harts of those afore him made so eminent and apparant in his eie, as they might be right sure he would never forget it....

Diverse write that Richard earle of Cambridge did not conspire with the lord Scroope and Thomas Graie for the murthering of king Henrie to please the French king withall, but onelie to the intent to exalt to the crowne his brother in law Edmund earle of March as heire to Lionell duke of Clarence: after the death of which earle of March, for diverse secret impediments, not able to have issue, the earle of Cambridge was sure that the crowne should come to him by his wife, and to his children, of hir begotten. And there-fore (as was thought) he rather confessed himselfe for need of monie to be corrupted by the French king, than he would declare his inward mind, and open his verie intent and secret purpose, which if it were espied, he saw plainlie that the earle of March should have tasted of the same cuppe that he had drunken, and what should have come to his owne children he much doubted. Therefore destitute of comfort and in despaire of life to save his children, he feined that tale, desiring rather to save his succession than himselfe, which he did in deed: for his sonne Richard duke of York not privilie but openlie claimed the crowne, and Edward his sonne both claimed it, and gained it, as after it shall appeare. Which thing if king Henrie had at this time either doubted, or foreseene, had never beene like to have come to passe, as Hall saith....

About the selfe same time the lord Cobham with his freends, whether as one of counsell in the conspiracie with the earle of Cambridge or not....

The same time, the lord Cobham, sir John Oldcastell, whilest he shifted from place to place to escape the hands of them, who he knew would be glad to laie hold on him, had conveied himselfe in secret wise into an husbandmans house, not farre from S. Albons, within the precinct of a lordship belonging to the abbat of that towne. The abbats servants getting knowledge hereof, came thither by night, but they missed their purpose, for he was gone; but they caught diverse of his men, whoome they caried streict to prison. The lord Cobham herewith was sore dismaied, for that some of them that were taken were such as he trusted most, being of counsell in all his devises. In the same place, were found books written in English, and some of those books in times past had beene trimlie gilt, limned, and beautified with images, the heads whereof had been scraped off, and in the Letanie they had boltted foorth the name of our ladie, and of other saints, till they came to the verse *Parce nobis Domine*. Diverse writings were found there also, in derogation of such honor as then was thought due to our ladie. The abbat of saint Albons sent the booke so disfigured with scrapings and blottings out, with other such writings as there were found, unto the king; who sent the booke againe to the archibishop, to shew the same in his sermons at Paules crosse in London, to the end that the citizens and other people of the realme might understand the purposes of those that then were called Lollards, to bring them further in discredit with the people....

About the same season was sir John Oldcastell, lord Cobham taken, in the countrie of Powes land, in the borders of Wales, within a lordship belonging to the lord Powes, not without danger and hurts of some that were at the taking of him: for they could not take him, till he was wounded himselfe.

At the same time, the states of the realme were assembled at London, for the levieng of monie, to furnish the kings great charges, which he was at about the maintenance of his wars in France: it was therefore determined, that the said sir John Oldcastell should be brought, and put to his triall, yer the assemblie brake up. The lord Powes therefore was sent to fetch him, who brought him to London in a litter, wounded as he was: herewith, being first laid fast in the Tower, shortlie after he was brought before the duke of Bedford, regent of the realme, and the other estates, where in the end he was condemned; and finallie was drawen from the Tower unto saint Giles field, and there hanged in a chaine by the middle, and after consumed with fire, the gallowes and all....

III. John Foxe, Acts and Monuments[2]

The Trouble and Persecution of the most valiant and worthy Martyr of Christ, Sir John Oldcastle, knight, Lord Cobham....

The chief and principal cause then of the assembling thereof, as recordeth the Chronicle of St. Alban's, was to repress the growing and spreading of the gospel, and especially to withstand the noble and worthy lord Cobham, who was then noted to be a principal favourer, receiver, and maintainer of those whom the bishop misnamed to be Lollards; especially in the dioceses of London, Rochester, and Hereford, setting them up to preach whom the bishops had not licensed, and sending them about to preach, which was against the constitution provincial, before remembered: holding also and teaching opinions of the sacraments, of images, of pilgrimage, of the keys and church of Rome, contrary and repugnant to the received determination of the Romish church, &c....

Among whom this noble knight, sir John Oldcastle, the lord Cobham, was complained of by the proctors of the clergy to be the chief principal. Him they accused, first, for a mighty maintainer of suspected preachers in the dioceses of London, Rochester, and Hereford, contrary to the minds of their ordinaries. Not only they affirmed him to have sent thither the said preachers, but also to have assisted them there by force of arms, notwithstanding their synodal constitution made before to the contrary. Last of all, they accused him that he was far otherwise in belief of the sacrament of the altar, of penance, of pilgrimage, of image-worshipping, and of the ecclesiastical power, than the holy church of Rome had taught many years before.

In the end it was concluded among them, that, without any further delay, process should be awarded out against him, as against a most pernicious heretic.

Some of that fellowship who were of more crafty experience than the others, thought it not best to have the matter rashly handled, but by some preparation made thereunto beforehand: considering the said lord Cobham was a man of great birth, and in favour at that time with the king, their counsel was to know first the king's mind, to save all things upright. This counsel was well accepted, and thereupon the archbishop Thomas Arundel, with his other bishops, and a great part of the clergy, went straitways unto the king then remaining at Kennington, and there laid forth most grievous complaints against the said lord Cobham, to his great infamy and blemish: being a man right godly. The king gently heard those blood-thirsty prelates, and far otherwise

---

[2] From John Foxe, The Acts and Monuments of John Foxe. Ed. Rev. George Townsend. (London: Seeley, Burnside and Seeley, 1843), Vol. III, 320, 321, 322-4, 325-6, 340-2, 348, 349-50, 350, 351-2, 541-2.

than became his princely dignity: notwithstanding requiring, and instantly desiring them, that in respect of his noble stock and knighthood, they should yet favourably deal with him; and that they would, if it were possible, without all rigour or extreme handling, reduce him again to the church's unity. He promised them also, that in case they were contented to take some deliberation, he himself would seriously commune the matter with him.

Anon after, the king sent for the said lord Cobham, and as soon as he was come, he called him secretly, admonishing him betwixt him and him, to submit himself to his mother the holy church, and, as an obedient child, to acknowledge himself culpable. Unto whom the christian knight made this answer: "You, most worthy prince," saith he, "I am always prompt and willing to obey, forasmuch as I know you a christian king, and the appointed minister of God, bearing the sword to the punishment of evil doers, and for safeguard of them that be virtuous. Unto you, next my eternal God, owe I my whole obedience, and submit thereunto, as I have done ever, all that I have, either of fortune or nature, ready at all times to fulfil whatsoever ye shall in the Lord command me. But, as touching the pope and his spiritualty, I owe them neither suit nor service, forasmuch as I know him by the Scriptures, to be the great Antichrist, the son of perditon, the open adversary of God, and the abomination standing in the holy place." When the king had heard this, with such like sentences more, he would talk no longer with him, but left him so utterly.

And as the archbishop resorted again unto him for an answer, he gave him his full authority to cite him, examine him, and punish him according to their devilish decrees, which they called, 'The Laws of holy Church.' Then the said archbishop, by the counsel of his other bishops and clergy, appointed to call before him sir John Oldcastle, the lord Cobham, and to cause him personally to appear, to answer to such suspect articles, as they should lay against him: so he sent forth his chief summoner, with a very sharp citation unto the castle of Cowling, where he at that time dwelt for his solace; and as the said summoner was come thither, he durst in no case enter the gates of so noble a man without his license, and therefore he returned home again, his message not done.

Then called the archbishop one John Butler unto him, who was then the doorkeeper of the king's privy chamber, and with him he covenanted, through promises and rewards, to have this matter craftily brought to pass under the king's name. Whereupon the said John Butler took the archbishop's summoner with him, and went unto the said lord Cobham, showing him, that it was the king's pleasure, that he should obey that citation; and so cited him fraudulently. Then said he to them in few words, that he in no case would consent to those most devilish practices of the priests. As they had informed the archbishop of that answer, and that it was for no man privately to cite him after that, without peril of life, he decreed by and by to have him cited by public process or open commandment; and, in all the haste possible, upon the Wednesday before the nativity of our Lady, in September, he commanded letters citatory to be set upon the great gates of the cathedral-church of Rochester, which was but three English miles from thence, charging him to appear personally before him at Ledis, the eleventh day of the same month and year, all excuses to the contrary set apart. Those letters were taken down anon after, by such as bore favour unto the lord Cobham, and so conveyed aside. After that the archbishop caused new letters to be set up on the nativity-day of our Lady, which also were rent down, and utterly consumed.

Then, forasmuch as he did not appear at the day appointed at Ledis (where he sat in consistory, as cruel as ever was Caiaphas, with his court of hypocrites about him), he judged him, denounced him, and condemned him, of most deep contumacy. After that, when he had been falsely informed by his hired spies, and other glozing glaverers, that the said lord Cobham had laughed him to scorn, disdained all his doings, maintained his old opinions, contemned the church's power, the dignity of a bishop, and the order of priesthood (for of all these was he then accused), in his moody madness, without just proof, did he openly excommunicate him. Yet was not with all this his fierce tyranny satisfied, but he commanded him to be cited afresh, to appear before him on the Saturday after the feast of St. Matthew the apostle, with these cruel threatenings added thereunto, that if he did not obey at the day, he would more extremely handle him. And to make himself more strong towards the performance thereof, he compelled the lay-power, by most terrible menacings of curses and interdictions, to assist him against that seditious apostate, schismatic, and heretic, the troubler of the public peace, that enemy of the realm, and great adversary of all holy church; for all these hateful names did he give him.

This most constant servant of the Lord, and worthy knight, sir John Oldcastle, the lord Cobham, beholding the unpeacable fury of Antichrist thus kindled against him, perceiving himself also compassed on every side with deadly dangers, he took paper and pen in hand, and so wrote a christian confession or reckoning of his faith.... both signing and sealing it with his own hand; wherein he also answered to the four chief articles that the archbishop laid against him. That done, he took the copy with him, and went therewith to the king, trusting to find mercy and favour at his hand....

This brief confession of his faith the lord Cobham wrote, as is mentioned before, and so took it with him to the court, offering it with all meekness unto the king, to read it over. The king would in no case receive it, but commanded it to be delivered unto them that should be his judges. Then desired he, in the king's presence, that a hundred knights and esquires might be suffered to come in upon his purgation, who he knew would clear him of all heresies. Moreover he offered himself, after the law of arms, to fight for life or death with any man living, christian or heathen, in the quarrel of his faith; the king and the lords of his council excepted. Finally, with all gentleness, he protested before all that were present, that he would refuse no manner of correction that should, after the laws of God, be ministered unto him; but that he would at all times, with all meekness, obey it. Notwithstanding all this the king suffered him to be summoned personally in his own privy chamber. Then said the lord Cobham to the king, that he had appealed from the archbishop to the pope of Rome, and therefore he ought, he said, in no case to be his judge. And having his appeal there at hand ready written, he showed it with all reverence to the king; wherewith the king was then much more displeased than afore, and said angrily to him, that he should not pursue his appeal; but rather he should tarry in hold, till such time as it were of the pope allowed. And then, would he or nild he, the archbishop should be his judge. Thus was there nothing allowed that the good lord Cobham had lawfully afore required: but, forasmuch as he would not be sworn in all things to submit himself to the church, and so take what penance the archbishop would enjoin him, he was arrested again at the king's commandment, and so led forth to the Tower of London, to keep his day (so was it then spoken), that the archbishop had appointed him afore in the king's chamber....

The First Examination of the Lord Cobham.

As the day of examination was come, which was the 23rd day of September, the Saturday after the feast of St. Matthew, Thomas Arundel, the archbishop, sitting in Caiaphas' room, in the chapter-house of Paul's, with Richard Clifford, bishop of London, and Henry Bolingbrook, bishop of Winchester; Sir Robert Morley, knight, and lieutenant of the Tower, brought personally before him the said lord Cobham, and there left him for the time; unto whom the archbishop said these words: "Sir John, in the last general convocation of the clergy of this our province, ye were detected of certain heresies, and, by sufficient witnesses, found culpable: whereupon ye were, by form of spiritual law, cited, and would in no case appear. In conclusion, upon your rebellious contumacy, ye were both privately and openly excommunicated. Notwithstanding we neither yet showed, ourselves unready to have given you absolution (nor yet do to this hour), would ye have meekly asked it." --Unto this the lord Cobham showed as though he had given no ear, having his mind otherwise occupied, and so desired no absolution; but said, he would gladly, before him and his brethren, make rehearsal of that faith which he held and intended always to stand to, if it would please them to license him thereunto....

And when the clergy perceived that policy would not help, but made more and more against them, then sought they out another false practice: they went unto the king with a most grievous complaint, like as they did afore, in his father's time, that in every quarter of the realm, by reason of Wickliff's opinions, and the said lord Cobham, were wonderful contentions, rumours, tumults, uproars, confederations, dissensions, divisions, differences, discords, harms, slanders, schisms, sects, seditions, perturbations, perils, unlawful assemblies, variances, strifes, fightings, rebellious rufflings, and daily insurrections. The church, they said, was hated. The diocesans were not obeyed. The ordinaries were not regarded. The spiritual officers, as suffragans, archdeacons, chancellors, doctors, commissaries, officials, deans, lawyers, scribes, and somners, were every where despised. The laws and liberties of holy church were trodden under foot. The christian faith was ruinously decayed. God's service was laughed to scorn. The spiritual jurisdiction, authority, honour, power, policy, laws, rites, ceremonies, curses, keys, censures, and canonical sanctions of the church, were had in utter contempt, so that all, in a manner, was come to naught.

And the cause of this was, that the heretics and lollards of Wickliff's opinion were suffered to preach abroad so boldly, to gather conventicles unto them, to keep schools in men's houses, to make books, compile treatises, and write ballads, to teach privately in angles and corners, as in woods, fields, meadows, pastures, groves, and in caves of the ground.

This would be, said they, a destruction to the commonwealth, a subversion to the land, and an utter decay of the king's estate royal, if remedy were not sought in time. And this was their policy, to couple the king's authority with what they had done in their former council, of craft, and so to make it, thereby, the stronger. For they perceived themselves very far too weak else, to follow against their enemies, what they had so largely enterprized. Upon this complaint, the king immediately called a parliament at Leicester. It might not, in those days, be holden at Westminster, for the great favour that the lord Cobham had, both in London and about the city. Yet were they deceived; what they doubted most, lighted the soonest upon them.

A bill was put in there again by the commons, against their continual wasting of the temporalties, like as it had been twice before, by procurement of the said lord Cobham, both in the days of king Richard II., A.D. 1395, and also of king Henry IV., A.D. 1410. Whereupon was grown all this malice afore specified; but this was then workmanly defeated by another proper of theirs: they put the king in remembrance to claim his right in France, and granted him thereunto a disme, with other great subsidy of money. Thus were Christ's people betrayed every way, and their lives bought and sold by these most cruel thieves....

In the Christmas following were sir Roger Acton, knight, master John Brown, esquire, sir John Beverly, a learned preacher, and divers others, attached, for quarrelling with certain priests, and so imprisoned; for all men at that time could not patiently suffer their blasphemous brags.

The complaint was made unto the king of them, that they had made a great assembly in St. Giles's field at London, purposing the destruction of the land, and the subversion of the common-wealth. As the king was thus informed, he erected a banner, saith Walden, with a cross thereupon; as the pope doth commonly by his legates, when he pretendeth to war against the Turks, and, with a great number of men, entered the same field, where he found no such company. Yet was the complaint judged true, because the bishops had spoken it at the information of their priests....

After all this, the sentence of death being given, the lord Cobham was sent away, sir Robert Morley carrying him again unto the Tower, where, after he had remained a certain space, in the night season (it is not known by what means), he escaped out, and fled into Wales, where he continued by the space of four years....

A DEFENCE OF THE LORD COBHAM, AGAINST NICHOLAS HARPSFIELD, SET OUT UNDER THE NAME OF ALANUS COPUS ANGLUS.

. . .

Now to the scope of Master Cope's matter, which is this: whether this aforesaid sir John Oldcastle, lord Cobham (first to begin with him) is rather to be commended for a martyr, or to be reproved for a traitor? and whether that I, in writing of him, and of sir Roger Acton, with others besides, in my former edition, have dealt fraudulently and corruptly, in commending them in these Acts and Monuments, or no? Touching the discussion hereof, first, I trust the gentle Master Cope, my friend, neither will, nor well can, deny any part of all that hitherto, touching the story of the lord Cobham, hath been premised; who yet all this while was neither traitor to his country, nor rebel to his prince, as by the course of his history hitherto the reader may well understand. First, in the time of king Henry IV., he was sent over to France to the duke of Orleans: he did obey. Afterwards, king Henry V. coming to the crown, he was of him likewise well liked and favoured, until the time that Thomas Arundel, with his clergy, complaining to the king, made bate between them. Then the lord Cobham, being cited by the archbishop, at his citation would not appear: but, sent for by the king, he obeyed and came. Being come, what lowly subjection he showed there to the king, the story declareth. Afterwards he yielded an obedient confession of his faith: it would not be received. Then did he appeal to the bishop of Rome, for which the king took great displeasure with him, and so was he repealed by the king to the archbishop, and committed to the Tower: which also he did obey. From thence he was brought to his examination once or twice: there, like a constant martyr, and witness of the truth, he stood to his confession, and that unto the very sentence of death defined against him. If this be not the effect of a true martyr, let Alanus Copus say what he will, or what he can. This I say, at least I doubt, whether the said Alanus Copus Anglus, put to the like trial himself, would venture so narrow a point of martyrdom for his religion, as this christian knight did for his: certes, it hath not yet appeared.

To proceed; after this deadly sentence was thus awarded against him, the said lord Cobham was then returned again unto the Tower, which he, with patience and meekness, did also obey; from which Tower if he afterwards by the Lord's providence did escape, whether hath Alanus Copus herein more to praise God for offering to him the benefit, or to blame the man for taking that which was offered?...

Thus, hitherto, I trust, the cause of the lord Cobham standeth firm and strong against all danger of just reprehension; who being, as ye have heard, so faithful and obedient to God, so submiss to his king, so sound in his doctrine, so constant in his cause, so afflicted for the truth, so ready and prepared to death, as we have sufficiently declared, not out of uncertain and doubtful chronicles, but out of the true originals and instruments remaining in ancient records: what lacketh now, or what should let to the contrary, but that he, declaring himself such a martyr, that is, a witness to the verity, for which also at last he suffered the fire, may, therefore, worthily be adorned with the title of martyr, which is in Greek as much as a witness-bearer?...

But, howsoever the intent and purpose was of these aforesaid confederates of the lord Cobham, whither to come, or what to do (seeing this is plain by records, as is aforesaid, that they were not yet come unto the place), how will Master Cope now justify his words, so confidently affirming, that they were there assembled seditiously together in the field of St. Giles against the king? And mark here, I beseech thee, gentle reader! how unlikely and untidely the points of this tail are tied and hanged together (I will not say without all substance of truth, but without all fashion of a cleanly lie); wherein these accusers in this matter seem to me to lack some part of Sinon's art, in conveying their narration so unartificially. First, say they, the king was come first, with his garrison, unto the field of St. Giles; and then, after the king was there encamped, consequently, the fellows of the lord Cobham (the captain being away) came, and were assembled, in the said field where the king was, against the king,...to the number of twenty thousand, and yet never a stroke in that field given! And furthermore, of all this twenty thousand aforesaid, never a man's name known but only three: to wit, sir Roger Acton, sir John Brown, and John Beverly, a preacher. How this gear is clampered together let the reader judge, and believe, as he seeth cause....

The Second Apprehension of the Lord Cobham.

Concerning sir John Oldcastle the lord Cobham, and of his first apprehension, with his whole story and life, sufficiently hath been expressed before, how he, being committed to the Tower, and was in Wales about the space of four years. In the mean time, a great sum of money was proclaimed by the king, to him that could take the said sir John Oldcastle, either quick or dead: who confederated with the lord Powis (who was at that time a great governor in Wales), feeding him with lordly gifts and promises, to accomplish their desire.

About the end of which four years being expired, the lord Powis, whether for love and greediness of the money, or whether for hatred of the true and sincere doctrine of Christ, seeking all manner of ways how to play the part of Judas, and outwardly pretending him great amity and favour, at length obtained his bloody purpose, and most cowardly and wretchedly took him, and in conclusion brought the lord Cobham bound up to London; which was about the year of our Lord 1417, and about the month of December; at which time there was a parliament assembled in London; for the relief of money the same time to be sent to the king, whom the bishops had sent out (as ye heard before) to fight in France. The records of which parliament do thus say: That on Tuesday the fourteenth day of December, and the nine and twentieth day of the said parliament, sir John Oldcastle, of Cowling in the county of Kent, knight, being outlawed (as is afore minded) in the King's Bench, and excommunicated before by the archbishop of Canterbury for heresy, was brought before the lords; and having heard his said convictions, answered not thereto in his excuse. Upon which record and process it was adjudged, that he should be taken as a traitor to the king and the realm; that he should be carried to the Tower of London, and from thence drawn through London, unto the new gallows in St. Giles without Temple-Bar, and there to be hanged, and burned hanging.

Thus, after long process, they condemned him again of heresy and treason, by force of the aforenamed act; he rendering thanks unto God, that he had so appointed him to suffer for his name's sake.

And, upon the day appointed, he was brought out of the tower with his arms bound behind him, having a very cheerful countenance. Then was he laid upon a hurdle, as though he had been a most heinous traitor to the crown, and so drawn forth into St. Giles's field, where they had set up a new pair of gallows. As he was coming to the place of execution, and was taken from the hurdle, he fell down devoutly upon his knees, desiring Almighty God to forgive his enemies. Then stood he up and beheld the multitude, exhorting them in most godly manner to follow the laws of God written in the Scriptures, and in any wise to beware of such teachers as they see contrary to Christ in their conversation and living; with many other special counsels. Then was he hanged up there by the middle in chains of iron, and so consumed alive in the fire, praising the name of God so long as his life lasted. In the end he commended his soul into the hands of God, and so departed hence most christianly, his body being resolved into ashes....

Thus have you heard the whole matter concerning the martyrdom of the good lord Cobham, as we have gathered it partly out of the collections of John Bale and others. As touching the pretensed treason of this lord Cobham, falsely ascribed unto him in his indictment, rising upon wrong suggestion and false surmise, and aggravated by rigour of words, rather than upon any ground of due probation, sufficiently hath been discoursed before in my defence of the said lord Cobham, against Alanus Copus; where again it is to be noted, as I said before, how by this it appeareth, that the lord Cobham was never executed by force of the indictment or outlawry, because if he had, he should then have been brought to the bar in the King's Bench, and there the judges should have demanded of him, what he could have said, why he should not have died; and then not showing sufficient cause for the discharge or delay of execution, the judges should have awarded and given the judgment of treason: which being not so, it is clear he was not executed upon the indictment. Besides, to prove that he was not executed upon the indictment and the outlawry, the manner of the execution proveth it, because it was neither the execution of a traitor, nor was the whole punishment thereof pronounced by the judge, as by due order of law was requisite.

Finally, as I said before, here I repeat again, that albeit the said lord Cobham was attainted of treason by the act, and that the king, the lords, and the commons, assented to the act; yet all that bindeth not in such sort (as if indeed he were no traitor) that any man may not, by search of the truth, utter and set forth sincerely and justly the very true and certain cause whereupon his execution did follow. Which seemeth by all circumstances and firm arguments to rise principally of his religion, which first brought him in hatred of the bishops; the bishops brought him in hatred of the king; the hatred of the king brought him to his death and martyrdom. And thus much for the death and execution of this worthy servant of Christ, the lord Cobham.

Bibliography

I. Editions of 1 Sir John Oldcastle (chronologically listed)

The first part / Of the true and hono- / rable historie of the life of Sir / John Old-castle, the good / Lord Cobham. London, 1600.

The First part / Of the true & hono- / rable history, of the Life of / Sir Iohn Old-castle, the good / Lord Cobham. London, 1600 [1619].

Shakespeare, William. Mr. William Shakespear Comedies, Histories, and Tragedies. London, 1664.

__________ Mr. William Shakespear's Comedies, Histories, and Tragedies. London, 1685.

__________ The Works of Mr William Shakespear. Ed. Nicholas Rowe. London, 1709. Vol. VI.

__________ The Works of Mr. William Shakespear. Ed. Alexander Pope. 2nd. ed. London, 1728. Vol. IX.

__________ The First Part of Sir John Oldcastle. London, 1734.

Malone, Edmond, ed. Supplement to the Edition of Shakespeare's Plays Published in 1778. London, 1780. Vol. II.

Scott, Sir Walter, ed. [conj.] The Ancient British Drama. Edinburgh: James Ballantyne and Co., 1810. Vol. I.

Simms, William Gilmore, ed. A Supplement to the Plays of William Shakespeare. New York: F.G. Cooledge & brother, 1848.

Tyrrell, Henry, ed. The Doubtful Plays of Shakespeare. London and New York: John Tallis and Co., n.d. [conj. 1851].

Hazlitt, William, ed. The Doubtful Plays of William Shakespeare. London: George Routledge and Sons, Limited, 1852.

Hopkinson, A.F., ed. The First Part of Sir John Oldcastle. London: M.E. Sims and Co., 1894.

MacArthur, John Robertson, ed. The First Part of Sir John Oldcastle. Diss. Chicago. Chicago: Scott, Foresman and Company, 1907.

Simpson, Percy, ed. The Life of Sir John Oldcastle. Malone Society Reprint, 1908.

Brooke, C.F. Tucker, ed. The Shakespeare Apocrypha. Oxford: Clarendon Press, 1908.

Drayton, Michael. The Works of Michael Drayton. Eds. J. William Hebel, Kathleen Tillotson, and Bernard H. Newdigate. Vols. I and V. Oxford: The Shakespeare Head Press, 1931 and 1941.

Kozlenko, William, ed. Disputed Plays of William Shakespeare. New York: Hawthorn Books, n.d. © 1974.

II. Primary Sources

i. Plays

Anon. The Famous History of Captain Thomas Stukeley. Ed. Judith C. Levinson. Malone Society Reprints, 1975.

__________ The History of Thomas Lord Cromwell. Ed. John S. Farmer. Tudor Facsimile Texts, 1911.

__________ The London Prodigal. Ed. John S. Farmer. Tudor Facsimile Texts, 1910.

__________ Look About You. Ed. W.W. Greg. Malone Society Reprints, 1913.

__________ The Merry Devil of Edmonton. Ed. John S. Farmer. Tudor Facsimile Texts, 1911.

__________ A Warning for Fair Women. Ed. John S. Farmer. Tudor Facsimile Texts, 1912.

Chapman, George. An Humorous Day's Mirth. Eds. W.W. Greg and David Nichol Smith. Malone Society Reprints, 1938.

Chettle, Henry and John Day. 1 The Blind Beggar of Bednal Green. Ed. John S. Farmer. Tudor Facsimile Texts, 1914.

Chettle, Henry and Anthony Munday. The Downfall of Robert Earl of Huntington. Ed. John S. Farmer. Tudor Facsimile Texts, 1913.

__________ The Death of Robert Earl of Huntington. Ed. John S. Farmer. Tudor Facsimile Texts, 1913.

Dekker, Thomas. The Dramatic Works of Thomas Dekker. Ed. Fredson Bowers. Vol. I. Cambridge: Cambridge Univ. Press, 1953.

Munday, Anthony. John a Kent & John a Cumber. Ed. Muriel St. Clare Byrne. Malone Society Reprints, 1928.

__________ et al. Sir Thomas More. Ed. W.W. Greg. Malone Society Reprints, 1911.

Peele, George. King Edward the First. Ed. W.W. Greg. Malone Society Reprints, 1911.

Shakespeare, William. The Complete Works of William Shakespeare. Ed. Peter Alexander. London and Glasgow: Collins, 1951.

Wilson, Robert. The Three Ladies of London. Ed. John S. Farmer. Tudor Facsimile Texts, 1911.

ii. Historical Works

Bale, John. Select Works of John Bale. Ed. Henry Christmas. Parker Society Publication. Vol. I. 1849.

Caradoc of Llancarfan. A Historie of Cambria. Corrector and augmentor David Powel. 1548; rpt. Amsterdam: Theatrum Orbis Terrarum Ltd. and New York: Da Capo Press, 1969.

Fabyan, Robert. The New Chronicles of England and France, In Two Parts. Ed. Henry Ellis. London: Printed for F.C. and J. Rivington, etc., 1811. Vol. II.

Foxe, John. The Acts and Monuments of John Foxe. Ed. Rev. George Townsend. London: Seeley, Burnside and Seeley, 1843. Vol. III.

Taylor, Frank and John S. Roskell, translators and eds. Gesta Henrici Quinti: The Deeds of Henry the Fifth. Oxford: Clarendon Press, 1975.

Hall, Edward. Hall's Chronicle. London: Printed for J. Johnson, etc., 1809.

Hayward, John. The First Part of the Life and Raigne of King Henrie the IIII. 1599; rpt. Amsterdam: Theatrum Orbis Terrarum and Norwood, N.J.: Walter J. Johnson Inc., 1975.

Holinshed, Raphael. Holinshed's Chronicles. Eds. R.S. Wallace and Alma Hansen. Oxford: Clarendon Press, 1923.

Howes, E. The Abridgement of the English Chronicle. London: 1610.

Stow, John. The Annales of England. London, 1592.

__________ The Chronicle of England. London, 1580.

Stow, John. Survey of London. Ed. Henry B. Wheatley. London: J.M. Dent & Sons Ltd., and New York: E.P. Dutton & Co., n.d.

iii. Other Works

Arber, Edward, ed. A Transcript of the Registers of the Company of Stationers of London; 1554-1640 A.D. Vol. III. London: privately printed, 1876.

Bacon, Francis. The Essays. 1625; rpt. Great Britain: Scolar Press, 1971.

Daniel, Samuel. The Civil Wars. Ed. Laurence Michel. New Haven: Yale Univ. Press, 1958.

Drayton, Michael. The Works of Michael Drayton. Eds. J. William Hebel, Kathleen Tillotson, and Bernard H. Newdigate. Vols. III and IV. Oxford: The Shakespeare Head Press, 1932 and 1933.

Greg, W.W., ed. Henslowe Papers. London: A.H. Bullen, 1907.

Foakes, R.A. and R.T. Rickert, eds. Henslowe's Diary. Cambridge: Cambridge Univ. Press, 1961.

Lambarde, William. A Perambulation of Kent. London, 1576.

Meres, Francis. Palladis Tamia. London, 1599.

Weever, John. The Mirror of Martyrs. London, 1601.

III. Secondary Sources

Abbott, E.A. A Shakespearean Grammar. 1869.

Adkins, Mary Grace Muse. "Sixteenth-Century Religious and Political Implications in Sir John Oldcastle." Univ. of Texas Studies in English, 22 (1942), 86-104.

Baldwin, T.W. "Nathaniel Field and Robert Wilson." MLN, 41 (1926), 32-34.

__________. The Organization and Personnel of the Shakespearean Company. 1927; rpt. New York: Russell and Russell, 1961.

Beckerman, Bernard. Shakespeare at the Globe, 1599-1609. New York: Macmillan Co., 1962.

Bennett, R.E. "The Parson of Wrotham in Sir John Oldcastle." MLN, 45 (1930), 142-44.

Bevington, David. Tudor Drama and Politics. Cambridge: Harvard Univ. Press, 1968.

Byrne, Muriel St. Clare. "Anthony Munday and his Books." The Library, 4th ser. 1 (1921), 225-55.

__________ "Anthony Munday's Spelling as a Literary Clue." The Library, 4th ser. 4 (1923), 9-23.

Chambers, E.K. The Elizabethan Stage. Oxford: Clarendon Press, 1923. Vols. II and III.

Collier, Jeremy. A Short View of the Immorality and Profaneness of the English Stage. 3rd ed. 1698; rpt. München-Allach: Wilhelm Fink Verlag, 1967.

Cottle, Basil, ed. Penguin Dictionary of Surnames. Great Britain: Penguin Books, 1967.

Craven, Alan E. "Simmes' Compositor A and Five Shakespeare Quartos." SB, 26 (1973), 37-60.

Creizenach, William. The English Drama in the Age of Shakespeare. Philadelphia: J.B. Lippincott Company and London: Sidgewick & Jackson, Limited, 1916.

Daniel, George. The Poems of George Daniel. Ed. Alexander B. Grosart. Boston, Lincolnshire: Robert Roberts, 1878. Vol. IV.

Ekwall, Eilert. Street Names of the City of London. Oxford: Clarendon Press, 1954.

Elton, G.R. The Tudor Constitution. Revised edn. Cambridge: Cambridge Univ. Press, 1965.

__________ England Under the Tudors. London: Methuen and Co. Ltd., 1974.

Ferguson, W. Craig. "The Compositors of Henry IV, Part 2, Much Ado About Nothing, The Shoemakers' Holiday, and The First Part of the Contention." SB, 13 (1960), 19-29.

Fleay, F.G. A Chronicle History of the Life and Work of William Shakespeare. New York: Scribners & Welford, 1886.

__________ A Biographical Chronicle of the English Drama. London: Reeves and Turner, 1891. Vol. II.

__________ A Chronicle History of the London Stage 1559-1642. New York: G.E. Stechert & Co., 1909.

Gibbs, Vicary, et al., eds. The Complete Peerage; or, A History of the House of Lords and all its members from the earliest times. Vol. VI. London: St. Catherine Press, 1926.

Gourvitch, I. "Robert Wilson 'The Elder' and 'The Younger'." N&Q, 150 (1926), 4-6.

Greg, W.W. "On Certain False Dates in Shakespearian Quartos." The Library, NS 9 (1908), 113-31, 381-409.

__________ The Shakespeare First Folio. Oxford: Clarendon Press, 1955.

__________ A Bibliography of the English Printed Drama to the Restoration. Vol. III. London: Oxford Univ. Press, 1957.

Hemingway, Samuel B. English Nativity Plays. 1909; rpt. New York: Russell and Russell Inc., 1964.

Hinman, Charlton. "Shakespeare's Text -- Then, Now, and Tomorrow." Shakespeare Survey, 18 (1965), 23-33.

Hotson, Leslie. "Anthony Mundy's Birth-Date." N&Q, 204 (1959), 2-4.

Jaggard, William. Shakespeare Bibliography. Stratford-on-Avon: The Shakespeare Head Press, 1911.

Jewkes, Wilfred T. Act Division in Elizabethan and Jacobean Plays 1583-1616. Hamden, Conn.: The Shoe String Press, 1958.

Juel-Jensen, Bent. "Michael Drayton and William Drummond of Hawthornden: A Lost Autograph Letter Rediscovered." The Library. 5th ser. 21 (1966), 328-30.

Kinsman, Robert C., ed. Poems. By John Skelton. Oxford: Clarendon Press, 1969.

Knight, Charles, ed. The Pictorial Edition of the Works of Shakespeare. London: Charles Knight and Co., 1838. Vol. III.

Koeppel, E. Studien über Shakespeare's Wirkung auf Zeitgenössische Dramatiker. 1905; rpt. Vaduz: Uranus Reprint Ltd., 1963.

Kökeritz, Helge. Shakespearian Pronunciation. New Haven and London: Yale Univ. Press, 1953.

Lloyd, Sir John Edward, et al., eds. The Dictionary of Welsh Biography Down to 1940. London, 1959.

Machlysaght, Edward. The Surnames of Ireland. Shannon, Ireland: Irish Univ. Press, 1969.

Malone, Edmond, ed. The Plays and Poems of William Shakespeare. London, 1790. Vol. I.

Mason, Oliver. The Gazeteer of England. Great Britain: Rowman & Littlefield, 1977.

Mithal, H.S.D. "The Two-Wilsons Controversy." N&Q, 204 (1959), 106-109.

Neale, J.E. The Elizabethan House of Commons. Rev. edn. Glasgow: Fontana/Collins, 1976.

Newdigate, Bernard H. Michael Drayton and his Circle. Oxford: The Shakespeare Head Press, 1941.

Notestein, Wallace. The English People on the Eve of Colonization, 1603-1630. New York: Harper & Row, 1954.

Partridge, A.C. Orthography in Shakespeare and Elizabethan Drama. Lincoln: Univ. of Nebraska Press, 1964.

Plomer, H.R. "The Printers of Shakespeare's Plays and Poems." The Library, NS 7 (1906), 149-66.

Pollard, A.W. Shakespeare Folios and Quartos. London: Methuen and Co., 1909.

Russan, Lilian and Ashmore. Historical Streets of London. New York: Thomas Y. Crowell Co., 1927.

Russell, Conrad. The Crisis of Parliaments: English History 1509-1660. Oxford: Oxford University Press, 1971.

Schlegel, A.W. Lectures on Dramatic Art and Literature. Trans. John Black. 2nd ed. rev. by A.J.W. Morrison. London: George Bell & Sons, 1900.

Sharpe, Robert B. The Real War of the Theatres. MLA Monograph Series. Vol. V. London: Oxford Univ. Press and Boston: D.C. Heath and Company, 1935.

Smith, Frank. A Genealogical Gazeteer of England. Baltimore: Genealogical Publishing Co., Inc., 1968.

Stephen, Sir Leslie and Sir Sidney Lee. The Dictionary of National Biography. Rev. edn. London: Oxford Univ. Press, 1921-22. Vols. I, VIII, IX, XI, XVI, XVII.

Stevenson, Allan H. "Shakespearian dated Watermarks." SB, 4 (1951-52), 159-64.

Tilley, Morris Palmer. A Dictionary of the Proverbs in England in the Sixteenth and Seventeenth Centuries. Ann Arbor: Univ. of Michigan Press, 1950.

Ulrici, Herman. Shakespeare's Dramatic Art. Trans. A.J.W. Morrison. London: Chapman, Brothers, 1846.

Waugh, W.T. "Sir John Oldcastle." English Historical Review, 20 (1905), 434-56, 637-58.

Withycombe, E.G. The Oxford Dictionary of English Christian Names. 3rd ed. Oxford: Clarendon Press, 1977.

Wooden, Warren W. "Recent Studies in Foxe." ELR, 11 (1981), 224-32.

Wright, Celeste Turner. Anthony Mundy: An Elizabethan Man of Letters. Univ. of California Publications in English. Vol. II. Berkeley: Univ. of California Press, 1928.

__________ "Young Anthony Mundy Again." SB, 56 (1959), 150-68.

IV. Unpublished Secondary Source

McMillin, Jr., Harvey Scott. "The Staging of Elizabethan Plays at the Rose Theatre." Diss. Stanford 1965.